Other books by Christopher S. Wren

Winners Got Scars Too:
The Life and Legends of Johnny Cash

Quotations from Chairman LBJ

with Jack Shepherd

Almanack of Poor Richard Nixon

with Jack Shepherd

The Super Summer of Jamie McBride
a novel

with Jack Shepherd

THE END OF THE LINE

The Failure of Communism in the Soviet Union and China
by **CHRISTOPHER S. WREN**

SIMON AND SCHUSTER
New York London Toronto Sydney Tokyo Singapore

Simon and Schuster
Simon & Schuster Building
Rockefeller Center
1230 Avenue of the Americas
New York, New York 10020

Designed by Laurie Jewell
Manufactured in the United States of America

1   3   5   7   9   10   8   6   4   2

Library of Congress Cataloging in Publication Data

Wren, Christopher S. (Christopher Sale),
The end of the line : the failure of communism in the Soviet Union
and China / by Christopher S. Wren.
p.   cm.
Includes bibliographical references (p.).
1. Communism—Soviet Union.   2. Communism—China.   3. Soviet
Union—Social conditions—1970-   4. China—Social conditions—1976-
I. Title.
HX313.5.W74   1990
335.43'0947—dc20   90-35021
                                                                                        CIP

ISBN 0-671-63864-5

To Jaqueline—

Wind and rain hurried spring's going,
whirling snow welcomes its return:
thousand foot high cliffs, ice-covered,
one flowering twig, beautiful there.

Beautiful, not competing for spring,
only calling that it is coming.
When mountain flowers are in full bloom,
she will be among them smiling.

—Mao Zedong

CONTENTS

INTRODUCTION:
THE REVOLUTION
HAS BEEN CANCELED
FOR LACK
OF INTEREST

▬▬▬▬▬▬▬▬▬▬▬▬▬

Do not believe we have forgotten
Marx, Engels, and Lenin. They
will not be forgotten until the
shrimp learn to sing.

—NIKITA S. KHRUSHCHEV
Soviet Communist Party leader
deposed in 1964[1]

All of us feel more deeply now
that without Marx's theory,
China could not possibly have
become what she is today.

—HU YAOBANG
Chinese Communist Party leader
deposed in 1987[2]

OUR FERRY BOAT HAD NAVIGATED the choppy currents of the Yellow River in a fine rain. My companion, Tony Walker, an Australian journalist, and I were traveling north through the back country of central China, and on the left bank of the old river port of Wuhu we looked for a train that could take us to Hefei, the capital of Anhui province. We had to cajole our tickets from the reluctant clerk at the station window. Foreigners were supposed to ride in the upholstered luxury of what the Chinese call soft class, and the next train out offered only the wooden benches of hard-class carriages, the lot of ordinary Chinese.

Hundreds of our fellow travelers pressed against metal barricades at the doors leading to the platforms. Some of them carried live ducks and chickens or staggered under the weight of mattresses and heavy sacks. As desperate as they were to get aboard, they made way as we wriggled around the barrier, assuming that, as foreigners, we were entitled to board first.

We had barely arranged ourselves on a worn bench of one carriage when the station's gates opened and the passengers fanned out across the platform, running for the best seats. It was clear that the train would be standing room only, a microcosm of China's overpopulation. The early arrivals grabbed their seats first, then hoisted through the open windows the baggage passed by their friends. Our Chinese companions displayed none of the annoyance that Western travelers evince when their space is invaded. They were content to have found room enough for themselves.

In an exception to the meticulous punctuality of the Chinese railway system, our train sat at the station until two men with the demeanor of authority pushed through the crowded car to confront us. One inquired if we were comfortable. The other apologized for the crowded conditions, which he regretted to say were *buxing* or unsuitable for China's foreign guests. More appropriate accommodations would be found. We didn't mind, I told him. The damp spring evening had turned cold and we would stay warm here, packed together. I also hoped for some candid conversation with the other passengers.

The two officials looked at each other with exasperation. More appropriate accommodations had already been arranged, the first man informed me, never mind the bother. The carriage grew silent as it became obvious that the train was not moving until we did. Reluctantly, we yielded our seats and followed our hosts. The carriage ahead to which we were escorted must have been as crowded as ours, but the train's crew was evicting the last of its occupants, some through the windows. When the train lurched out of the station, we found ourselves the only occupants of an otherwise empty carriage.

The trip to Hefei took four hours but it seemed to last all

night. As I stamped my feet to stay warm, I looked back to our old carriage. It looked snug and warm, judging by the steamed-up windows. I would have moved back, but our bene-factors had locked the doors.

Our train journey from Wuhu to Hefei became a metaphor for the sojourn of a Westerner in a Communist country. In the more than seven years I spent reporting in the Soviet Union and China, this simultaneous coddling and isolation proved my most consistent frustration. Yet it also left me free as an outsider to watch what was unfolding around me because I had no personal stake in the outcome. Like a traveler stranded high and dry on a rock in midstream of an imminent flash flood, I had a vantage point from which to witness the coming deluge without being submerged by it.

The obsolescence of Communism was apparent well be-fore the Berlin Wall came tumbling down or Chinese troops assaulted Tiananmen Square, leaving in the wake of their bat-tle tanks martyrs who died not for Marxism but for Western-style democracy. Deng Xiaoping jeopardized China's economic modernization program, flouted world opinion in persecuting the pro-democracy demonstrators, who had the talent and ed-ucation needed to make his reforms succeed, and sacrificed his designated heirs—Hu Yaobang in 1987 and Zhao Ziyang in 1989—to salvage a rotting Party apparatus that often as not tried to undercut his reforms.[3] In Eastern Europe, Communism became so unpopular that the leaders of East Germany were subsequently revealed to have been packing concealed pistols as they went about the Party's business. The Communist Party, which rode to power around the world on the dreams of hundreds of millions of ordinary people, showed that their aspirations in the end counted for less than its own survival. The Soviet revolutionary Leon Trotsky would have under-stood. "The dictatorship of the Communist Party," Trotsky wrote after breaking with Stalin, "is maintained by recourse to every form of violence."[4]

In the Soviet Union, Mikhail Sergeievich Gorbachev la-bored to overcome economic stagnation and ethnic antago-nism in the face of opposition from inside his own Communist

Party. To build his constituency, he tolerated an unprecedented public outspokenness—or *glasnost*—that revealed startling examples of the Soviet Union's inability to feed and care for its citizens. He made unprecedented adjustments in the Soviet political structure. But for all his courage in moving much farther than Deng, Gorbachev wanted change to lead to more efficient production and improved living standards under basically the same system. The consequence has been reforms imposed from the top, not rising from below as in Eastern Europe. Gorbachev set out to revitalize the tired old world, not usher in a brave new one.[5]

Perhaps Karl Marx, now reposing in London's Highgate Cemetery, within sound of the tennis balls being whacked on the public courts at Waterlow Park, got it right after all when he predicted intensification of the class struggle, though he could not have anticipated that the exploiting class desperately fending off its overthrow by the proletariat a century and a half later would be filled with Communists, not capitalists. Where Marxism took root, it has been revealed as an idea whose time has come and gone. And that is what this book is about as it focuses upon the Soviet Union and China, where I was eyewitness to the impending failure of the grand experiment called Communism.

As a journalist in Moscow and Beijing, engaged in what we presume to call history on the run, I lived daily with the contradictions of Communism when it first began losing control. By inviting you to travel as my companion back through the Soviet Union and China and see what I saw, I hope that you may appreciate how the *Communist Manifesto*'s observation that history "has only established new classes, new conditions of oppression, new forms of struggle in place of the old ones" was borne out in the very societies that took Marx's name.[6] This historical phenomenon, arguably the most significant of the twentieth century, is difficult to encompass in newspaper headlines or the television evening news, but its sharpening dialectics affect us all because the consequences could shake even the foundations of Western democracies. In a nuclear age, a dying or self-destructive Communist state could prove no less dangerous than a dynamic, aggressive one.

I started writing this book after departing Beijing, when the Soviet Union showed little sign of following China's lead in reform. That Moscow has overtaken Beijing on the flight from ideological orthodoxy has confirmed that true believers now accept that Communism does not work, even if they have nothing with which to replace it. Consequently, when I describe conditions and situations in one country, they are generally pertinent to the other, whether by comparison or contrast.

Though some time has elapsed since my tours in the Soviet Union—from October 1973 to October 1977—and China—from October 1981 to December 1984—I am struck by how little the problems of Communism have changed since I left Moscow and Beijing, or in the intervals between three other working trips I made to the Soviet Union between 1967 and 1988. In talking to Russian and Chinese expatriates and in scanning the official and dissident press, I kept coming across the same complaints about privilege, corruption, sloth, and the stifling of egalitarianism. This consistency with what I reported has encouraged me to put subsequent developments in the context of my own serendipitous experiences.

My perceptions of Communism in crisis were acquired in visits to all fifteen republics of the Soviet Union, including Siberia and the Soviet Far East, as well as to twenty-nine of China's thirty-one provinces, autonomous regions, and municipalities. Other assignments for The New York Times took me into Eastern Europe, where I reported from Poland, East Germany, Hungary, Czechoslovakia, and Rumania, and to Mongolia. The rejection of Marxism in Eastern Europe has confirmed my thesis, but I concentrate here on the Soviet Union and China because they are the two largest experiments in an unraveling ideology that can neither succeed nor endure.

It is only fair to the reader that I summarize some opinions that I hope to make more persuasive anecdotally, for my proposition will be understood better if it entertains in the course of informing:

What the reformers embarked upon in China and the So-

viet Union is bold, even startling, but it is not a revolution
that Marx, Lenin, or Mao would have advocated because it is
not the violent overthrow and destruction of the established
order. The popular rebellions in Eastern Europe have been more
consistent with their calls to arms.

The Soviet Union and China arrived at the necessity for
change from different directions and backgrounds—China
from the chaos of the Cultural Revolution and the Soviet
Union from economic and social stagnation—but they have
nearly identical aims: to survive by pulling back from disaster
caused by the monumental misrule of the Party. Deng Xiaoping and Mikhail Gorbachev gained world celebrity for trying
to bootstrap their countries out of the morass without scrap-
ping the socialist system altogether. Despite a preoccupation
with plans and targets of both their countries, neither leader
spelled out a coherent new vision of the future such as Karl
Marx and Friedrich Engels forecast in their *Communist Manifesto*. Whatever works will be evolutionary at best.

The foremost obstacle to the arrival of true communism,
that utopian final stage of socialism, is the Communist Party.
Hijacked from the idealists by opportunists, the Party has
botched its vanguard role assigned by Lenin. Absolute power
has corrupted the Party absolutely, breeding contempt for the
masses, life-styles befitting degenerate imperial aristocracies,
self-interest, venality, and official deception, all of which belie
the *Communist Manifesto*'s claim that Communists "have no
interests separate and apart from those of the proletariat as a
whole." Though the Party promises to weed out criminal and
incompetent members, they hang on. The legacy has been
distrust and resentment from the broad masses, who were portrayed for years as content with, even ardent about, the institutionalized inequality of the status quo.

It is ironic that Gorbachev and Deng, when they acted
most forcefully against the Party's vested interests, might have
won public office in a landslide in an unfettered, pluralistic
election. But this has not been the accepted Communist route
to power, whether because its leaders are unaccustomed to

explaining their actions or because they do not trust what the official press says about their popularity.

The reforms attempted so far are breathtaking in their Soviet or Chinese context, but they would hardly shake up a Western democracy. Making ideological hacks stop fiddling with the economy, letting farmers decide for themselves what to grow, paying honest wages for honest labor, providing a little more truth in packaging, whether in produce or the press, and allowing people to choose their leaders get taken pretty much for granted in the West. The argument inside the Kremlin and Zhongnanhai, its Chinese equivalent, is waged not over whether the existing system must change, but over how to go about changing it without leaving the Party altogether irrelevant. The Russians and Chinese agree that their system is not delivering, yet many want to believe that socialism, which has produced some of the lowest living standards on their respective continents, remains superior to capitalism.

The Communist system has been brutal, inefficient, and intolerant of individual rights, but out of revolutionary chaos it did create stability in its time. Under Marxism-Leninism, the Soviet Union was transformed into a major industrial nation, a nuclear power and a rival of the United States. China sloughed off its own colonial shackles ("The Chinese people have stood up," Mao Zedong proclaimed in 1949), bootstrapped itself into the industrial age, and built its own atomic bombs and space satellites. The Communist state gave Russians and Chinese national dignity and unprecedented services in health, education, and social welfare, though of uneven quality and at a cost hard to sustain. Whether a freer, more market-oriented political system would have done better can be debated. The Soviet Union and China have grown adept at lurching from one economic disaster to the next, but their squandering of natural and human resources could not last forever.

Directives issued from the center of a Communist monolith will not transform the system at its grass roots. Provincial Soviet and Chinese officials need not choose between embracing and rejecting reforms unenforced by arbitrary repression. They need only ignore them. What this means is that the Soviet and Chinese leadership today cannot turn around their countries as swiftly as Stalin or Mao did by physically eliminating opponents.

The surprise isn't that Communism collapsed so abruptly, but that it lasted so long. The ideology that rallied converts to the barricades has proven wrong in its predictions and irrelevant in its solutions. Popular enthusiasm has been replaced by apathy and resentment. The old fraternalism has given way to self-interest, opportunism, and cynicism. A new class, or caste, of exploiters has revealed itself. And the revolution has been canceled for lack of interest, leaving its apostles scrambling for alternatives to shore up what they created. There is nothing here to defy logic. Forty years before the blood of students crying out for democracy washed the stones of Tiananmen Square, Chairman Mao observed: "Classes struggle, some classes triumph, others are eliminated. Such is history, such is the history of civilization for thousands of years."[7]

The similarities of the Soviet Union and China extend to the physical trappings of a system that set the twentieth century's standard for totalitarianism. In Moscow, my family and I lived at Sadovo-Samotechnaya inside a compound for foreigners, segregated from the Russian people by armed police guards from the Committee for State Security, or KGB. The automobile I drove had a coded license plate that identified me as an American correspondent. My Russian neighbors were discouraged, sometimes to the point of intimidation, from meeting or talking to me, though this has relaxed somewhat under *glasnost.*

In Beijing, we lived at Jianguomenwai, also inside a compound built for foreigners, guarded by the People's Armed Police Force. My car there also carried a distinguishing license plate, and Chinese were inhibited from associating with me, except on an approved basis. Beneath these similarities, the Soviet Union and China of course have real differences. But like the layers of an onion, within them appeared subtler similarities, which again is what this book is about.

I do not pretend to offer a definitive work of Kremlinology or Sinology. I am a journalist, not a scholar, though I hope the book will complement more academic studies of the Soviet Union and China. Most of the information I draw upon went into my daily reporting for *The New York Times*, but some also appeared in other articles I wrote for magazines as diverse as *Harper's* and *TV Guide*. My research has been reorganized and written afresh here. Some material has not appeared before, whether for lack of time or concern that it would jeopardize others; I do not believe it will now.

I could not have enjoyed my life under Communism without the loving companionship of my wife, Jaqueline, and our children, Celia and Chris, who shared in the material shortage and sensory abundance and who contributed their own experiences. Jack Shepherd and Martin Goldman were unstinting in their encouragement and set high standards in their passion for good writing. Sterling Lord saw the potential of my subject, even in tentative outline. I am grateful to the MacDowell Colony in Peterborough, New Hampshire, and especially to Roz Putnam and Chris Barnes, for the pine-scented solitude given me to work on this book. A. M. Rosenthal, the former executive editor of *The New York Times*, entrusted me with two of his most prestigious foreign bureaus. Max Frankel, the present executive editor of *The Times*, and Joseph Lelyveld, the managing editor, cared enough about my quixotic project to let me finish while they saved another plum assignment for me in South Africa. Frank Stankus played midwife in extracting my manuscript from a perverse computer. And Alice Mayhew and David Shipley, my editors at Simon and Schuster, sharpened the book's focus and proposed significant improvements.

Before my posting in Moscow and Beijing, I was fortunate to have learned Russian and Chinese, the former at Dartmouth College and the University of Edinburgh and the latter in the Chinese Language Project at Cambridge University on a year's sabbatical provided by *The New York Times*. These marvelous languages became my best tools for cutting through the official insulation and enhancing my understanding of and affection for the people who speak them. Everyone introduced in these pages is real, though occasionally I had to alter some minor detail of their identities to protect them if they told me more than the authorities would allow. There are no fictitious or composite personalities here, and I make clear if I am compelled to change a name or significant fact about an acquaintance.

If living with Communism for more than seven years left me critical of the system, I harbor no such feelings toward the Russians and Chinese themselves, many of whom went out of their way to open their lives to an outsider. I never lacked for real friends, though the secret police limited their number, and I regret that I cannot accord them the limelight that they deserve. For every ideologue, hypocrite, and informer I met, someone else surfaced with an integrity and humanity that caught me unaware. The official bombast was offset by unofficial flashes of sometimes outrageous humor. Not everyone I met was brave, but those who displayed courage did so in such abundance that it seemed to compensate for the timidity of others.

Our life in Moscow and Beijing was not always monotonous or hard, though both qualities existed in some measure. Reporters are prone to focus on the more dramatic negative features of the societies they cover, to the slighting of subtler positive ones. Where the Communist system has worked, I try to acknowledge it but without suspending judgment.

And now, in the exhortation of the early Soviet poet Aleksandr Blok, "with your whole body, with your whole heart, with your whole conscience, listen to the Revolution"—and let me show you what it wrought in the Soviet Union and China.

1

IF IT WORKS, WE'LL CALL IT SOCIALISM: SALVAGING AN IDEOLOGY

▬ ▬ ▬ ▬ ▬ ▬ ▬ ▬ ▬ ▬ ▬ ▬ ▬ ▬

> Why do I constantly sit with
> volumes of Lenin, looking
> through them, looking for
> approaches? Because it is never
> too late to consult with Lenin.
>
> —MIKHAIL S. GORBACHEV[1]

> We have to develop Marxism and
> Mao Zedong Thought.
> Otherwise, they will become
> ossified.
>
> —DENG XIAOPING[2]

THE ROAD TO CHAIRMAN MAO'S HOUSE begins in Changsha, Hunan's provincial capital, and leads some fifty miles through the red-dirt countryside, with scrub pines and rice fields shining in the morning sun. Outdated Maoist slogans show through the whitewash of the small brick farmhouses that line the road: "In industry, learn from Daqing; in agriculture, learn from Dazhai." In 1964, Chairman Mao selected both places as models for China's agricultural and industrial development. But Daqing, the Manchurian oilfield, got overpumped and now needs Western technology to scour what little oil is left. And Dazhai, a model production brigade in northern Shanxi province, faked its production figures, which had set impossible standards for the country's 53,000 agricultural communes.

The village of Shaoshan lies in a snug valley surrounded by a rim of rolling hills. Here, in one of its sprawling tile-roof homesteads overlooking a small pond, Mao Zedong was born in 1893.

Once this rural pocket of south-central China was hallowed ground, visited by thousands of pilgrims. At the height of the Cultural Revolution, seventy thousand Red Guards reportedly converged upon Shaoshan in a single day. Since Chairman Mao's death in 1976, the crowds have thinned down to a few hundred visitors a day.

"In the Cultural Revolution, people came here to worship Mao Zedong," recalled Fu Changming, a local girl who worked as a guide. "He was like the image of a god, of an idol. Now many of them just come to understand Mao Zedong's life and China's modern history."

The rules for visitors are posted outside the large house where the Mao family lived. "Maintain seriousness," the Chinese characters exhort. "No smoking. No spitting. Don't move the furniture. No climbing trees and picking fruit. No carving on the bamboo and wood." That leaves the visitors, who seem more curious than fervent, with little to do but traipse through submissively and then head for the local gift shop to buy machine-embroidered portraits of Mao and badges, not just the familiar metallic profile on a red enamel background but also fat plastic buttons with the chairman in a Red Army cap smiling disembodied over the bucolic village.

Fu Changming led the morning tour, stopping in the long kitchen. "Here Mao helped his mother do the cooking," she told us. "The wooden buckets are original. So is the kitchen cupboard. In the spring of 1921 it was very cold. Mao sat with his brothers around the fire"—here her small hand fluttered toward the fireplace—"and encouraged them to join the revolution. His brothers all died for the Chinese revolution."

The house, built in a U shape, with the farm buildings next door, had five and a half rooms. "It was almost like a rich peasant's family," the guide conceded. The house had been refurnished with replicas of the furniture thought to have surrounded Mao as a child. The Nationalists had destroyed most of the original pieces when they confiscated the home in 1929. A little prodding elicited the disclosure that other pieces were carted off by local peasants, who were ordered later to bring them back. So Mao's bed was genuine; the bedding and mosquito netting on it were not. We were led through Mao's small bedroom and into his parents' bedroom, which still had their old double bed. "His father was very strict with the children and hot-tempered," Miss Fu told us. "He died in 1920 of typhoid at the age of fifty."

A reception room had been converted into a small museum, replete with the *Communist Manifesto*'s parting shot: "Workers of the world, unite." Portraits of Mao's revolutionary comrades—Liu Shaoqi, Peng Dehuai, and Zhu De—hung along one wall. When Mao had turned on Liu, Peng, and Zhu, their pictures were removed, leaving Lin Biao, Mao's heir apparent, conspicuously on display. In 1971, according to the official version, Lin died fleeing an abortive coup attempt against Mao.

"After Liu Shaoqi and Peng Dehuai were rehabilitated, they put their pictures back," Miss Fu said. "The pictures of Lin Biao were taken away."

Mao's father acquired a little over three and a half acres of land, an index of some prosperity in those days, some of which is now cultivated by Tang Ruiyin, a chatty middle-aged country woman who lives in the farmhouse on the other side of the pond. "Chairman Mao was the savior of us poor farmers," she volunteered. She did not need much encouragement to reminisce about the times when visitors swarmed over Shaoshan like locusts. "During the Cultural Revolution, some Red Guards slept on the floor and in our loft because they didn't have any other place to sleep," she said. "They had red books and kept saying, 'May Chairman Mao live ten thousand years.' "

I asked whether the Red Guards made a nuisance of themselves, as was their habit on rampages elsewhere. Miss Tang had found them rather nice young people. "They were very disciplined and respectful. They paid for their food. They

helped carry water up from the pond and gather the firewood."
Moreover, she reflected, "Because they were guests of Chairman Mao, you had to treat them nicely."

Miss Tang's husband, a retired soldier, was now an electrician working on a project in another village. They were what
people called a "half-noodle" family, because only she grew
the rice while he held down a state job. Her three children
were grown. I sympathized that it must be hard to do the
farmwork by herself.

Not really, Miss Tang said, because she paid laborers to
plant and reap her rice. Most of the time she could cope, "but
in harvest time, I cannot do it all by myself, so I invite others
to help me. They get a pack of cigarettes, two yuan a day"—
about sixty cents—"and three meals to bring in the crops."

So hired hands were again doing the stoop labor on the
old Mao homestead. When Chairman Mao was alive, peasants
who tried to employ others were accused of exploiting them.
Miss Tang found my surprise silly.

"The system of hiring people from another area is quite
different from exploiting the peasants in the old days," she
snorted. "They were forced to work for the landlord and sometimes he paid them nothing. Now some people are happy to
help others overcome their difficulties. Paying them two yuan
and a pack of cigarettes and their meals is quite fair."

Before the Third Plenum—the popular shorthand for the
Central Committee's plenary session in December 1978,
which laid the foundation for the agricultural reforms—Miss
Tang said she received only 330 pounds of rice a year for working in the collective. For a few years, she had to buy some of
her rice to eat. Now, by sowing two crops a year on her paddies,
she reaped nearly a ton and a half of rice, and after the state
took its quota, she was left with more than thirteen hundred
pounds for herself.

"Since the Third Plenum, the individual responsibility
system started in China and all the farmers here are getting
richer. They have distributed the land to the farmers so the
rice output is going up. People are freer to have sideline oc-

cupations, to raise chickens and pigs and ducks," Miss Tang said. Under Mao, we both knew, farmers who raised their own livestock were publicly denounced as the "tail of capitalism" and often punished for it.

"Mao's policy was to organize many people into agricultural communes, so very few people were free to work for themselves. Now, very many people are free to work as they please. All the farmers here respect Mao Zedong because he distributed the land to the poor peasants. But now they have the land to produce what they like.

"In the early days of the responsibility system, I had some doubts myself, because I couldn't see the point of it. But now I have seen with my own eyes that production is getting better.

"Mao Zedong paved the way for Communist power in the country. But now Mao Zedong is dead," Miss Tang said. "His successors are continuing the policies and they are not against Mao Zedong's ideas. But if we follow their new system closely, we can get a new idea of China."

To hear this coming from Miss Tang, who was a farmer and not a philosopher, suggested how easily many Chinese reconciled the new realities of change with the old verities. "If it works, we'll call it socialism; if it doesn't, we'll call it capitalism," one Party official confided.

Any journalist covering the Communist world finds that the gap between rhetoric and reality begins with its ideology, which itself has been the product of an ongoing revisionism. Marx's self-styled heirs—Vladimir Ilyich Lenin, Joseph Stalin, and Mao Zedong—bent his tenets to their eclectic purposes just as he had bent the writings of the nineteenth-century German philosophers Georg Hegel and Ludwig Feuerbach.

The Communist Manifesto that Karl Marx and Friedrich Engels published in 1848 declared that "the history of all hitherto existing society is the history of class struggles" and that "What the bourgeoisie—or capitalist class—produces, above all, is its own gravediggers. Its fall and the victory of the proletariat are equally inevitable." They expected the proletariat, by which they meant workers who lived by selling their labor, to grow in numbers and strength until isolated confrontations with their capitalist bosses merged into a single victorious revolution.

Lenin believed that the proletariat could not pull off this revolution by itself. To realize Marx's "dictatorship of the proletariat," Lenin argued, required a tight, disciplined vanguard of revolutionaries, meaning the Communist Party.[3] Lenin's view of the Party's leading role was used to justify its selfish domination of all aspects of life in Communist countries. Marx and Engels had assumed that once classes were abolished, the state would wither away. Lenin willed it—and the Party—to flourish and proliferate.

The contribution of Iosif Vissarionovich Dzhugashvili, better known as Stalin, to the dogma of Marxism-Leninism was simplistic, serving to rationalize the country's rapid industrialization and the cruelties he inflicted on the Russian people. As millions of them disappeared into prison cells and labor camps, the ideology became whatever Stalin said it was, synonymous with the dark terrors of totalitarianism overlaid with a glittering *kult lichnosti,* or cult of personality. Under Stalin, Marx's presumption that the state would wither away became extinct.

On the other side of the world, Mao Zedong was putting his own spin on Marxism. He broadened Marx's definition of the urban proletariat—translated into Chinese as *wuchan jieji,* or class without property—to encompass millions of poor farmers. Mao wrote for China as he knew it, an ancient empire fallen on hard times, abused by corrupt rulers and humiliated by foreigners, groping for some exit from its misery. Mao called the Chinese "poor and blank," but these frailties only encouraged him. "Poverty gives rise to the desire for change, the desire for action and the desire for revolution," he argued, while on the blankness of China's masses "the freshest and most beautiful characters can be written, the freshest and most beautiful pictures can be painted."[4]

Fanaticism and pragmatism dwelled together in Mao's personality. While accepting Lenin's leading role for the Communist Party, Mao also introduced the "mass line," as he termed the collective aspirations and wisdom of the Chinese people. He meant that power should flow both ways, up from the bottom as well as down from the top. "The masses are the real heroes, while we ourselves are often childish and ignorant, and without this understanding it is impossible to acquire even the most rudimentary knowledge,"[5] he wrote in 1941. Yet Mao, like Stalin, came to believe in his own personality cult. Once he was in power, his edicts became more erratic, his intolerance more fearsome. Mao let his deft prose be truncated into the little red book mindlessly brandished by the Red Guards.

It was this legacy that Deng Xiaoping disowned, but subtly and selectively. He dismantled the people's communes that Mao created in 1958 to harness not just agriculture but the peasants themselves. The communes reverted to the traditional *xiangs* or rural townships, and the production brigades became villages again. Collective labor gave way to family sharecropping. Sideline occupations, once condemned as capitalist, were actively encouraged. Word spread in China that revolutionary sacrifice was out. Real glory lay in getting rich. Even the ascendancy of the conservatives in the wake of the 1989 democratic protests did not roll back these momentous deviations from Maoism, for a simple reason: a Communist country, however orthodox, has to feed itself.

Marx's dream of proletarian internationalism, a brotherhood of the working class, which subsequently rationalized supporting Communist movements and meddling in insurrections overseas, gave way to a preoccupation with internal problems in both Moscow and Beijing. They talked no longer of exporting revolution but of importing Western technology and management techniques. China's new internationalism smacked more of the ancient philosopher Mencius: confine yourself to building the perfect society at home that other nations will want to emulate. The spartan garrison state was evolving into a consumer society. The personality cult around Mao was scrapped in favor of power sharing, but strictly within the Party.

To slough off the dead weight of Marxist orthodoxy meant minimizing the hero worship without impugning the founding fathers. With characteristic ingenuity, the Chinese dispensed with Mao. The Russians tried to ignore Stalin, finding him impossible to turn to any advantage. "Marxism-Leninism was always flexible. Only under Stalin did it become inflexible," said a Soviet editor, who told me that Gorbachev was trying to restore the old dynamism. He left me to infer that Khrushchev, Brezhnev, Andropov, and Chernenko had not gotten around to it during their collective three decades of power. The Russians stopped short of reducing Lenin to fully human dimensions.

The demythologization of Mao did not begin immediately after his death in 1976. Hua Guofeng, his chosen heir, made clear in a major policy statement in February 1977 that "we will resolutely uphold whatever policy decisions Chairman Mao made and unswervingly follow whatever instructions Chairman Mao gave." Such admirable devotion had already brought China to the brink of economic and social disaster and made it the laughingstock of the world. Hua Guofeng's "two whatevers," as they came to be called, did not hearten those impatient to get the country moving again. Deng Xiaoping was just emerging from his second period of official disgrace, but he called such blind obedience absurd. "Comrade Mao Zedong himself said repeatedly that some of his own statements were wrong," Deng told his supporters back in May 1977. "He said that no one can avoid making mistakes in his work unless he does none at all." In time, Deng's new pragmatism solidified into a dogmatism of its own.

Compared to the tortuous verbiage of Marx, Mao's writings were such a model of clarity and exposition that when I studied Chinese at Cambridge one of my tutors would quote Mao to press home some point of Chinese grammar. "A revolution is not a dinner party," he wrote and went on to prove it. But his writings became so voluminous as to justify just about anything. The ideological guideposts Mao left for Chinese Communism were reduced by Deng to three selective slogans: "Seek truth from facts" implicitly repudiated the dogmatism of Marx's *Capital* and the little red book of Chairman Mao. "Practice is the sole criterion of truth" meant that a policy's ideological correctness depends only on whether it works. "Emancipate the mind from dogma" gave the Party and people an excuse to try new things. "The fundamental point of Mao Zedong Thought is seeking truth from facts and integrating the universal truth of Marxism-Leninism with the concrete practice of the Chinese revolution," Deng said back in 1978. Like Zen Buddhism, the new ideology threw the questions back at the questioner, but without granting him real freedom to think.

The approach reminded me of a fable written some years ago by Ai Qing, probably China's finest modern poet and a prominent victim of Mao's Anti-Rightist Campaign in 1957, which Deng carried out. Ai's fable told of a young man who asked an old hunter to show him how to shoot birds. The hunter agreed but his pupil proved a lousy shot. Not only did he fail to shoot a bird on the wing, he could not even hit a bird sitting on a tree branch. In desperation, the old hunter told his pupil to fire his gun at a large piece of cardboard. "When you have done that," the hunter said, "draw a bird around each hole."

In the Soviet Union as well as in China, this tinkering stopped consciously short of impinging on the Party's primacy. In a 1987 speech republished by the Soviet dissident magazine *Glasnost*, the Yugoslav Marxist Milovan Djilas observed that Gorbachev's reforms had yet to shake "the 'holy trinity' of the Communist universe," which he defined as the state, ideology, and socialist ownership, all united in the Party's monopolistic rule. "This monolithic trinity is the system, the very core of the system, even though for the sake of self-preservation Communist leaders have adapted somewhat and continue to adapt to specific national features."[6] Dissecting the guts of this system is tantamount to self-destruction.

One tightrope artist walking the high wire of the Party's guiding ideology was Su Shaozhi. When I met him in Beijing in 1984, Professor Su was director of the Institute of Marxism-Leninism–Mao-Zedong-Thought, which was responsible for reconciling China's changes with Maoist thought. When bonds were floated in Shanghai, condominiums sold in Canton, or private restaurants opened in Wuhan, Su's institute had the unenviable task of explaining why these reforms were not heresies.

I came to hear Professor Su lecture at the Chinese Journalists' Association. In his rumpled blue tunic, Su looked like the semi-literate Party hacks I kept encountering in China. I underestimated him, for Su had a talent for making sense of the stilted verbiage of Chinese Communism. He had actually read Marx, though he reminded his audience that "there are no Marxist quotations for what we are doing now. If we used quotations, we would be dogmatic."

Su repeated Deng's aphorism that it did not matter whether a cat was black or white as long as it caught mice.[7] "It can be a black cat or a white cat, but it must be a cat, not a dog," Su said. I hadn't heard that twist before, and I wrote it down. "For us, socialism means a cat," Su insisted.

"I wish to add that there are not only many roads leading to socialism," he continued. "Even under socialism, there should be more than one solution. There are many states with different social systems.

"The debate over what is a socialist system is still going on. But several points need no challenging. There must be public ownership of the means of production; the distribution to each according to his work; the workers, peasants, and intellectuals as the masters of the country, and socialist democracy," Su said. "Since we have public ownership of the means of production and distribution to each according to his work, these guarantees will not lead to capitalism and a new exploiting class."

Su had recently helped draft the Party's plan for an overhaul of China's urban economy. "During the formulation of the Party document, we didn't make any special effort to find quotations from Marx and Lenin," Su said. "You find quotations from Marx and Lenin in dogmatism, and dogmatism came to its highest point in the Cultural Revolution, when everyone waved a little red book."

Su addressed his questioners with more frankness than I had heard from any other Party theoretician. In rapid succession, he demolished the hoary Maoist clichés that it is better to be Red than expert, that whatever Mao said and did should be followed, and that the Party was striding down the only road to socialism. Someone asked him to clarify the confusion over Mao Zedong Thought, which had less and less to do with the man whose name it bore.

"Many foreign friends cannot make the distinction between Mao Zedong Thought and the thought of Mao Zedong as an individual," Su agreed. "The thought of Mao Zedong as an individual had many mistakes, especially in his later years. But as far as Mao Zedong Thought goes, we regard it as a serious ideology that excludes the ideological mistakes of Mao Zedong himself. That is why we say, Persist in Mao Zedong Thought. It means we should persist in seeking truth from facts, in the line for the masses and in self-reliance."

Su Shaozhi had formulated the ingenious theory, declared gospel at the 13th Party Congress in 1987, that China was still in the initial stages of socialism. Back in 1958, the *People's Daily* promised that even octogenarians would live to see Communism, the utopian stage of socialism. No longer. Professor Su gave the leadership license to try just about anything on grounds that China was in a transitional period of trial and error.[8]

"The ultimate goal of China's future development is Communism, but it is a long way off," Su assured us. "It will take centuries."

Su Shaozhi subsequently earned the kind of reward that the system bestows on its best and brightest. In the wake of the student protests in late 1986, he was sacked as a theoretician and told to hand in his Party membership card. As I heard it, Su consented to quit his institute but not his beloved Party. Why he fell from favor was never explained. By one account, he offended the hard-liners by contending that the Party suffered from lingering Stalinism. Subsequent events were to prove him right. So Deng Xiaoping, who valued Party discipline foremost, threw the conservatives his most articulate ideologist; Chinese call it "sacrificing the rook to save the queen."

I wonder if Su had been too diligent about finding strands of Marxist logic for what the reformers were doing. Chinese Marxism, whatever that means today, was safer tucked deep inside the bosom of the Party. Su made a comeback as co-author of a bold article in the *People's Daily* in March 1988. To cope with the future, it argued, China needed more democratic elections, stronger legal safeguards, and a competitive market economy free from bureaucratic interference. The article presaged some of the demands of China's ill-fated democracy movement. So I was relieved to learn that Su Shaozhi, having fled Deng Xiaoping's crackdown on pluralistic thought in 1989, was alive and well and living in Chicago.

Whenever I wanted to measure the promise of Marxism against what it was delivering in the Soviet Union, I drove out to the sparsely furnished walk-up flat of Roy Medvedev, a dissident Soviet historian, in Moscow's western suburbs. Medvedev, a gentle-spoken scholar whose father had died in the Stalinist purges, was the only Marxist I had met who was willing to discuss his convictions honestly. He argued that Marxism was never meant to be a hard and fast ideology. In fact, Marx disparaged ideologies as "false consciousness."[9] What he had tried to do, Medvedev said, was work out a scientific rationale for the social and economic change he witnessed around him. This coincided with the rise of the working class, the emergence of political labels, and the subsequent revolutionary upheaval, which created conditions for the dogmatization of Marxism as a political cult that had little in common with what Marx was originally trying to say.

Paying lip service to this cult, I realized, offered Communism its continuity. Stalin claimed to be faithful to Marx and Lenin even as he scythed down those more loyal than he to the ideals of Marxism-Leninism. Medvedev observed that Stalin fed parasitically on Marxist ideas but never practiced them.

The Soviet and Chinese leaderships have been reluctant to expose totally the abuses of their predecessors. In October

1984, the Chinese Party's Central Committee blamed the economic and social disasters of Mao's Cultural Revolution and
Great Leap Forward, in which millions died, on "the influence
of left-deviationist errors in the Party's guiding ideology." Leonid Brezhnev described Stalin's purges, which killed up to
twenty million Russians, as "certain violations of socialist
legality"—as if the grim dictator had done nothing worse than
run a red light. Gorbachev was more honest. He sanctioned
the most devastating repudiation of Stalinism that I ever saw—
a 1988 Soviet television documentary, titled simply *Trial*, in
which several elderly Bolsheviks eloquently testified to the
cruelties that Stalin had inflicted on them and their purged
comrades.

But to probe too deeply into the past might raise doubts
about the Party's legitimacy and competence as the self-
appointed political vanguard. It has been far easier to fiddle
with history, which the earlier leaders were never hesitant to
do. In China, I collected different prints of a well-known photograph from the 1960s that showed a smiling Chairman Mao,
hands clasped in front of his baggy tunic, greeting an equally
smiling Prime Minister Zhou Enlai, who clutched a large bouquet of flowers. In the background was a Soviet-made airplane
on which Zhou had returned from a diplomatic trip. It was the
kind of public display of vanguard camaraderie that Marxist
regimes love. Only the cast of characters kept changing, depending on which picture you saw.

The original black-and-white photograph showed President Liu Shaoqi wedged in alongside Chairman Mao, while a
bespectacled Zhu De, the father of the Red Army, looked on.
A subsequent print included Zhu but not Liu, who got airbrushed out after Mao purged him and locked him up in a bank
vault in Kaifeng, where he died in 1969. The scene without
Liu was later issued in color on a postage stamp. After Deng
had Liu posthumously rehabilitated, the original picture with
Liu appeared and the doctored one was withdrawn. I assumed
this ended the matter until I came across a new propaganda
poster in western China. It was an artist's rendition of the

same airport scene, but this time Deng Xiaoping, holding a large bouquet of flowers, had materialized alongside Zhu and Zhou.

Cutting and pasting history is nothing new for a society that treats the future as certain and only the past as unpredictable. One of the most famous photographs of Lenin, taken in Moscow's Sverdlov Square on May 5, 1920, showed Trotsky and Kamenev standing beside Lenin's podium. They got painted out of the picture after Stalin purged them. Another piece of ubiquitous political art I acquired in the People's Republic of Mongolia showed Sukhe Bator, its first Communist leader, entering Lenin's Kremlin study bearing traditional gifts of bread and silk. The Soviet leader was rising from his chair in welcome, but only in the painting. Though Sukhe Bator did visit Moscow once, there is no evidence that he ever met Lenin.

After Khrushchev denounced Stalin in his secret speech at the 20th Soviet Party Congress in February 1956, the dead dictator was removed from the tomb on Red Square that he shared with Lenin and planted in a less conspicuous grave at the Kremlin Wall, where he could be overlooked. The Chinese took a characteristically different approach: Mao's embalmed corpse remains on display inside a crystal sarcophagus, but now he shares the mausoleum built for him in Tiananmen Square with the memorabilia of Liu Shaoqi, Zhou Enlai, and Zhu De. It was as if the Russians had left Stalin in Lenin's mausoleum but also made room for his archenemies Leon Trotsky and Nikolai Bukharin.

On the anniversary of Mao's ninetieth birthday in December 1983, the foreign press was invited to the opening of Mao's expanded mausoleum. I went because it was not every day that one had a chance to witness history remade. Mao's aura at first seemed undimmed. We were confronted in the lobby by a white marble statue of the Chinese leader, larger than life and surrounded by a forest of potted palms, miniature citrus trees, ferns, and fresh flowers. Further inside, we encountered pictures of Mao with Stalin, Ho Chi Minh, Kim Il Sung, Nicolae Ceausescu, and Edgar Snow. Copies of Mao's books in English, Russian, Mongolian, Arabic, and other languages familiar and exotic were on display. So were some personal possessions—a heavy woolen coat with fur collar, a Red Army cap, a leather briefcase, an old dressing gown, his reading glasses, and a Ping-Pong ball with two paddles. Samples of his distinctive calligraphy lay on a central table.

Mao himself was preserved under glass in an adjoining room, colorless down to his distinctive chin mole and draped in a red flag with a Communist hammer and sickle. The spectacle of Mao's body on display is a novelty for the Chinese because the government encourages cremation to save land for farming. After Mao died on September 9, 1976, his supporters wanted him displayed in state like Lenin, but they could find no undertakers who knew how to embalm the body. Eventually they sought help from Vietnam, then still a fraternal ally. The Vietnamese specialist (one popular story in Beijing claims he was a taxidermist) was dispatched, but he performed the task so poorly that the mausoleum closes periodically to repair the "incredible shrinking Mao," as Western correspondents irreverently nicknamed the corpse. Officials are not unmindful of the rumors. Gao Liang, a senior cadre of the Party's Propaganda Department, paused during a briefing for reporters on Mao's ninetieth birthday to assure us that "the remains of Comrade Mao Zedong are very well preserved."

There are no remains of Zhou Enlai or Zhu De, who were cremated. So was Liu Shaoqi, though a crematory worker claimed to have saved his ashes. But the three revolutionary heroes were given their own memorial rooms inside the mausoleum. The displays, filled with yellowing photographs and whatever else could be retrieved, seem deftly done considering that the memorabilia was assembled more than a decade after their deaths.

Here were the reading spectacles and embroidered skullcap of the intellectual Liu Shaoqi, and somewhere amid the photo captions a notation that he had been "wrongly criticized" in the Cultural Revolution—although there was no mention that his persecutor lay in the sarcophagus next door. Another room had Zhou Enlai's blue woolen jacket, binoculars, and dispatch case from his guerrilla years, a red woolen blanket that kept him warm through the winter of 1932, and a row of sharpened pencils that he supposedly used. Beyond the next door was Zhu De's bemedaled marshal's uniform, his field glasses and Mauser pistol, and a tattered battle flag that stressed his commander's role in the Chinese civil war. Again, there was no mention that the grand old warrior who forged the ragtag Communist guerrillas into a triumphant fighting machine was vilified during the Cultural Revolution for cultivating orchids in his retirement.

Liu Shaoqi, Zhou Enlai, and Zhu De merited this beatification, but the effect on a visitor was to dilute the legend of Mao Zedong, just as his teachings were reduced to the Party's "historical experience and collective wisdom." This hallowed ground had become a bus stop for tourists, complete with souvenir kiosk, and before leaving Chairman Mao, I bought a flimsy desk thermometer and a box of wooden chopsticks stamped with the Chinese characters for "Mao Zedong Memorial Hall." The thermometer broke, but our family uses the sturdy chopsticks when we order takeout Chinese food.

By comparison, my earlier visit to the mausoleum of Vladimir Ilyich Lenin in Moscow seemed like a descent into the crypt of the Church of the Holy Sepulchre in Jerusalem. On winter days, I would watch hundreds of Russians file off their buses and queue for hours in the snow, sleet, and wind of Red Square to glimpse the relic of the founder of the world's first Communist state. The slogans on countless Soviet billboards—"Lenin lived, Lenin is living, Lenin shall live"—proclaimed his resurrection.

I made my pilgrimage on a warmer day in June, in the company of the American artist Norman Rockwell, who had come to Moscow for some magazine illustrations, and his wife, Molly. Like other Western tourists, we were allowed to jump the line, which stretched across the cobblestones to the GUM department store on the far side of Red Square. Somber young soldiers wearing the blue epaulets and brass Cyrillic initials of the KGB's élite troops guarded the tomb entrance. We were paired up and enjoined from even whispering as we descended the stairs into the air-conditioned crypt. The coolness seemed refreshing after the sultry heat outside, but we were given little time to enjoy it.

The visitors filed around the sarcophagus, in which the Messiah of Communism lay wearing a dark suit with a red necktie. Victor Serge, a Russian contemporary of Lenin, wrote that "his blue eyes often twinkle with mischief . . . . He laughs freely; he looks gay and even tempered."[10] Death had taken away his spontaneity, and here Lenin looked as mortal as the rest of us.

The interior lighting of the crypt was subdued and the crowd so reverent that I felt the momentary urge to cross myself. But we were given no time to linger. The guards, stern as monks, hurried us through the chamber and out through another flight of stairs. Only back in the bright sunlight of Red Square were we free to speak.

"What did you think?" I asked the Rockwells, relieved to break the heavy silence.

A sly grin crossed Norman Rockwell's face. "Wax," he announced.

Marxism has survived, however tattered, as the fig leaf with which the Soviet Union and China cover a spiritual nakedness. They have nothing with which to replace Marxism beyond the uncomfortable alternatives of religion, nationalism, and consumerism. In 1988, *Pravda* published a thoughtful letter by a Party member of sixteen years' standing named Selivanov, who lamented that the Soviet Union had few heroes left. "This has a particularly negative influence on young people, who have the most need for positive heroes," Selivanov wrote. "So far, judging by the brand labels on clothes and shoes worn by young people, the sports equipment they buy and television programs they view, the only heroes available to them are Western heroes and Western films."[11]

Heroes pose no small problem for a monolithic party that seeks to lead and inspire through example, for the real idealists like Moscow's original Bolsheviks and Beijing's Long Marchers have pretty much faded away. When I was driving around Moscow one afternoon in late 1977, I picked up a pair of Russian students hitchhiking and our discussion turned to the subject of heroes. They revered the late John F. Kennedy, they said, but none of their own politicians. "Then whom do you admire in your country?" I asked. "Only Vysotsky," one of them replied. He meant Vladimir Vysotsky, a ruggedly handsome actor and folksinger with a devoted following among Soviet youth. The student said they admired Vysotsky for not compromising on his honesty, least of all in his songs. I asked them to name another Soviet hero, but they said they couldn't think of one, not even among their cosmonauts. They were right about Vysotsky, for after he died on July 25, 1980, at the age of forty-two, thousands of unanticipated mourners turned his simple funeral into a near riot. The Soviet authorities, which had allowed only five of his songs to be recorded, moved to co-opt Vysotsky posthumously and issued his records in the thousands. Vysotsky's widow, the French actress Marina Vlady, observed that he was not treated so decently when he was alive. A decade later, I asked some Russian teenagers the same question: their hero was invariably Mikhail Gorbachev.

The Chinese I knew initially admired Deng for his boldness, but they did not worship him as many had Chairman Mao. Some intellectuals blamed Deng for having led the Anti-Rightist Campaign in 1957 that punished educated Chinese who had taken Mao at his word to "let a hundred flowers bloom, a thousand schools of thought contend." Deng's subsequent repression of the democracy movement would not have surprised them, as it did so many Westerners. "I believe that no liberalization of any kind should exist," Deng Xiaoping told a Central Committee meeting in 1987, two years before he sent battle tanks to crush the students demonstrating in Tiananmen Square.

One of the criteria for socialist heroism is that it conform to the Party's changing needs, which means that the most reliable heroes are dead ones. During my assignment in China, the authorities tried to make a hero out of Zhang Hua, a twenty-four-year-old medical student who had jumped into a nightsoil pit to save an elderly peasant overcome by the fumes. The pits are filled with human and animal excrement, commonly used to fertilize crops and sometimes to produce some methane gas for cooking. Zhang fainted from the methane fumes too, and died after a passing dairy worker pulled him out.

Zhang Hua's death followed the classic Maoist scenario of a citizen serving the people at the cost of his life, but it touched off a heated exchange of letters in the Chinese press. The argument raged over whether the life of a potential young doctor was worth that of an ignorant old peasant. One university student likened Zhang's sacrifice to bartering gold for a stone. Another asked whether China's youth should really aspire to die in a pit full of shit. A reader retorted that peasants like the old man, by dint of their sweat, provided money for the state to educate future doctors.

Nobody seemed to give much thought to Wang Baoan, the dairy worker who had wrestled the unconscious Zhang Hua out of the pit. He took the same risks but the government did not make him a national hero. A Chinese friend in Beijing explained that survivors, because of their human frailties, were less useful to the ideology.

Nonetheless, Party ideologists held up as another role model a sunny young woman named Zhang Haidi, who was paralyzed from the waist down but nonetheless led a busy life from her wheelchair. Disabled young people elsewhere have done no less, but the Party was proprietary in its insistence that Zhang's pluck resulted from her Communist convictions. When a Japanese film released in China portrayed a similarly crippled heroine who overcame her handicap, the *Yangcheng Evening News* (*Yangcheng Wanbao*) in Canton compared the heroine (named Dianzi in Chinese) to Zhang Haidi and was promptly rebuked by the *China Youth Newspaper* (*Zhongguo Qingnian Bao*) for not distinguishing between mere courage and the valor inspired by Marxism-Leninism–Mao Zedong Thought.

The Chinese press dredged up other heroes as worthy of emulation. There was Zhou Yongli, a Manchurian steelworker who moved his bedroll and toothbrush to the foundry and fulfilled his production quotas for the next nine years, but nobody I knew wanted to be like him. There was Yu Shuzhen, a forty-six-year-old mezzo-soprano in Tianjin, who voluntarily relinquished her opera roles to a much younger woman, though people thought her gesture shortsighted. Tu Yuyun, a worker at a Suzhou silk factory, handed over an inheritance worth thousands of dollars to the state, whereupon co-workers ridiculed her as stupid or conniving. Tu tearfully told the *Workers' Daily* newspaper she didn't expect her generosity to foster so much antagonism.

I suppose my favorite socialist hero was a worker in Shanghai, Chen Yanfei, because she sounded more like the rest of us. Chen was five months pregnant when she dove into fetid Suzhou Creek to save a woman who had tried to drown herself. After Chen swam back to shore, she found her handbag had been stolen. And then she caught a cold.

There remain defenders of Mao and Stalin in China and the Soviet Union who wax nostalgic for the familiar old verities, but they are too seasoned in the guerrilla war of ideology to mount a frontal counterattack on the reformers. Their campaign of subversion has been waged allegorically in the official press and with a subtlety lost on anyone unaccustomed to reading between the lines. Reporters are hard-pressed to identify most opponents of reform until they declare themselves, as in China's crackdown on democratic aspirations in 1989. This habit is hardly new. Chairman Mao launched his Cultural Revolution after Wu Han, a playwright and deputy mayor of Beijing, dramatized an obscure Ming Dynasty tale in 1965 about an upright official unfairly sacked by a megalomaniacal ruler. Mao realized that the play, *Hai Jui Dismissed from Office*, was a veiled attack on himself for firing Peng Dehuai, a respected old Red Army marshal, and unleashed his minions on Wu Han.

When I was in China in 1983, Bai Hua, an army playwright who had been criticized for his film script *Unrequited Love*, about a returning overseas Chinese hounded to death by radicals, rebounded with a play called *The Shining Spear of the King of Wu and the Sword of the King of Yueh*. This allegory about the corruption of an imperial ruler 2,500 years ago caught on because the Chinese accepted that the tyrant was really the late Chairman Mao. On my visit to Moscow five years later, a theater on downtown Gorky Street had dramatized *Heart of a Dog*, Mikhail Bulgakov's long-suppressed novel, in which a stray mongrel becomes a loutish Soviet commissar after being implanted with the pituitary gland of an executed hoodlum. The satirical play became popular with Moscow theatergoers, who recognized in it the arrogance of unlettered Soviet officials.

The Chinese actor Ying Ruocheng told me that he hoped creativity in the arts would move beyond what he called this "literature of conspiracy and historiography of insinuation." The latter survived in the official press, where an omitted name or sentence remained more significant than everything else that appeared, even under the unprecedented proliferation of information called *glasnost* in the Soviet Union.

One October afternoon in Beijing, a Hungarian journalist telephoned to alert me to an article that he had read in the latest issue of the Shanghai newspaper *Liberation Daily* (*Jiefang Ribao*). I wasn't sure what the fuss was about. The article in Shanghai's Party organ seemed to be discussing courtesy, the theme of a civic campaign that month. Under Mao, crude manners had been elevated to a virtue, and Deng wanted Chinese to behave a little more politely. But as my Hungarian friend pointed out one seemingly innocuous passage after another, it became apparent that the article, which was reprinted from the *Liberation Army Daily* (*Jiefangjun Ribao*), the official armed-forces newspaper, was nothing less than an attack by hard-liners on Deng Xiaoping's reforms.[12]

The article, by Zhao Yiya, an army propagandist, made a Maoist differentiation between what was proletarian and bourgeois in China's "spiritual civilization." "Take courtesy, for example," Zhao wrote. "Ours is based on equality and fraternity. Their 'courtesy,' however, is merely a 'veil' that covers their scrambling for fame and profit and jockeying for position." The article went on to complain about "the laxity and weakness of the leadership over the ideological front" and suggest that Deng's open-door policy was letting in subversive Western values and breaking down ideological standards. This subject, no matter how elliptically written, could not have been addressed in a Party newspaper without the support of higher-ups unhappy about efforts to reacquaint China with the outside world.

Deng Xiaoping reacted fast and Shanghai's *Liberation Daily* later retracted its article for having been "a grave political and organizational error" that perpetuated "severe theoretical and ideological mistakes."[13] Courtesy could not be dismissed as bourgeois, the newspaper now realized, because "courtesy is a method through which people communicate with each other . . . and has certain general characteristics in all societies." The retraction acknowledged that Zhao Yiya's article "actually propagates a 'leftist viewpoint,' " and that its sudden appearance in two major newspapers on the same day showed that "among a small number of comrades in the Party and the army, the influence of left deviation does exist." The *Liberation Army Daily*, in turn, confessed to having spread "erroneous views without giving facts or reasons." With that, everyone seemed to let the matter drop. Significantly, the reemergence of the conservatives in 1989 was accomplished by the same public attacks on "bourgeois liberalization," the code words for Western democratic values.

In the spring of 1988, a similar drama was played out in the Soviet Union. *Soviet Russia (Sovetskaya Rossiya)*, the official government organ of the Russian Republic, published a lengthy letter from Nina Andreyeva, a high school chemistry teacher in Leningrad, despairing that the new policies of *perestroika* were pulling the Soviet Union away from its anchor of socialism. Her letter, titled "I Shall Not Give Up My Principles," defended Stalin as a leader who merited "honor and dignity" as one of "socialism's trailblazers." Miss Andreyeva complained that young Russians were suffering from "ideological confusion" and a "loss of political bearings" because socialism was being discredited under *glasnost*.[14]

Andreyeva did not explicitly attack the new leadership for its policies, as a letter to a Western newspaper would have done, but the publication of her letter frightened intellectuals whom I visited in Moscow only two months later, not least because it appeared when Gorbachev was leaving on an official visit to Yugoslavia. The poet Yevgeny Yevtushenko, for one, feared that such an article in *Soviet Russia*, which has a conservative reputation, presaged a coup d'état by hard-liners. The letter stood unrebutted for three weeks while Moscow buzzed with rumors.

Then, in early April, *Pravda* replied with an editorial labeling the Andreyeva letter a manifesto of the anti-*perestroika* forces. The Party newspaper charged that the letter lacked "a scientific approach to the whole problem" and constituted an attempt, "little by little, to gradually revise Party decisions." Gorbachev's policy of *perestroika*, *Pravda* contended, was "firmly based upon the concepts of Marxism and Leninism."[15]

Soviet Russia was compelled to retreat from its espousal of the Andreyeva letter and reprint the *Pravda* editorial. The Moscow correspondent for the Italian Communist Party newspaper *L'Unita* reported that he had read Miss Andreyeva's original letter, and that only five of its eighteen pages had appeared without changes, while key new passages were inserted. "It seems that there is someone behind Andreyeva who wants to make his political business with her hands," said the weekly *Moscow News*, an active supporter of Gorbachev. Nina Andreyeva, who does teach chemistry in Leningrad, promptly dropped from sight, though she has resurfaced since to defend her conservative views.

The prevailing assumption in Moscow was that Gorbachev's opponents printed the doctored letter to troll for broader support and failed to find it. But Russians, having seen greater enigmas under Stalin and Brezhnev, differed over whether Gorbachev had waited to see how many enemies would surface or had found more backing for the letter than he could deal with immediately. "There were three weeks of stagnation between the publication of the article in *Soviet Russia* and the reply in *Pravda*," said Vladimir Nadein, the letters editor of the government newspaper *Izvestia*, when we discussed the incident in his office. Nadein thought the interval had been "very helpful for our political life" because it frightened people into realizing what could happen if the enemies of *perestroika* triumphed. "If there were no such three weeks of stagnation, it should have been invented," Nadein quipped. In the old days, it would have been.[16]

Some Soviet and Chinese reformers, anticipating criticism for going too far or too fast, vied with conservatives in cloaking themselves in the red banner of socialism, much as American politicians in an election year love to embrace the American flag.

Zhou Yang, an ideologist of some enlightenment, touched off a furor in 1983 when he suggested at a symposium on Karl Marx that alienation, meaning the estrangement of an individual from the society around him, could exist in China. "Socialist society is undoubtedly superior to capitalist society, but this by no means says that there is no alienation in socialist society," Zhou told his audience of Chinese writers and artists. ". . . Only by admitting that there is alienation will we be able to overcome alienation." Zhou was suggesting that the writers and artists in his audience portray life more realistically. It came as no surprise that socialists might feel alienation too; it was chronic among homesick young Chinese sent to the countryside during the Cultural Revolution.

But Zhou, an adviser to the Party's Propaganda Department, had strayed beyond the parameters of permissible interpretation. The old ideological journal *Red Flag* trotted out the cliché that alienation was impossible under socialism. It took eight months to pull the inevitable *zi wo piping* or self-criticism out of Zhou Yang. In an interview with the New China News Agency that was promptly reprinted on the front page of the *Guangming Daily*, a newspaper read by intellectuals, Zhou confessed to having been imprudent in his "shortcomings and mistakes" and inattentive to "the detrimental effect of bourgeois ideas from outside." And, he groveled, "I did not pay proper attention to drawing a clear line ideologically between Marxist and bourgeois views on this question."[17] As far as I know, this got him off the hook.

Zhou Yang's climbdown was hardly unique. About the

time I left Beijing in December 1984, the *People's Daily* published an editorial about Marx that was rash enough to echo what many Party members were saying privately.

"There have been tremendous changes since his ideas were formed," the editorial said of Marx. "Some of his ideas are no longer suited to today's situation, because Marx never experienced these times, nor did Engels or Lenin. And they never came across the problems we face today. So one cannot expect the works of Marx and Lenin, written in their time, to solve today's problems."[18]

Such candor recalled the wisecrack of Hu Yaobang, the Party chief sacked in early 1987, that Marx never saw a light bulb, Engels never saw an airplane, and neither of them ever visited China. To hear the same thing from the Party's own organ must have been too much, for three days later the *People's Daily* ran a front-page correction, explaining that the sentence should have ended: ". . . to solve all of today's problems."[19]

It did not identify what problems Marxism-Leninism could still solve.

Perhaps the most reliable barometer of the climate of reform in the Soviet Union and China is their receptivity to foreigners, who are less inhibited about remarking upon such inconsistencies. After Mao died in 1976, Beijing stopped making it a crime to listen to the Voice of America (though it did expel two of its reporters after the 1989 disturbances). A decade later, Moscow ceased jamming most Western radio broadcasts. Yet the old suspicions are not sloughed off so easily, for historical Russia and China were closed societies long before the Communists seized power, and this has clouded their outlook on the world today.

The Russians and Chinese themselves rationalized their xenophobia as a reaction to Western colonial interference, notably the Allied intervention against the Bolsheviks in the Russian Civil War of 1918–20, and the Western encroachments that followed China's humiliating defeat in the Opium Wars of the 1840s. Yet centuries before these intrusions, the Russians and Chinese feared foreigners, who were often synony-mous with invaders. "I am struck by the excessive uneasiness of the Russians concerning the opinion that a foreigner might have of them . . . ," wrote the Marquis de Custine, a peripatetic nineteenth-century French nobleman, whose observations about Czarist Russia in 1839 keep being rediscovered by West-ern correspondents. "The impression that their country must make on the mind of a traveler disturbs them endlessly."[20] And Thomas Taylor Meadows, a British traveler in China in 1847, reported of the Chinese: "Their exclusion of foreigners and confinement to their own country has, by depriving them of all opportunities of making comparisons, sadly circum-scribed their ideas."

Though China and the Soviet Union have since turned to the West for grain to feed their people and technology to mod-ernize their economy, they have not abandoned the kind of mistrust that caused the Great Wall to be built. Foreign jour-nalists have become particular targets, I suspect, because we get paid to report when the emperor has stopped wearing clothes.

Sidney Rittenberg, an American who spent sixteen years in Chinese prisons during two xenophobic campaigns, attrib-uted China's fear of outsiders to the peasant mentality of those who fought its revolution. "Chairman Mao used to say that Party cadres were afraid of two things: intellectuals and for-eigners. It's a feature of peasant consciousness," Rittenberg told me, though he thought that they were trying to overcome it. Rittenberg's insight recalled an observation by Karl A. Witt-fogel, author of *Oriental Despotism*, that the Russian Bolshe-vik revolutionaries, after winning their revolution in 1917, turned anti-Western partly in reaction to the pro-Western sen-timents of their rivals for power.[21]

This traditional xenophobia was reinforced by the Com-munist tendency to lump the world into morally unequal parts—socialist and capitalist, progressive and reactionary, self-less and exploitive, good and evil. The suspicion of outsiders, which sometimes approaches paranoia, undermines the Com-munist claim to universal brotherhood, capsuled in the concluding cry of the *Communist Manifesto*: "Workers of the world, unite!"

The paradox of embracing humanity in general while distrusting individuals who come from beyond the borders was one of the first things to strike me in Moscow and Beijing. "We have friends all over the world," declared a slogan written large in Chairman Mao's gold calligraphy on a wall inside the Beijing Hotel, but ordinary Chinese were kept out lest they mix with their visiting foreign friends.[22] Indeed, I saw some guidelines promulgated by the Chinese Ministry of Education for its schools. One directed that a third grader be trained not to tag after or accept gifts from foreigners.

The foreigners-only compounds where we were billeted in Moscow and Beijing were like dormitories for international graduate students, with a notable exception. Here, armed guards at the gates would intercept and interrogate locals who wanted to see us. We got our friends inside by driving them through the gates at a brisk speed.

Our movements around Moscow were likewise confined to a twenty-five-mile radius emanating from the Kremlin. In Beijing, similar areas were posted with warning signs in Chinese, Russian, and English. The cities open to foreigners were limited, though during my tour in China more were made accessible. Such constraints on foreigners, which extended to the guarded compounds in which we were assigned to live, were not invented by the Communists. Czar Ivan IV, better known as Ivan the Terrible, had a quarter, literally called Chinatown, where foreign traders were confined in the sixteenth century. And Chinese emperors had similar enclaves for foreign merchants outside their city walls.

The twentieth century's contribution to this isolation of foreigners included police checkpoints to control automobile travel outside the open cities. On my second visit to the Soviet Union in 1967, I was permitted to drive a Volga sedan some twelve hundred miles from Leningrad to the Caucasus, virtually the length of European Russia, but I had to preplan the mileage of my trip in order to arrive at an approved Intourist hotel each evening. Otherwise, GAI, the Soviet highway police, would be alerted to search for me. Nearly a decade later, my family and I stopped to picnic in a pasture on a day's drive from Moscow to the Volga River town of Yaroslavl; we had barely unpacked the sandwiches when a police car pulled up and ordered us to get moving again. Foreigners were not permitted to stop on the Yaroslavl road, the policeman said.

From Beijing, I sometimes drove to interviews in Tianjin, a city of grimy factories about sixty miles away, and had to submit my car and personal documents to police checkpoints set up at the outskirts of both cities. On our initial trip, our first bureau translator, Wu Qianwei, turned around after one stop and asked, "Is this how your checkpoints for foreigners work in the United States?" When Jaqueline told him that we didn't have any checkpoints, he sniffed and lapsed into sullen silence as if to let us know he was not so naïve. The notion that any country would let foreigners run loose within its borders seemed to strike Wu as preposterous.

Even today, many Chinese, and Russians too, believe such segregation of foreigners is not only normal but preferable. Their own apartments are cramped and dingy compared to what they perceive are palatial American homes, or even the comparatively commodious flats inside our compounds. Their food is more monotonous and worse quality than what is lavished on the tourists. Beyond this an assumption has persisted that foreigners are happier by themselves.

In Moscow, the travel agency Intourist, which supervises virtually every aspect of a visitor's stay in the Soviet Union, phoned our office to announce that it was hosting a typical Russian New Year Eve's party for foreigners only in a nightclub of the Intourist Hotel, which was also for foreigners. Jaqueline and I had already been invited over by some Russian friends, so I declined. The voice on the other end of the phone commiserated with a sigh that I would miss a chance to learn how the Russians celebrated their favorite holiday.

After Tony Walker, my Australian journalist friend, and I arrived at Hefei, we slipped out of our hotel to lunch downtown at one of the "masses" restaurants that dishes up food cheap on tables shared among noisy customers. While we applied our chopsticks to the dishes of stringy pork, greens, and rice—even here, a separate table had been cleared for us—a stocky policeman in a white jacket scrutinized us from another table as he poked his teeth with a wooden toothpick. Hefei was a city of great starers, but he seemed so intent that I wondered if we were under surveillance. When he and his friends left, the policeman paused at our table to ask why we didn't like the food at our hotel. I explained that we wanted to try something different. He acted bewildered. Foreign friends always ate in their hotel, he said, and walked out shaking his head. In cities like Beijing, the most popular "masses" restaurants have rooms set apart, usually upstairs, for foreigners to dine by themselves.

To learn what is going on, journalists have to part the curtains drawn around them, sometimes literally. I was flying back to Beijing one afternoon, and as I waited in the spacious departure lounge of Canton's airport, the ground staff of the state airline, CAAC, began to peer through the large windows in a state of agitation. Something was amiss. Then one man in a blue jacket pointed at me. "There's a foreign guest," he shouted. Immediately, several others ran over and yanked the heavy curtains at either end of the window facing the runway. I managed a glimpse of a CAAC jetliner descending for a landing before they blocked my view. When the passengers from the jetliner filed into the lounge, I could not understand their animated Cantonese, but I found a woman who explained in standard Chinese that the flight had experienced engine problems and made an emergency landing. The first reaction of the CAAC staffers in the departure lounge was to hide the potential crash from a foreigner.

Such behavior underscores a basic difference between Western tradition and the values ingrained among the Russians and Chinese. "We proceed in broad daylight; they advance under cover: the game is one-sided," lamented the Marquis de Custine on his visit to Russia a century and a half ago, though he might have been writing about China too. "The ignorance in which they leave us blinds us; our sincerity enlightens them; we have the weakness of loquacity; they have the strength of secrecy."

This obsession with secrecy led the Soviet Union for half a century to put errors in its maps to fool foreigners (I never uncovered this fakery in Chinese maps).[23] A town in a Soviet atlas might be deliberately located on the wrong bank of a river, several hundred miles away or missing altogether. The only reliable map of Moscow I found was drawn by the U.S. Central Intelligence Agency from satellite photographs. It was so valued by the Russians that a copy hung on the wall of Moscow's automobile club. Not until 1989 did the Soviet Union start producing accurate maps. The previous distortion, explained the official press agency Tass, "was one of the manifestations of the policy of secrecy, which quite often covered up lawlessness and arbitrariness."

Much has been made of the "Potemkin villages" named for Prince Grigory Potemkin, an eighteenth-century statesman and sometime lover of Catherine II, who had façades erected in some Crimean villages to mask their poverty from the Austrian and Polish sovereigns whom Catherine accompanied on a tour in 1787. The habit persisted in Russia and China of letting foreigners see only what the authorities want them to see.

In China, I once flew to Wuhan, a major industrial city on the Yangtze River. I had no trouble spotting its notorious air pollution, which had just been the subject of a scathing article in the People's Daily. As we drove downtown from the outlying airport, smog hung like a menacing rain cloud over the city. I asked the guide who had met me how Wuhan was handling its pollution. Wuhan didn't have any pollution, he replied. I pointed out how dirty the horizon looked in front of our car. "Well, I don't see it," my guide said. After I reminded him of the article days earlier in the Communist Party's official organ, the guide lapsed into sullen silence.

In the Soviet Union as well as in China, my requests to venture outside the approved parameters for foreigners were scrutinized for some hidden agenda. I once decided to do a story about garbage. I was intrigued by some statistics in *Pravda* disclosing that each Russian city dweller discarded about 660 pounds of garbage a year, which was less than half of what New Yorkers threw away. Russians were frugal consumers and had not yet been introduced to disposable packaging. I asked to visit an experimental plant that was converting nearly a quarter of Leningrad's garbage into farm compost, fuel, and other salvageable by-products. Leningrad had become a pioneer in recycling Soviet trash and I thought such Russian ingenuity might make a positive story to offset the articles I had been writing about dissidents.

I did not anticipate the alarms that my request set off. The Leningrad city officials, convinced that I would ridicule them, grilled me at length. "Can't you find something better to write about Leningrad?" the deputy mayor asked. They grudgingly acceded to my request after I explained my project. I was driven to the dump a half-dozen miles away, where Leningrad's director of sanitation services showed me about with the sort of enthusiasm normally reserved for Soviet space triumphs. We watched as the garbage was loaded into mammoth two-hundred-foot-long rotating drums that fermented it for two days. We poked over the flaky brown compost that would be sold to hothouses to grow vegetables during the long Russian winter. But my Soviet hosts never did understand why I was preoccupied with garbage in so elegant a city, famed for its canals, monuments, and ballet.

Sometimes I found the authorities would go to the other extreme and give a visitor what they assumed he expected. When President Reagan visited China in 1984, he made a brief tour of Shanghai's suburbs. It was May Day, the hallowed Communist holiday, and those of us covering Reagan's visit doubted he would see anyone working. But the peasants were indeed diligently toiling in the fields when the President drove by. As soon as his motor cavalcade disappeared, of course, they dropped their hoes and ambled home.

James Rusk, a friend from the *Globe and Mail* of Toronto, came up with an even more startling example of this humor-the-barbarians mentality a couple of years later. Jim was cov-

ering the visit to China of Rick Hansen, a Canadian paraplegic
who was pushing himself around the world in a wheelchair.
The Chinese greeted Hansen with particular warmth because
Deng Xiaoping's son, Deng Pufang, was also left paralyzed
below the waist after Red Guards forced him out of a window
at Beijing University during the Cultural Revolution. When
Hansen arrived in Shanghai, nine or ten Chinese athletes in
wheelchairs were waiting to greet him at a local stadium. After
Hansen had left, Jim learned from a Canadian diplomat, "the
purported wheelchair athletes got up, folded their chairs, and
walked away."

It was not just a matter of official duplicity. It also revealed
the extent of separateness ingrained in most Russians and
Chinese, whose lives remain unviolated by the foreigners they
watch come and go. At first, I objected to being treated as an
alien, but as I learned to work around the segregation, riding
the subway in Moscow or a bicycle in Beijing, it no longer
struck me as malicious and occasionally I took it as a com-
pliment.

In late 1984, I journeyed out to the Ningxia-Hui Autonomous Region, an arid slice of northwestern China normally
closed to foreigners because of its extreme poverty. I traveled
by minibus south to Tongxin County, which found a fleeting
place in history as a rest stop for the Red Army during its Long
March, the epic Communist trek that the American writer
Edgar Snow presented in his classic book *Red Star Over China*.

The county magistrate, Su Hongyou, invited me to lunch
and produced a delicious banquet that I feared Tongxin could
not afford, for its per capita cash income was hardly more than
$30 a year. Assuming I would not have come so far if the
authorities hadn't sanctioned it, Su spoke about the local problems without the polite equivocation of Beijing's bureaucrats,
and his blunt concern for the local people touched me.

Su leaned across with his chopsticks to find me another
piece of crispy chicken from the platter and remarked almost
as an afterthought, "You know, you are the second American
correspondent to visit us." This upset me. I had secretly
planned my trip to this remote corner of China and assumed

that none of my colleagues in Beijing knew. As Su talked on
I hardly listened, obsessed with figuring out who had scooped
me. When the meal was over, I could not contain my curiosity.
I asked the magistrate with as much indifference as I could
muster who the other correspondent was. He replied ingen-
uously: "Edgar Snow was here in 1936."

2

WHAT WAS THE SUBJECT OF YOUR SILENCE? LOSING CONTROL IN A TOTALITARIAN STATE

▬ ▬ ▬ ▬ ▬ ▬ ▬ ▬ ▬ ▬ ▬ ▬ ▬ ▬ ▬

There is no getting around the
fact that no socialist state in the
post–World War Two era has
been successful, and neither has
our own socialist experiment of
thirty-odd years.

—FANG LIZHI
Chinese dissident, 1986[1]

Nearly seventy years of Soviet
history, filled with horrible and
revolting events against the background of entirely inappropriate
official cheerfulness, give me reason to doubt the ability of the
Communist Party of the Soviet
Union to lead the country on its
own.

—ANATOLY ZAVERNYAYEV
Soviet dissident, 1987[2]

WHEN VENIAMIN LEVICH, a corresponding member
of the Soviet Academy of Sciences, was being punished for
applying to emigrate to Israel, I used to drop into his second-
floor apartment on Lenin Prospect for no other reason than
that he and his wife, Tanya, were one of the most congenial
couples I knew in Moscow. After a few months, I didn't bother
to keep my visits a secret. A nosy old woman, perched on a

hard chair just inside the building's entrance, logged my arrivals and departures, probably augmenting her meager pension
with the pittance paid her for informing on Levich and his
acquaintances. We assumed that Levich's flat was thoroughly
wiretapped by the Committee for State Security, or KGB.
Whenever our conversation took a delicate turn, Levich
pointed toward the ceiling, a grin crossed his cherubic face,
and he pulled from the clutter of his desk an indispensable toy
donated by some earlier visitor. It was a "magic slate," a piece
of bright red American cardboard decorated with dancing rab-
bits and ducklings, with a kind of plastic sheet that could be
written upon with a blunt instrument. When you were finished, you pulled up the plastic sheet and your writing vanished. These Western imports were put to serious use in just
about every dissident's flat in Moscow.

I was not the only one to visit Levich. Many Western
scientists who came to Moscow found their way to Levich's
apartment, not just because he had been one of the Soviet
Union's pioneers in magneto-hydrodynamics but also because
his official nonexistence had won the sympathy of the Western
scientific community. Most of his colleagues at the Soviet
Academy of Sciences refused to have anything to do with him
for fear of damaging their own careers, so this gracious physical
chemist relied on the kindness of foreigners to tell him what
was happening in science since he had been fired from his
institute and forbidden to travel abroad.

One evening, a visiting French physicist dropped by the
apartment, and the two men plunged into a discussion of
magneto-hydrodynamics. Levich did not want to have the formal charge of spilling state secrets added to his troubles, so
the two scientists scribbled on the little cardboard slate for
nearly an hour as they compared their theories. The next day,
two husky plainclothesmen intercepted Levich on the street
and drove him down to the KGB's office at Kuznetsky Most
for a chat. The interrogator told Levich that the KGB knew
about his French visitor. Then he leaned across his desk.

"Tell us, Comrade Levich," the interrogator prompted.
"What was the subject of your silence?"

Levich laughed uproariously when he told me the story at a Russian restaurant in New York after he had gained his freedom. I laughed too but I found the question more significant than ludicrous, because Professor Levich and his magic slate had reduced the dreaded secret police to having to ask it.

Any Western visitor to the Soviet Union and China comes forewarned about the inherently totalitarian nature of modern Communism. When the ideology is no longer novel enough to mesmerize believers and disenchantment sets in, the Party protects its vanguard role by resorting to what it does best: control rather than inspire.

The Czech writer Milan Kundera explained it this way to Philip Roth: "Totalitarianism is not only hell, but also the dream of paradise—the age-old dream of a world where everybody would live in harmony, united by a single common will and faith, without secrets from one another . . . . Once the dream of paradise starts to turn into reality, however, here and there people begin to crop up who stand in its way, and so the rulers of paradise must build a little gulag on the side of Eden. In the course of time this gulag grows ever bigger and more perfect, while the adjoining paradise gets ever smaller and poorer."[3]

But once the control founders or is relaxed, as has happened in the Soviet Union and China, the centrifugal reaction can give rise to the kind of chaos unleashed by the revival of ethnic nationalism in the Soviet Union from the Baltics to the Caucasus. It has become no less apparent in the tensions between the state and the individual that have frustrated Moscow's attempts to curb alcohol abuse and Beijing's drive to enforce birth control, both of which I will deal with more fully.

In 1948, when Stalin's terror had not yet subsided and Mao's terror had not yet begun in China, George Orwell published *1984*, his vivid novel about totalitarianism.[4] When 1984 arrived and I was living in Beijing, the spartan Maoist garrison state had given way to a Dengist society of bustling farmers' markets, joint industrial ventures with Western companies, marriage introduction bureaus and muscle-building contests.

In Moscow, the Kremlin's gray old men—Leonid Brezhnev, Yuri Andropov, Mikhail Suslov, and later Konstantin Chernenko—were dropping dead one after another ("Have you a pass, comrade?" a Russian joke had the KGB guard demanding of a mourner at Chernenko's funeral. "I have a season pass, comrade," was the retort) as the Soviet Union slouched toward the more enlightened rule of the younger Mikhail Gorbachev.

This is not to say that Orwell got it wrong. The Soviet Union and China once offered ample justification for the futuristic pessimism of *1984*. The double-think mentality was evident in Lenin's assertion in 1920 that "we destroy in order to build better." The mindless worship of Orwell's Big Brother thrived in the cults of personality surrounding Stalin and Mao. Modern China's best-known hymn proclaimed:

> The East Is Red. The sun has emerged.
> China has brought forth a Mao Zedong.

Everyone seemed to have been caught up in the nightmare. In Beijing, I talked one evening with a high school teacher of considerable sophistication about the Maoist persecution of educated Chinese back in the Cultural Revolution. My acquaintance confessed that he had been a Red Guard himself and that his contingent accused their own teacher at school of lagging behind the bold pace of Chinese Communism. "So then what happened?" I asked. My acquaintance gave a brittle laugh. "Oh, we nailed his feet to the floor," he said, as if he were talking about some adolescent prank.

Roy Medvedev told a story about Vyacheslav Molotov, Stalin's Foreign Minister. Molotov attended a Politburo meeting that voted to arrest his wife, Polina Zhemchuzhina, whom the xenophobic Stalin distrusted because she was Jewish and had a brother living in Connecticut. According to Medvedev, Molotov abstained from voting, but he did nothing to prevent the Politburo from sending his wife to prison and possible death. Years later, she was sent home rehabilitated and Molotov joyfully embraced her. A visitor later asked how he could have let them jail the woman he loved. "Because I am a member of the Politburo and I must obey Party discipline," Molotov reportedly replied.[5]

Blind obedience makes a certain urgent sense in a new state, whose rulers want to accomplish everything as quickly as possible. Lenin believed that the masses could not be trusted to act in their own interest. In his essay "What Is to Be Done?" he wrote that "there must be a hard core of professional revolutionaries leading the way and keeping the workers under tutelage." Without ruthless control, Stalin could not have industrialized the Soviet Union in the 1930s, and Mao could not have brought hundreds of millions of peasants to heel in the 1950s. For all the human pain they inflicted, the intent of the early Bolsheviks and Maoists was not necessarily malicious.

Yet totalitarianism has gone out of fashion, if one excepts the last two countries that still believe in Communism—Albania and North Korea. It may have been the futility of an ideology that numbed the mind while failing to fill the stomach, or the burgeoning of a state bureaucracy that was supposed to have withered away, or the disintegration of the international Communist movement, which left Moscow and Beijing looking a little irrelevant. It may have been the replacement of true believers and martyrs with government pencil pushers and Party straphangers or maybe the sheer exhaustion of trying to march the reluctant masses into a future that the Leninist vanguard realized wouldn't work.

The changes preceded Deng's and Gorbachev's decisions to temper arbitrary political and economic theories with a little common sense. Years before the people's communes were formally dismantled in China, peasants in the backcountry of Anhui province took advantage of the chaos of the Cultural Revolution to divide up the land and go back to household farming. And more than a decade before the Soviet press was emboldened by Gorbachev to discuss which way the Soviet Union should go and how far, I read *samizdat* essays, painstakingly typed and surreptitiously circulated on onionskin paper, by three dissident thinkers—Aleksandr Solzhenitsyn,

Andrei Sakharov, and Roy Medvedev—who vigorously debated its direction. They raised the first voices of *perestroika*.

The cruelty diminished partly because of Western revulsion but more likely because it didn't seem that necessary. Stalin had his rivals tried and shot. Mao dispatched China's President, Liu Shaoqi, into solitary confinement in Kaifeng. Such was the fear Mao inspired that when Liu was dying of illness in 1969 his captors did not fetch a doctor for fear that they might be punished; it was safer to do nothing. And such was the terror of Stalin that when he himself died in 1953 his servants held off checking his bedroom for hours for fear of disturbing his rest.

Soviet and Chinese leaders learned to deal less ruthlessly with the losers in subsequent power struggles, no doubt mindful that they could find themselves in the same predicament. Nikita Khrushchev sent Georgi Malenkov, Stalin's heir, off to run an obscure hydroelectric station in Soviet Central Asia. Khrushchev in 1964 and Hua Guofeng, Deng's predecessor, in 1987 were merely shoved by their enemies into premature retirement, as was Zhao Ziyang in 1989. Mao's widow Jiang Qing was sentenced to death in 1980, but two years later her sentence was commuted to life imprisonment, though she displayed no contrition.

Dissidents who challenge the system may go to labor camps or mental asylums but not to the firing squad. And secret police may have to justify their arbitrary conduct. The Soviet Union and China have mellowed, and not everyone approves of this reordering of society. An elderly Russian agreed that people suffered in the disciplined years under Stalin, but, she said, they also had something to believe in. Now Russians had grown selfish and promiscuous, she lamented, because "there is neither faith nor fear." The moral vacuum she alluded to contributed to the resurgence of religion discussed later in this book.

In the old days, ordinary citizens watched themselves and each other for fear of being denounced to the secret police. The most notorious informer in Stalin's Russia was Pavlik Morozov, who at thirteen turned in his own father as a class enemy for conspiring to hold back some grain from the state. The other peasants lynched him and little Pavlik was pronounced a model for other children to emulate. The last time I was in Moscow, a statue of Pavlik was still standing atop a ten-foot pedestal in Moscow's Children's Park. But the Russians I knew loathed him for having undermined the family as a haven of trust and his demythification seemed inevitable, even before the magazine *Youth* (*Yunost*) declared him a symbol "of legalized and romanticized treachery" in 1988. Now the Soviet government says it no longer pays attention to anonymous denunciations.

Though the Chinese resumed worrying about what the neighbors think as a result of Beijing's repression of liberal dissent, Russians at this writing were more willing to speak their mind. The surveillance of the KGB became a subject of cautious amusement in Moscow. One joke I heard had a Muscovite discovering that his pet parrot had flown the cage and promptly calling the KGB. "I want to report that my parrot has been stolen," the owner declared, "and I want to tell you that I do not share his opinions."

Letting go poses a real dilemma for the Party apparatus. A Moscow scientist told me once what it took for him to visit a university in the West. He needed a formal invitation. He had to submit four copies, ostensibly to his superior but actually for the KGB, if the invitation was in Russian. If it was in English, he had to include eight copies in Russian translation, with an affidavit from a recognized linguistics scholar attesting that the translation was accurate. The director of his institute had to sign all copies before forwarding them to the authorities for a decision. The director, he added, needed higher permission to make more than five photocopies of any document.

"They like to control the information. They like to control everything," agreed Efrem Yankelevich, a computer specialist and Yelena Bonner Sakharov's son-in-law. "The ideal picture of the world they have in mind is that nothing is happening without their consent."

The sentinels of totalitarianism did not anticipate the technological advances of the photocopier, videocassette recorder, computer, and satellite disc. When nationalist demonstrations swept Armenia in 1988, the Soviet authorities sealed off the republic to foreign travelers. Dissidents taped what happened with small video cameras and smuggled the footage to Western television networks to air on prime-time news programs. During the flurry of pro-democracy protests in Beijing in 1989, Chinese students living overseas used fax machines to telephone in Western newspaper reports to their friends showing how the protests were playing abroad.

Yevgeny Levich, an astrophysicist who is Veniamin Levich's son, believed the headaches for the Kremlin had just begun. "The Soviet authorities need computers in order to modernize," he told me. "But computers threaten Communist control, because they depend on a free exchange of information, which is incompatible with Soviet secrecy."

The Soviet Union stopped jamming most foreign radio broadcasts in May 1987 not out of altruism but because so many Russians were finding ways to tune in, and the Soviet jamming cost more than what Western countries spent on the actual broadcasts. Friends told me how they cut back the grinding static by sticking their radio in a common kitchen pot. A respected commentator at *Pravda* confided to me that he listened to the Voice of America while he shaved to learn what was happening in the world. A newspaper editor in Kaluga, a town south of Moscow, over lunch defended the superiority of socialism by taunting me with the details of the Watergate scandal. I had never seen the Soviet press report some things he told me and asked him how he knew. After a pause, the editor admitted sheepishly, "I listen to the Voice of America."

This was not unusual, especially among educated Soviet citizens. A poll by the Soviet Academy of Social Sciences in the western Ukraine in 1983 showed that, despite jamming, nearly 20 percent of people there regularly followed the Voice of America and West Germany's Deutsche Welle. The press agency Tass reported the number of VOA listeners declined to 10 percent in 1987 once the Soviet media grew more candid under Gorbachev, a point the VOA contested. China stopped jamming the Voice of America and the British Broadcasting Corporation because letting Chinese listen to the English-language programs was deemed a good way to improve their English, which would help the country's modernization. Listenership was so widespread that after the 1989 suppression of dissent the Chinese authorities, fearful of having the truth heard, resumed selective jamming.

It amused me to hear American right-wingers inveigh against the infiltration of Communist values into the United States, when the traffic has run so conspicuously in the other direction. The West has subverted Communist society, not deliberately with political ideas but quite accidentally with rock music, videotapes, fast food, blue jeans, and tee-shirts emblazoned with nonsensical slogans. The hunger for Western-style goods among those who have known only shortages is so great that when I went out cross-country skiing in Moscow's Lenin Hills one winter evening, a Russian skier overtook me to plead that I sell him my Finnish skis and poles on the spot, ignoring my insistence that I needed them to get back to my car. Siberian teenagers tried to buy my Levi's off me in the street. At a small club in Riga's suburbs, I heard a rock guitarist perform "Have You Ever Seen the Rain?" as masterfully as Creedence Clearwater Revival. I went up later to congratulate the Latvian singer on his excellent English, only to discover that he didn't speak a word of it. He had painstakingly memorized the lyrics from a bootlegged cassette.

Inevitably, this fascination with the West spilled over into politics. On a long train trip from Moscow to Novosibirsk, I struck up a conversation with three amiable middle-aged men in baggy blue track suits who seemed intrigued to meet an American journalist. On the last night of our journey, they invited me into their compartment to share some watery Russian beer and *vobla*, a kind of small fish dried to a crisp and munched like pretzels, and we stayed up most of the night talking. They plied me with questions about the United States and what Americans really thought and felt, never mind what their own press reported. When they learned that I knew Andrei Sakharov, they begged me to tell them about him. Was he a renegade or did his ideas make sense? When we pulled into Novosibirsk the next afternoon, I saw my three beer-drinking buddies emerge from their compartment in the brown dress uniforms of Soviet Army colonels.

It was not hard to fall into such discussions on trains or airplanes, where Soviet citizens felt they had a pretext to talk. Their first questions usually involved how much I earned, how much my clothes cost, and what kind of car I owned. I never had such conversations with Chinese travelers, whether because my Chinese was not as good or because they were too wary. But it was impossible to stroll along the waterfront Bund in Shanghai without being approached by some amiable youths practicing their English and asking how to get visas to visit the United States.

Westerners tend to think of the Soviet and Chinese political systems as monolithic. And by Western standards they are, with no democratic checks and balances. Yet the directives announced so confidently in Moscow and Beijing may be given only lip service or ignored altogether in the provinces, particularly if they threaten to undercut the authority of regional Party warlords. The reforms devised at the top have to filter down through layers of bureaucracy as dense as hard-packed sand, and that can take a long time.

Russia and China share a proverb, "Heaven is high and the emperor (or czar) is far away."[6] I never failed to be surprised by the independence I encountered outside their capitals. Sometimes I carefully arranged appointments in advance through the Chinese Foreign Ministry, only to find local officials brushing aside Beijing's instructions and refusing to cooperate once I arrived. And occasionally, with the connivance of local authorities who hoped that publicity might bring a little prosperity, I slipped into backwater areas nominally closed to foreigners. The Cantonese in southern China took pride in flouting the ideological constraints of Beijing and looked to Hong Kong for inspiration. But in Xian, a city in northern China, I heard "The East Is Red" playing on the street loudspeakers years after Deng Xiaoping removed Chairman Mao from his pedestal.

For all their denunciations of colonialism, the Soviet Union and China are the world's surviving colonial empires. Their "great power chauvinism," as Lenin would call it, was less obvious because it expanded overland and not overseas. Unlike much smaller Britain, their empires were vast enough to annex neighbors less conspicuously, much as the United States took its southwestern territories from Mexico. As reform loosened the grip of the Soviet and Chinese governments, the dormant forces of nationalism awakened, creating nightmares for Gorbachev in the Caucasian and Baltic republics, and for Deng in more remote Tibet.

With Russians eventually comprising only half of the Soviet population, the Communist Party and the Russian language constituted the glue that held the unwieldy Soviet empire together; when one failed, the other was irrelevant for placating antagonistic neighbors like the Armenians and Azerbaijanis. Visiting the polyglot republics on the Soviet Union's periphery, I was struck by the absence of the kind of fondness for Russian that one finds for French or English in the former colonies of Africa. The Kremlin also miscalculated in proclaiming a constitutional right for its ethnic republics to secede, though no procedure was spelled out for doing so, thereby leaving in place a legal justification for declarations of independence by Lithuania and other takers.

In China, the Uighurs who populated Xinjiang province stubbornly kept their watches set to an informal local time, ignoring government instructions that the entire country, which should logically span at least four time zones, be run on Beijing's time. The Party slogans I read daubed on walls in Urumqi warning inhabitants against both "petty chauvinism" by the Chinese Asian minorities and "great Han chauvinism" by the Chinese confirmed their fragile coexistence, which erupted periodically in ethnic riots that were promptly crushed by the People's Liberation Army.

Nationalistic self-interest was always there, hidden beneath a veneer of Communist fraternalism that finally cracked. "Scratch many a communist and you will find a Great Russian chauvinist," Lenin told a Party Congress more than seven decades ago.[7] Though Russians run the Soviet Union, some of my Russian acquaintances complained that they had been denied their own academy of science and other trappings of ethnicity granted the outlying republics. The sprawling Russian Federation and its capital, Moscow, had been preempted by the larger Soviet bureaucracy, they said. And they objected violently to being called Soviet. "The West talks about Soviet ballet and Russian tanks, when it should be Russian ballet and Soviet tanks," an intellectual in Moscow complained.

This Russian chauvinism, which Stalin in his essay on Marxism and the National Question called three quarters of the Soviet Union's nationalities problem, manifests an alarming intolerance that has ominous ramifications for whatever society fills the vacuum left by the moribund Communist system. The anti-Semitism of the Russian nationalist movement Pamyat (Memory) has been reported, but its racism is more extreme. An artist active in Pamyat would grip my shoulder as he rambled on emotionally about the *belaya raza* or white race, by which he meant the Russians, whom he saw threatened with extinction by hordes of Uzbeks, Kazakhs, and other non-Slavic minorities, not to mention the Jews. Our white skin ordained Russians and Americans to be natural allies, he insisted, brushing aside my demurrals.

As my spoken Russian grew more fluent, I found myself patronized in Moscow by Russians who mistook me for Latvian and given misdirections in Riga by Latvians who assumed I was Russian. I met Russians who had lived fifteen years in Tallinn without learning a few words of Estonian. And almost everywhere, the Soviet Union's minorities were quietly marching to tunes of their own choice, even as they professed to keep step with their Russian elder brothers. On my first visit to Armenia in 1974, I met some students at a concert in Yerevan and they insisted on accompanying me back to my hotel. As we walked through Lenin Square at midnight, I heard folk music blaring from loudspeakers atop the pink tufa building that housed Party headquarters. "Your singer sounds very much like our Bob Dylan," I remarked politely. The students laughed. "That *is* Bob Dylan," one said.

A few years ago, Ding Ling, the venerable widow of Prime Minister Zhou Enlai, expressed her distress over the flippancy with which she heard some young Chinese greet the singing of a patriotic hymn, "Without the Communist Party, There Would Be No New China." Instead of joining in, she reported, they snickered or cracked jokes. The official press fussed over her complaint and agreed that the ideological ardor of Chinese youth was flagging.

I sympathized with both Ding Ling and the young people she criticized. The old-timers remembered how grim life was before the Communists took over. The youngsters, born too late to experience such conditions, measured their lives not by the yardstick of history but of geography, with what they knew of the richer world beyond China. This generation gap lay at the core of the Party's declining moral authority, and it elicited contradictory responses to the lyrics by Huo Xing, which stirred the souls of aging revolutionaries but not their grandchildren:

> Without the Communist Party there would be no New China.
> Without the Communist Party there would be no New China.
> The Communist Party toils for the nation.
> The Communist Party devotes itself wholeheartedly to saving
>   China.
> It pointed out to the people the way to Liberation.
> It kept up the war of resistance against Japan for eight-odd years.
> It improved the people's livelihood.
> It established base areas behind enemy lines.
> It practiced democracy, which has many advantages.
> Without the Communist Party there would be no New China.
> Without the Communist Party there would be no New China.[8]

I heard one Chinese scholar who is now well into his thirties explain the problem like this after he came to study at Harvard University. "I believed in Communism. I went out and picked up grain on the streets. I helped coolies pull their coal carts and I visited the blind," he said. "It's the younger generations that don't believe. The generations behind us missed that part of political indoctrination. And then the poverty of the country came home. For them, the images of the feudal old society are remote, so they have a very different perspective."

But he went on to blame the Party's own incompetence for compounding the credibility gap. "The process of indoctrination has been made mechanical," he said. "It is required in schools and colleges, and even in college it is the most hated course." I knew that the propaganda had alienated most young people. An American I knew studying at a university in Beijing was taken by a Chinese friend to one mandatory political-study session, from which foreign students are normally exempted. As the lecturer droned on about some obscure detail of dialectical materialism, she said, most students seemed to be reading along dutifully. Then she noticed that tucked inside the open textbooks were novels, magazines, even the penny comics that are sold on Chinese street corners. Some students in the back passed notes and others slept. "No one's paying attention," she whispered to a Chinese friend. "Would you?" came the reply.

In 1986, the *People's Daily* conceded that the ideological courses being taught in Chinese universities and schools were tedious and unpopular: "The universal comment now is that students of higher learning feel indifferent toward Marxist theory. They have no interest. And a small number of students even show abhorrence and antagonism toward it." The mandatory lectures were allowed to fall into limbo until 1989, when the Party revived them in an effort to counter the substantial student support of the democracy protests. A law student I met at Shanghai's prestigious Fudan University estimated that no more than 10 percent of his fellow students believed in Communism. "I believe, but I'm in the minority," he volunteered.

Many young Chinese woke up when intellectuals like

Fang Lizhi and Liu Binyan began posing intelligent questions about the applicability of Marxism. For a while, it appeared that, to dredge up Chairman Mao's old adage, a hundred flowers might blossom and a thousand schools of thought contend. But the Party, worried at what would happen to its monopoly, took away Fang's Party card, stripped him of academic tenure at the University of Science and Technology in Hefei, and, after the 1989 protests, made him a wanted criminal. Liu Binyan, a popular investigative reporter, was fired from the *People's Daily*.

Another Chinese student in the United States told me that he and his friends had been excited about the new approaches that Fang and others were suggesting. They even foresaw a dynamic revival of Marxism. But, he said, "When the liberal Marxists offered their new interpretations, they were severely criticized by the Party. So today young people put all kinds of Marxism in the same trash can."

The inflexibility of ideological indoctrination, which has since been revived, was brought home one autumn afternoon in 1983 when I visited Qinghua University, a Beijing institution that has been called China's MIT. I was permitted to interview some selected students. Such was Qinghua University's reputation for ideological reliability that 94 percent of the undergraduates belonged to the Communist Youth League and another 2 percent had received their Party cards. "The students here are stable ideologically," explained an instructor named Sung, who was monitoring our meeting. "Their enthusiasm is on the rise."

I asked the students what they thought about the latest campaign being waged against "spiritual pollution," the Party's code word for unwelcome Western values and trends. An earnest young engineering student named Wang volunteered that he and his classmates were struggling resolutely against it. "All these things will never catch on here," he assured me, his spectacles and crew cut bobbing for emphasis. "Personally, I think that things like wearing long hair and dancing to disco music are not that popular even in Western countries. I think many decent people don't like long hair."

"What is wrong with long hair?" I asked him.

Wang looked at me dumbfounded. I repeated my question and pointed to a hirsute portrait of Karl Marx fortuitously hanging on the classroom wall. "Didn't Karl Marx have long hair?" I said.

Wang swiveled around to look first at Marx and then for his ideology instructor, who had slipped out of the classroom. Panic unfolded across his face. A chubby girl named Liu tried to rescue Wang. "I think different nations have their own backgrounds or traditions, so it is just a matter of tradition," she said. Her explanation seemed to end in a question mark. A heavy silence settled upon the room.

Sung, their ideology instructor, walked back in, and they all chattered too fast for me to follow. With an indulgent smile, Sung sorted it out. "Long hair is not a matter of whether it is long or short. It is a matter of whether or not we carry out a policy of hard work. In recent years, some students were rather weak-willed. Dancing itself is all right, but what we need to do is work harder." I followed the contrast between dancing and hard work, but I still couldn't see how long hair fit in, given the kind of hours that Marx spent laboring over his voluminous *Capital* when he might have been at the barbershop. But the Qinghua students nodded happily.

Perhaps they kept bolder opinions to themselves. With room at university for barely 4 percent of China's high school graduates, the students were not likely to jeopardize their élite situation with a casual visitor. What struck me first about the tragic sit-ins in Tiananmen Square in the spring of 1989 was that the student protesters had the most to lose, and those who sacrificed their privileged status to a dream about democracy would end up assigned to menial, dead-end jobs.

Deng Xiaoping's purification drives may have reassured conservatives that economic reform would not undercut the Party's control, but the confused responses from the grass-roots cadres were often farcical. When I lived in Beijing, a woman with long black hair was stopped from entering a municipal office by the doorkeeper, who pointed to an edict posted on the wall forbidding women office employees to wear long hair, makeup, or jewelry. Though she didn't work there, she had to pull her hair into a ponytail with a rubber band that he provided. When she completed her errand and was leaving the office, the doorkeeper took back the rubber band. It was all the more ludicrous because the *China Youth* newspaper had just assured its readers there was nothing wrong with fashionable hair styles and bright clothing.

Sillier salvos have been fired in the Party's offensives against "spiritual pollution" and "bourgeois liberalization." Some army commanders tore photographs of fully clothed young women out of magazines sent to their units, lest their troops be distracted by sexual fantasies. And once at the Xidan department store in Beijing, salesmen were ordered to trim back "strange hair styles" and saleswomen to remove earrings, lipstick, and eyebrow pencil. Such unhealthy artifices, the management explained, would "entice certain customers with unhealthy thoughts to tease the employees and distract them from working well."

My favorite souvenir from the ideological crusades was a lavender-jacketed booklet put out by the People's Music Press in Beijing titled *How to Distinguish Decadent Songs*. The primer warned about the "quivering rhythm" and the "unclear, loose, drunken pronunciation" peculiar to imported pop music. It described most songs from Taiwan and Hong Kong as "low and dirty" and complained that "they don't express working-class sentiments" or indicate the singer's class status. "What they sing about," the primer said, "is deformed love in a colonial or semi-colonial society."

The editors went on—in all seriousness—to catalogue Western musical perversions. Jazz, the booklet advised, "forces people to accept what is unexpected, the abnormal beat. Dancing to this kind of music is like having nervous spasms." The distinguishing features of 1950s rock and roll were "a frenzied beat, neighing-like singing and a simple melody." Rock music of the 1960s poured out "a kind of passion for the bewildering, the vague, the numb, and the impetuous." Disco music, it said, had a "rapid beat like a war drum" and gave an excuse "for the dancer to do whatever will express his feverish mood."

Chinese musical tastes had come a long way from the golden oldies on the Maoist hit parade like "Medical Teams in Tanzania" and "The Nightsoil Collectors Are Descending the Mountain." Unlike the Soviet youths I met who loved the cacophony of heavy metal and punk rock—in 1989, Western heavy-metal bands were invited to perform in Moscow—young Chinese were hardly being lured, toes tapping and fingers snapping, down the road to bourgeois perdition. They doted on saccharine tunes like "Do Re Mi" from *The Sound of Music* and the cowboy standard "Red River Valley." Their tastes got no raunchier than John Denver or The Carpenters. Still, their elders foresaw a potential for ruin in any Western tune. A student in Beijing whose younger brother asked him to borrow a tape of folksongs by Peter, Paul, and Mary from his classmates told of being scolded by their father. "Be careful of all this love, love, love," the old man admonished. "Studying is more important."

It seemed human nature that the ideological attacks on pop culture would only whet the curiosity of the masses. Li Guiying, a popular singer, used to perform a sentimental song about love in the countryside. "It wasn't a very good song, but it was attacked as spiritual pollution," Ni Yuxian told me. "So every time she performed, the audience wouldn't let her leave the stage without singing the song." The smuggled cassettes of Deng Lijun, a button-cute pop singer from Taiwan, became even more popular on the black market after her love songs were denounced as similarly tainted. And a friend on vacation in the Yangtze River city of Wuhan reported back that crowds were jamming a local theater after rumors spread that the Japanese film being shown would be removed as spiritually polluting. Instead, the film, which she found disappointing after lining up to see it, was held over for an extra month to meet the increased demand.

The counterproductivity of ideological indoctrination was described by Wang Bingzhang, a slender, intense physician from Beijing who grew up under Mao Zedong: "Ideological education began as soon as you entered school, from the age of six or seven, even from birth. The first character I learned to write was 'Mao.' The first sentence I learned to write was 'Long live Chairman Mao.' You can teach this at church because God is God. But Chairman Mao was not God," Wang said. "I think the ideological education of the Communist Party failed completely." It did for Wang, a former Young Pioneer and Red Guard, who ended up in New York publishing the dissident magazine *China Spring*.

His disillusionment set in when Mao's protégé Lin Biao was killed after failing in a plot to overthrow his patron in 1971. "We used to cheer, 'Long live Chairman Mao and good health to Vice Chairman Lin Biao,'" Wang said. "Then suddenly we were told to criticize Lin Biao."

Wang illustrated the damage of such hypocrisy with a Chinese *xiaohua*, or fable, about an old monk and his novice who lived in a temple on a steep mountainside. "The most dangerous thing in the world is a woman," the old monk warned. "Never touch her or talk to her. A woman is as dangerous as a tiger." One day, the novice hiked down the mountain to fetch water and fell with his yoke and buckets. A lovely young girl found him and solicitously bound up his injuries. So pleasant an encounter led the young novice to assume, "If a woman is like a tiger, then a tiger must be very nearly like a woman." Later on the mountain, the young monk met a tiger, and when he tried to befriend it, Wang said, the tiger attempted to eat him, and he barely escaped, to realize that the old monk was wrong.[9]

"This is just like the ideological education of the Communist Party," Wang concluded. "When we realized that the reality was different, then the faith of young people in the system was weakened. And now there is no faith in the Communist Party."

Two campaigns mounted by the Soviet Union and China in recent years that fell short of their well-intentioned goals illustrate the sort of difficulties that a Communist government has enforcing its will when it can no longer offer a consistent ideology and has stopped dominating its citizens through fear.

In May 1985, when Mikhail S. Gorbachev launched his drive on alcoholism, he declared war on a Russian tradition. He was not the first Communist leader to grapple with drunkenness. The old Bolshevik V. A. Ovseyenko, who used the pseudonym of Antonov, wrote of the bacchanal that followed the seizure of the Winter Palace in the Bolshevik Revolution in 1917: "The Preobrazhensky regiment got completely drunk while guarding the wine cellars of the Palace. . . . The Pavlovsky regiment did not withstand the temptation either. . . . Mixed picked guards were sent; they too got drunk. . . . The fire brigades got drunk. . . . The whole city was infected by this drinking madness."[10]

The Bolsheviks debated whether to keep the Czar's prohibition on alcohol that had been promulgated without great success in World War One. After Lenin died in 1924, Stalin legalized the distilling and sale of liquor as a state monopoly. Vodka, because it generated revenue, was better than "the bondage of foreign capital," Stalin argued.

The eventual consequence was widespread drunkenness. The Russians I saw tossed back their vodka not in moderation but with a vengeance. When I stayed at a Soviet hotel on Saturday night in the Brezhnev era, I inevitably watched some drunken brawl in which knuckles cracked against bone and boots thumped against ribs. A birthday party I joined at a restaurant in Kishinev ended when a guest lifted his head from a stupor to find someone nuzzling his wife. The interloper was slugged so hard that he fell over the bandstand. The police arrested the brawlers and hauled off the musicians as witnesses. A Novosti Press Agency journalist accompanying me in the Central Asian city of Tashkent excused himself one afternoon to have a quick drink with a local reporter, and returned with his front teeth knocked out. In a bar in Itkol, a Caucasian ski resort, I saw one quarrelsome drinker slam another headfirst onto the concrete floor. The other patrons checked the victim's pulse, covered his bloody head with his coat, and resumed drinking. I assumed I was eyewitness to a murder and cleared out. When I came back, the man I had taken for dead was sitting back at the bar with his assailant. They were weeping as they shared a fresh bottle of Georgian brandy.

Any occasion became a pretext for a drink. In Minsk, Jim Jackson, a fellow correspondent, and I were interviewing some veterans of the guerrilla war against Hitler. A table had been set up near their old forest hideout and the light lunch was obscured by bottles of a local 120-proof vodka flavored with buffalo grass. The interview left me hung over for three days, but I took comfort in outlasting our handler from the Belorussian Foreign Ministry, who mumbled before he slid under the table, "Whom do you report to in the FBI?"

Among Soviet males, it was considered wimpish to avoid a drinking bout. I don't like hard liquor, and my reluctance to participate was taken as an insult. On a trip through Moldavia, a Soviet republic on the Rumanian border, I stayed up late one night accommodating some collective farmers who offered platitudinous toasts with raw brandy. By the time I arrived at another collective farm the next evening I was nursing a splitting headache and sour stomach. When we sat down to dinner, one of my hosts filled the water glasses to the brim with brandy. He proposed a toast that his house not be struck by lightning. I declined as politely as I could. "You want my house to be hit by lightning?" he asked incredulously. I said I was not feeling well. The others begged me not to offend him by abstaining. "We must cement the friendship among our two peoples," one farmer whispered. "The United States of America wants my house destroyed by lightning," my host concluded morosely. He grew more antagonistic as he downed each glass. Overcome by nausea, I excused myself from the banquet. Thereafter I carried a fake certificate claiming that alcohol endangered my health. It worked, for no Soviet citizen wanted a dying foreigner on his hands.

My own experiences offer a superficial glimpse into the damage alcohol causes Soviet society. A study I found reported that drunks accounted for 73.9 percent of murders, 76.4 percent of rapes, and 90.9 percent of acts of hooliganism in the Russian

Federation, which includes European Russia and Siberia. It appeared in 1971, but I doubt the statistics improved by the time Gorbachev cracked down, for per capita consumption of vodka in the Soviet Union doubled between 1965 and 1985, and wine consumption quadrupled, according to Abel Aganbegyan, a leading economist. By 1987, over 4.5 million alcoholics were registered with the police and health authorities.

Given the extent to which drinking permeated the fabric of the nation, curtailing alcohol abuse was one of Gorbachev's more courageous decisions. His predecessors failed to do anything because liquor sales earned the state billions of rubles and soaked up excess income in a society short of consumer goods. Like Orwell's Victory Gin in *1984*, vodka had become a socially accepted escape from the surrounding drabness.

Gorbachev did not confine himself to half measures. State distilleries, breweries, and wineries were ordered to cut their production and bottle more nonalcoholic beverages. Many liquor stores shut down, while others had to curtail their hours. Customers were limited to two bottles a visit. Restaurants were forbidden to serve liquor at lunch, and official receptions were reduced to offering orange drink and Borzomi mineral water. Russians took to referring to their Party's General Secretary in a pun as "Mineral Secretary" Gorbachev.

On the surface, it seemed to work. The government reported that the annual consumption of alcoholic beverages in 1986 plummeted from 8.4 to 4.4 liters a person. "Losses of working time due to absenteeism have dropped," *Pravda* said in June 1987. "The number of individuals taken to medical sobering-up stations has decreased by one-third, and the number of crimes committed by intoxicated persons has fallen by 28 percent." Injuries from traffic accidents dropped. For the first time in two decades, the average life expectancy of Russians rose. Gorbachev claimed that his temperance campaign saved 300,000 lives in 1986 alone.[11]

But the same years saw an increase in alcohol poisoning as thirsty Russians guzzled cologne, shaving lotion, mouthwash, and insect repellant. *Izvestia* blamed a toothpaste shortage on some alcoholics who were swallowing tubefuls in anticipation of a high. In March 1988, *Izvestia* reported that over ten thousand people died from drinking alcoholic substitutes.

The real traffic was in *samogon*, or Russian moonshine. Drinking home brew was also hazardous because it often contained metal oxides and other unfiltered additives, but stills proliferated in cramped apartment kitchens and rural backyards, and sugar disappeared from store shelves across the Soviet Union. Do-it-yourself distilling grew so popular that when *Working Woman* (*Rabotnitsa*) magazine inadvertently printed a recipe for a yeast culture, the dowdy Soviet homemaking monthly sold out and became a hot item on Moscow's black market.

During a chat with Muscovites in August 1987, Mikhail Gorbachev revealed that per capita sugar consumption had reached ninety-nine pounds a year, half again as much as an overfed American consumed. "As for where all the sugar is going, you can guess," Gorbachev said. ". . . It's going to make *samogon*."[12]

As with Prohibition in the United States, Gorbachev's war on alcohol helped the wrong people become rich. According to *Izvestia* in March 1987, the police nabbed one moonshiner, a woman named Arzamasova, who had hoarded half a ton of sugar. Criminals carted off 140,000 rubles, about $190,000, worth of sugar from a refinery in Dzhambul with the connivance of its manager. Farm families collectively operated stills, and near Vinnitsa, a moonshiner built a watchtower in the forest near his still to look out for police. In Leningrad, the police seized two thousand bottles of alcohol brewed in the homes of the Soviet Union's most sophisticated city.

The disappearance of sugar from the shops created new ordeals for the long-suffering Soviet consumer. A teetotaler in Kiev's suburbs wrote *Pravda* to complain that his family no longer had any sugar for tea. Residents of two other Ukrainian villages, who had been putting up with shortages of meat and milk, threatened to boycott an upcoming election of legislators to the Supreme Soviet unless they got sugar. The nervous officials drove two pounds of sugar to every villager. In February

1988, the government introduced sugar rationing for the first time, I was told, since World War Two.

In a year and a half of the sobriety campaign, the police reported that some 900,000 homemade stills were confiscated or voluntarily dismantled and nearly 700,000 gallons of liquor and beer destroyed. And yet, warned Aleksandr Vlasov, a Deputy Minister of Internal Affairs, "the incidence of this evil is not falling, but on the contrary, is growing in many areas of the country." His statistics on the moonshiners were revealing. In 1986 alone, courts convicted more than 130,000 Soviet citizens of making alcohol; 70,000 others were punished administratively. Over half were under thirty years of age, while only a fifth were pensioners, who traditionally brewed their own. The new lawbreakers were not just younger but were often better educated, and over half of them were women. About 4,700 belonged to the Party or its Komsomol youth branch. In the first half of 1987, moonshining convictions jumped again, by 39 percent.

Such disregard of the law reflected other weaknesses of Soviet society. Russians spend so much time in line that some found it quicker to brew their own alcohol. In 1988, near Moscow's Belorussky Station at noon, I saw nearly a hundred men and women waiting in a sullen queue for their neighborhood liquor store to open. One newspaper estimated that the usual waiting line for vodka averaged three hundred people. A report in the newspaper *Soviet Russia (Sovetskaya Rossiya)* told of an old woman killed in the crush of nearly one thousand desperate customers outside a liquor store in Petrozavodsk.

Alcohol, moreover, was not only used for drinking. A bottle of vodka had become a coinage more valued than the Soviet ruble, for it helped get a better cut of meat from the butcher, persuade a plumber to fix a leaky toilet, or reward a clerk who had set aside a pair of imported stockings. When vodka began disappearing from circulation, *samogon* filled this essential need. In Tula province south of Moscow, more than half of those convicted of selling *samogon* said they made it to buy such mundane services.

In the face of such opposition, the Party's Central Committee conceded in 1987 that "we have not managed to create a broad front in the struggle against drunkenness everywhere." Some Party members assigned to crack down on drinking, it reported, "are themselves partial to this vice." Police enforcement was haphazard; 32,800 stills were destroyed in one Russian province, but only 15 in another. *Pravda* identified three far-flung areas—Karelia on the Finnish border, Poltava in the western Ukraine, and Krasnodar in southern Russia—where it said the offensive against alcohol had virtually ceased.

The Gorbachev regime did not abandon the crusade, but it scaled back. Constraints on serving liquor were relaxed in hotels and restaurants. And plans were announced to reopen liquor stores in Moscow and Leningrad, in part to put the bootleggers out of business. The real solution, of course, was to create the kind of society that Russians would want to live in sober.

China's drive to restrain the growth of its population provides another vivid example of a Communist regime's struggle with individual will. Though the Chinese make up more than a fifth of the world's population, they live on only 7 percent of its arable land. Because Chairman Mao viewed his burgeoning population as an asset, China's population swelled by an average of 2.6 percent a year between 1966 and 1980, more than three times the American growth rate.[13]

A feeble attempt at family planning in the 1960s collapsed under the onslaught of the Cultural Revolution. When Deng Xiaoping took control of the Party, he realized that progress would be futile without birth control. The 1982 census showed that China's population had nearly doubled to 1 billion in the first thirty-three years of Communist power, and so a ceiling of 1.2 billion Chinese by the year 2000 was officially declared. To delay births, the minimum age for marriage had been set at twenty-two years for men and twenty years for women. Now a nationwide campaign promulgated the ideal of one child per family. Billboards across China showed an apple-cheeked, well-dressed tot caressed by beaming parents under the slogan "Papa, Mama, and me." The single-child policy was envisioned as necessary for only one generation.

As I traveled around China, officials showed me smiling young couples who had pledged to limit themselves to a single child. They were rewarded with fancy certificates, priority in housing, generous maternity leaves, even cash bonuses. But the family-planning program contained a stick as well as a carrot, and it was wielded by local cadres concerned foremost with the birth-control targets assigned to their areas. Tales emerged of the persecution of women who refused to sign the pledge, of forced sterilizations, of abortions in the last months of pregnancy, and of female infanticide. The modern birth-control program collided with traditional values of the Chinese, who cherished large families with lots of sons.

On a trip to Canton, a lively city not far from Hong Kong, I inquired how the family-planning drive was going in Guang-dong province, which occupies 2 percent of China's land but has 6 percent of its population. I spent a day in Canton's Yuexiu district, where the family-planning campaign was especially active. Some of its enterprises had set quotas for the number of babies their female employees were allowed to have. At the Wuyang electric-fan factory, the director, Zhang Zhiqiang, ex-plained, "Our plan for this year is eighteen babies. We have two so far, and five women are pregnant." From Zhang's en-thusiasm, I inferred that the other eleven were busy copulating to meet the deadline.

Some enterprises maintained charts on the menstrual cycles of their working women, posted signup lists for those wanting to have children, and arranged free abortions, with two weeks off, for those who had gotten pregnant without the boss's permission. Working women were allowed seventeen days off to have intrauterine devices inserted or, if they got sterilized, twenty days off, with 40 yuan for supplemental food. At the Wuyang factory, benefits passed down to the unborn child; as long as he had no brother or sister, he would receive a gift of 10 yuan on national holidays. If he got sick, his parents could leave their jobs to nurse him without forfeiting their monthly performance bonuses.

But couples in Yuexiu district who ignored the single-child policy might have 10 percent of their wages withheld until their youngest child turned fourteen. Elsewhere in China, this penalty was increased to 15 or 20 percent of a worker's salary. And women unwilling to undergo abortions or sterilization were targeted for what one family-planning cadre euphemistically called "painstaking and careful ideological work, ten times or even twenty times with a person." It sounded like the old "struggle sessions" of the Cultural Revolution, when victims were verbally battered into submission. Privacy of the most intimate kind went out the window once the state entered the bedroom, but the drive seemed successful. "The biggest problem is the old habits of seven thousand years," said Li Hanbo, a deputy chief of Guangdong's family-planning office, with an understatement I did not appreciate at the time. "People put too much emphasis on having sons."

But the peasants were not so compliant, and the family-planning campaign among them was described as "arduous" by a cadre named Li. "One of the reasons for high growth is that we have too many families having three or more children," he told me. They amounted to nearly a quarter of all families under his jurisdiction. Ideological persuasion, Li said, didn't always work. "On the average, it takes ten times to persuade each person, but the most difficult people can need one hundred times," he said. He estimated it cost more to talk someone out of having a child than to rear it to adolescence.

"It's a hard job to persuade the masses about family planning," Li said. "People who don't like it can go so far as to swear at or beat the cadres who come to persuade them. We tell our cadres to fear no hardships and not to fight back if they get beaten up." Promulgating the virtues of a one-child family was not a cushy job.

The stubborn resistance was encouraged by the new responsibility system in agriculture, which rewarded peasants according to how much they produced, and this reinforced the farmer's conviction that he needed sturdy sons to help him work the land. "People feel it would be difficult for a daughter to do the job," explained Li. So if a farm couple had a daughter, they had little hesitation about trying again for a son. Beyond this consideration lay the more enduring belief that many children offer the best insurance against a poor and lonely old age. "The general problem with a majority of people is that they fear that their future will not be guaranteed when they get old," the family planning cadre said. "We have to admit that this is a practical as well as an ideological problem." China's few old-age homes tend to be bleak places; the Chinese prefer to complete their lives surrounded by caring offspring.

Fines were not a deterrent in the countryside, because a farmer with sons to help him grow more under the agricultural reforms could come out ahead even after he paid the penalties for their birth. Small children were useful tending the ducks or sheep that brought in sideline income. So family-planning authorities in Guangdong compromised; if a peasant's first child was a daughter, or if the baby son had a physical defect, they let the couple try again. They decided that peasants were entitled to two children but not three, and in time this relaxation spread through rural China, where 80 percent of the Chinese live. Fishermen were similarly exempted because, a spokesman for the State Family Planning Commission explained, "traditionally it's rare for girls to go to sea."

The one-child limit was also waived for non-Han ethnic minorities, who make up about 7 percent of China's population, as a way of assuring their loyalty. Uighurs in the desert of Chinese Central Asia, Tibetans in the snow-capped Himalayas, and Dais in the rain forests bordering Indochina were permitted to have two children, and sometimes officials looked the other way when they had more. When I visited the island of Hainan, its ethnic Li minority was expanding by 3.6 percent a year, and the Miaos by 4.1 percent, two of the highest population-growth rates in the world. A young Li peasant tending rubber trees in a mountain village told me he thought that "we are allowed to have four children, but no more than four."

The disparities caused resentments. A Han doctor treating Vietnamese refugees who were being resettled in Yunnan province said in disgust that "they want to produce a child in China as a souvenir." If they refused to practice birth control, he said, "there is nothing we can do." And at Emei Shan, a ten-thousand-foot-high mountain in Sichuan revered by Buddhists, a wiry peasant porter who carried my pack said he and his wife had obeyed the Party's call to postpone marriage while their friends got married and had children. He waited too long, he said bitterly, and the government fined him for having a second child. He was earning money to pay the fine—83 yuan a year for seven years—by carrying devout old ladies on his back to Emei Shan's summit.

Yet enforcement of the single-child rule was so lax elsewhere that I read of one cadre in Guangdong who was tossed out of the Party only after his wife gave birth to their seventh child. In the end, the single-child policy was enforced mostly among newlyweds in the cities because, family-planning officials said, it was easier to convince women who were better educated. By 1984, the government revealed that only 21 percent of Chinese women of childbearing age had just one child.

Once persuasion failed, coercion took over, with sometimes grim consequences. In Canton, I heard of abortions performed on women in their final month of pregnancy, sometimes in the delivery room. A Chinese surgeon told about a young Cantonese wife who gave birth to twins. Obeying the single-child policy, a nurse dutifully suffocated one of them. Another nurse came in later and, assuming the first child had been taken to the nursery, unwittingly smothered the second.

A Hong Kong magazine with good contacts on the mainland reported that in some districts of Guangdong pregnant women were abducted on the street and trucked off for abortions to meet the local targets. It cited an incident in which one women subjected to an involuntary abortion turned out not to be pregnant, just fat. The family-planning cadres whom I interviewed seemed sensitive about what they called these false rumors.

Such "deviations," as a senior official described them, were caused by cadres who met sterilization and abortion quotas like any other assigned target. A health worker at Beijing Medical College told me about young women who were browbeaten into consenting to sterilization while they lay groggy from childbirth on the delivery table. Abortion statistics were kept confidential because of their sensitivity, but an unpublished study showed that one urban district in Beijing counted seventy-four abortions for every hundred births, while a county in the suburbs had eighty-four abortions for every hundred births. There were persistent reports that abortions outnumbered live births in some parts of China but I could never confirm them.

There was no doubt that women were encouraged, if not compelled, to be fitted with contraceptive devices, mostly a stainless-steel ring inserted in the uterus. Over half of the Chinese women practicing birth control used intrauterine devices and another 30 percent were sterilized. The rest used birth-control pills and condoms or relied on the vasectomies of their husbands.[14]

The intrauterine rings experienced a high failure rate, ostensibly because they were improperly inserted by medical workers. One study attributed up to a third of the abortions to the failures of these devices. But one expert admitted that "some women secretly take them out and then get pregnant." I read of a peasant who went to jail after he ripped out his wife's coil so they could have another child; she hemorrhaged and nearly died.

The traditional Chinese preference for sons has led to a rash of infanticides, as unwanted first daughters are drowned or abandoned outdoors. In one village in Hefei province, 85 percent of its births recorded in a single year were boys. Some husbands, under pressure at work to observe family planning, blamed their wives for not bearing sons. Wife battering increased. One woman in Heilongjiang province was brain-damaged by a blow from her irate husband when she had a girl instead of a boy.[15] A few women killed themselves in despair, though others were resourceful enough to deposit unwanted daughters on the doorstep of the local Party headquarters for the cadres to worry about.

Other births went unregistered, because parents wouldn't admit to them or local authorities refused to accept that the babies were born. An official in the Public Security Ministry was quoted by the *China Daily* as saying that China had one million such children without residence registrations. This meant that they would grow up lacking documents needed to get subsidized food, housing, jobs, or schooling.[16]

Among those couples who confined themselves to one child, there emerged another unexpected side effect—the spoiled brat. The love and attention once spread among many children in a large family was focused on the single child. In some kindergartens, the only children were given more sweets than their classmates or were allowed to go home early while the others did the cleaning-up chores. A physician at Shanghai Children's Hospital found that the only children were getting obese because their mothers stuffed them with rich food and candy. And a father in Beijing who grew up in a large family told me he didn't know how to discipline an only child. "Before, you could say: 'Look at your brother, look at your sister,' " he said. "Now there is no one else for comparison."

The one-child policy made it harder to space out marriages, another practice used by the government to hold down the population. When the Year of the Dragon arrived in February 1988, many Chinese rushed to get married and conceive quickly, because children born under the sign of the dragon were supposedly blessed with greater intelligence and good fortune. Potential grandparents were accused of arranging marriages for their children to seize the felicitous occasion for the sake of eugenics.[17]

China's family-planning campaign was not a disaster, only a disappointment. In 1988, the State Statistical Bureau reported that without such stringent measures, 104 million more babies would have been born over the previous decade. But the Chinese grew weary of the calls for restraint. "Nearly 90 percent of the people want more than one child in the countryside, and at least half of the city dwellers do too," the People's Daily reported. As uncontrolled births of the 1960s increased the number of women of childbearing age to nearly 300 million, the country braced for another baby boom. China's people were advised to eat less meat and more rice, to make the country's food resources stretch farther.[18]

With such disappointments, it is not hard to understand why the reformers in the Soviet Union and China could not conceive of total democracy, because freedom of the individual clashes with the goals, and entrenched self-interest, of the Party. Deng Xiaoping and Mikhail Gorbachev, both career Communists who rose through Party ranks, meant to overhaul the system, not preside over its demise, as Deng's suppression of dissent showed in 1989. "Our government does not give us democracy by loosening our bonds a little," said Fang Lizhi. "It gives us only freedom to writhe."

3

UNCLE LEI FENG IS DEAD: CASTE AND PRIVILEGE IN A CLASSLESS SOCIETY

▬▬▬▬▬▬▬▬▬▬▬▬▬▬▬

At no time and in no circumstances should a Communist place his personal interests first; he should subordinate them to the interests of the nation and of the masses.

—MAO ZEDONG
to followers, 1941[1]

On rainy days, leading comrades driving cars should pay attention not to splash rainwater on pedestrians.

—Radio announcement in Harbin,
Manchuria, 1983

IN THE HALCYON DAYS of Mao Zedong and for an embarrassingly long time thereafter, the model Communist was Lei Feng, a simple soldier who died in the bloom of youth on August 15, 1962. Lei Feng did not fall in battle like tens of thousands of other young Chinese. His martyrdom was less glorious; he was flattened by a telephone pole. He had been teaching a comrade how to drive a truck. His pupil backed into the pole, which fell on Lei Feng. Mao Zedong had argued eloquently that any death, however trivial, was as weighty as Taishan, the sacred Chinese mountain, if it came in the cause of good, while any death, if it happened in the service of evil, was as light and inconsequential as a feather.

Good soldier Lei's real contribution, however, came only after his death, when the Maoist ideologues determined that he had been secretly performing all kinds of good deeds. As evidence, they produced photographs of a grinning Lei Feng busy darning a fellow soldier's socks, teaching an old man to read, playing with children, and befriending China's ethnic minorities. His posthumous promoters announced the discovery of a diary in which Lei Feng, a Communist Party member, of course, had jotted down his good deeds together with uplifting thoughts about Chairman Mao. Before long, two traveling exhibitions, each with its own original copy of the diary, were touring China to promulgate the legend of Lei Feng.

It was ideological overkill, what the Chinese call "drawing a snake and adding feet." In a kind of Communist Golden Rule, the Chinese were exhorted to learn from Lei Feng—"xuexi Lei Feng"—and devote themselves to others. Since upward mobility in a classless society doesn't work that way, younger Chinese in time came to view Lei Feng with the same bemused contempt that their Russian peers felt toward Pavlik Morozov, the boy who betrayed his parents to the Stalinist authorities.

Most Chinese would find a simple cook in Shandong province a more authentic hero. The cook (I never learned her name) was assigned to work for some cadres, or Party functionaries, in Linshu County, one of the poorest and most backward parts of the province. The officials were digging into a fourteen-course banquet with their chopsticks when the irate cook marched out of the kitchen and overturned one of the tables in protest against the extravagance. What happened to her is not clear, but she was subsequently supported by many of the locals and, a couple of months later, by some newspapers in Beijing.[2]

The gluttony of the Communist cadres, who learned not from Lei Feng but from the greedy pigs in Orwell's *Animal Farm*, was not confined to Shandong. One of my first articles in China in 1981 featured Wang Lei, China's Minister of Commerce, who took his friends to dine gratis in Beijing's best restaurants until one of the chefs blew the whistle. The government made an example of Wang and he resigned shortly thereafter, but within months Party cadres were again feasting on bird's-nest soup, sea slugs, and Peking duck while most other Chinese got through the day on little more than a few bowls of rice. In one memorable meal, some Party officials inspecting a livestock research station in Yunnan province devoured six of its experimentally bred pigs, which they washed down with seventy large bottles of beer. Six years after the gourmand Wang Lei was told to pay for his meals, the *People's Daily* lamented that "the long-standing trend of sumptuous banquets at public expense has been rampant around the country in spite of the Party's repeated bans and frequent criticism in the press. Patient persuasion, outright condemnation, and even doctors' warnings have proved utterly useless."

Freeloading officials may not be unique to a Communist society, but they provide one of the more vivid examples of the Revolution's betrayal. Such misconduct led the Soviet Union and China to what would seem the impossible: the creation in an ostensibly classless society of two distinct and mutually antagonistic classes—the Party and the people.

It is not surprising that ordinary Russians and Chinese, confronted daily with such high-handed behavior, develop a contempt for the Party apparatus. In Beijing, I went to see a film comedy about some lazy Manchurian peasants who were finally motivated by the agricultural reforms. The pretty young ingénue, fetching in denim overalls and pigtails, initially snubbed the hero by turning up her nose and telling him, "No girl in our village wants to be seen out with a Party member." The audience sitting around me in the darkened theater cheered and clapped.

The Communists came to power in China on a pledge of honesty and frugality. The Three Main Rules of Discipline issued by the People's Liberation Army at the height of the civil war in 1947 were: (1) Obey orders in all your actions; (2) Do not take a single needle or piece of thread from the masses;

(3) Turn in everything captured. A family-planning official from Shandong who had fought in the PLA as a teenager told me how he and the other combat-weary infantrymen slept on the sidewalks of newly liberated Shanghai, forbidden by their commissars to move indoors with local residents lest they be compared to the retreating Nationalist troops who had looted and bullied civilians.

In 1945, Mao Zedong wrote from the caves of Yanan: "Hard work is like a load placed before us, challenging us to shoulder it. Some loads are light, some heavy. Some people prefer the light to the heavy; that is not a good attitude. Some comrades are different; they leave ease and comfort to others and take the heavy loads themselves; they are the first to bear hardships, the last to enjoy comfort. They are good comrades. We should all learn from their Communist spirit."[3] In short, "*xuexi* Lei Feng."

Some older Chinese shared an honest nostalgia for Lei Feng, or rather for what he represented. Deng Xiaoping, barely back from official disgrace in 1975, blamed the decline in behavior on the Cultural Revolution, which had dragged out for nearly a decade. "Formerly, when army comrades rode a bus, they would make a point of offering their seats to elderly people or women carrying babies," he told a meeting of the Party's Central Military Commission. "But now some of them don't bother to do that. I have heard of a case where a soldier riding a bus did not offer his seat to a woman with a baby even when it began to cry. Seeing this, an old man commented, 'Uncle Lei Feng isn't around anymore.' " The Lei-Feng-Is-Dead remark contradicted the official myth of proletarian selflessness and helped send Deng back into disgrace a second time.[4]

The myth of Communist sacrifice is perpetuated even in the face of contradictory reality. Zhu Muzhi, a Party spokesman, reminded those of us covering China's 12th Party Congress that "Party members must be the first to bear hardships and the last to enjoy luxuries. They absolutely must never use public office for personal gain at the expense of the public." Ni Yuxian, a writer jailed during the Cultural Revolution, scoffed at this when I met him later. "It's not true anymore," he told me. "The Party is the first to enjoy privileges and the last to suffer hardships."

Indeed, it is this selfishness and not economic backwardness that poses the most formidable obstacle to decisive change in China and the Soviet Union. Not only is the élite reluctant to give up its privileges; sometimes it has forgotten why it should. Boris N. Yeltsin, Moscow's former Party chief, endeared himself to Muskovites by riding the subway and queueing up in the shops. "If there is a shortage of something in our society, then everybody should feel it," Yeltsin told a Latvian newspaper in August 1988, nine months after he was fired for questioning the slow pace of reform. "A leader in the agricultural industry who gets the finest foods delivered to his home is never going to put his heart into the battle for the production program. For him the problem has long since been solved."

The Communists demanded absolute power in Russia and China with the promise that they would remain answerable to the people. Lenin accused self-important Party members of "Communist conceit." In his oration at Lenin's funeral in 1924, Stalin declared: "In departing from us, Comrade Lenin ordained that we should hold high and keep pure the dignity of Party members; we vow to you, Comrade Lenin, that we shall fulfill your command with honor."

What followed instead was the rise of the "new class," which the Yugoslav Marxist Milovan Djilas defined as "those who have special privileges and economic preference because of the administrative monopoly they hold."[5] A person's class in Marxist terms denoted his relationship to the means of production. Since production in the Soviet Union and China is owned by everyone, at least in theory, class distinctions no longer exist. This dialectic, of course, has fallen victim to the schizophrenia afflicting the rest of the ideology.

Perhaps caste is the better definition for the ruling élite. The Soviet *apparatchiki* and the Chinese *ganbu* or cadres are both governed by a codification of status—the Russians call it *nomenklatura*, the Chinese *zhiwu mincheng biao*—that assigns responsibilities and attendant rewards to officials according to their positions and political reliability. The details of this "feudal socialism," as the Chinese poet Ye Wenfu labeled it, may constitute the most sensitive, and worst-kept, secret of a Communist society, in which the Marxist ideal, "From each according to his ability; to each according to his need," came to mean ". . . to each according to his connections."

A middle-aged scientist friend in Moscow said Russia had changed less since Czarist times than meets the eye. "The biggest difference is that the highest leaders now conceal their privileges," he said. "The old Russian leadership had palaces. The current leadership doesn't show anything. A high official doesn't ride in a golden carriage, he goes about in a Chaika [limousine]. You'll never see the dacha of a Politburo official, though they are luxurious inside. He will dress in a simple suit or jacket. He doesn't go out shopping. He phones out and has it sent in."

And there are castes within castes. A Soviet Party Congress I covered had four segregated buffets for hungry delegates. In descending order of importance, there was a luxury dining room for Politburo members and visiting foreign Communist leaders, a buffet for Central Committee members, another for local Party secretaries and less-important foreign Communist guests, and finally a buffet for ordinary delegates with nothing better than a Party card. A Russian journalist I knew compared it to a multi-class cruise ship; fellow travelers in deluxe class could go slumming on the lower decks (there was no indication they ever did), but to invite someone upstairs was prohibited. I was told a similar segregation existed at the buffets for Party functionaries inside the Kremlin.

Though much has been written about the mandarins of Communism, the scope of their privileges is barely fathomed in the West, where such prerogatives would be taken for granted. While workers wait ten years or more for flats of their own, the élite have first shot at new apartments. As the masses queue up for shoddy shoes, stringy meat, and overage cabbages, the cadres buy food and clothing at restricted stores. Caste determines one's eligibility to fly on airliners or take a train without being wedged all night on the wooden benches in hard class. It includes VIP lounges with plush sofas and hot tea and tables in popular restaurants like the Aragvi in Moscow or the Beiyuan in Canton. The heady prominence of being more equal than others in an egalitarian society itself constitutes a perquisite that this caste would never relinquish willingly.

The poet Yevgeny Yevtushenko created a furor when he told a gathering of Soviet writers in December 1985 that "any sort of closed distribution of foods and goods is morally impermissible, including the special coupons for souvenir kiosks that lie in the pocket of every delegate to this congress, myself included." Yevtushenko said aloud what the others knew: that while many ordinary Russians contended with rationed butter and meat, the literary élite found both available at the special stores hidden from public view. His observation was sensitive enough to be deleted by the *Literary Gazette* (*Lituraturnaya Gazeta*) when it published his speech. Two and a half years later, when I visited Yevtushenko at his wooden dacha set among the graceful birches of the suburban writers' colony at Peredelkino, his Mercedes luxury sedan was parked in the yard and cassettes of recent American films sat piled on a dining-room table next to a Japanese videocassette recorder.

More senior Party and government officials in the Soviet Union and China have staffs of servants paid by the state (those in Beijing tend to prefer young Cantonese girls because their limited fluency in Mandarin Chinese makes them less likely to spill family secrets). They read foreign news reports and books and watch films ruled too decadent for lesser comrades. And they are allowed passports, and the necessary dollars or yen, to travel abroad. When the élite fall sick, they are treated in special facilities, like the Kremlin Clinic in Moscow or the Capital Hospital in Beijing. Once they die, they are likely to be buried apart from the masses to whom they have purportedly dedicated their lives.

Ordinary Chinese bicycle to work and Russians cram into the subway, but the Party cadres ordained to serve them are chauffeured in Shanghai, Chaika, or Volga sedans, or, if they rank high enough, hand-tooled Hongqis and Zils fitted with prissy curtains across the side and back windows. Moscow's main thoroughfares boast a special "Chaika lane" down the middle, reserved for the Chaikas and Zils carrying senior officials. Their limousines can turn left at intersections where other cars must continue straight and make a legal U-turn, or *razvorot*, at designated spots later. The story is that a Politburo member was thrown from his seat when his Zil braked for an ordinary car making a left turn; as a result most left turns in downtown Moscow were declared illegal. "Even a driver of a Zil or Chaika is an officer and a policeman has to salute him," explained a Russian friend when I asked why the capital's otherwise nasty traffic cops behaved so deferentially toward limousines. Beijing needs no such traffic segregation, because almost all the cars on the road are official. But the Chinese leaders travel by underground tunnel from their guarded red-walled compound at Zhongnanhai to functions at the Great Hall of the People without having to expose themselves to public view.

While any automobile is a prized item in Communist countries, cars with chauffeurs carry much greater status. It was not uncommon when I lived in Moscow and Beijing to see idle Volgas and Chaikas or Toyotas and Shanghais lined up for hours in front of government buildings while their drivers chatted and smoked, polished the fenders or napped in the front seats. Back in 1974, Yevgeny N. Trubitsyn, then the Russian Federation's Minister of Automotive Transport, suggested that officials learn to drive themselves around, so their drivers could be reassigned to buses and taxis. "A manager behind the steering wheel?" marveled the *Literary Gazette*. Trubitsyn conceded that eliminating chauffeurs would pose "a whole tangle of psychological problems" for Soviet officials. But in Western countries, he testified, "I personally saw company managers, company directors, and even government ministers drive their own personal cars." The bureaucrats dug in their heels, of course. After Gorbachev took over, he ordered that some government cars be sold off to taxi fleets or the public. He also made other chauffeur-driven cars remove their flashing lights and sirens, which were used to scatter pedestrians at Moscow's intersections.

Privacy is a luxury in both the Soviet Union and China, where housing shortages are chronic. In Moscow, we were permitted to drive twenty miles into the countryside, to a river beach at Uspenskoye reserved for foreigners. The hour-long drive carried us through forests broken by roads leading off to official summer residences. At almost every intersection, a policeman ensured that travelers didn't stray from the main road. In the Chinese seaside resort of Beidaihe, similar villas for senior officials were tucked well back into the scrub pines. I don't know which were more elaborate because we were kept away from all of them.

The facilities that I did see compared favorably with anything in the West. Jaqueline and I traveled to southeastern Guangdong province for a story on agricultural reform. In Zhongshan, the hotel manager offered us a suite used by the late Ye Jianying, who had served as China's tacit head of state. Our quarters, larger than our Beijing apartment, included two plush bedrooms with king-sized beds, a color television tuned to Hong Kong stations, a gracious courtyard with small garden and a sunken tile bathtub with gilded faucets that was the size of a small swimming pool. On the island of Hainan, I stayed at a gracious old rest house set among gardens on a rubber-tree plantation. Before her arrest, Jiang Qing, Mao's wife, liked to stay there for the tranquillity, I was told, and no wonder. While she was in residence, all motor traffic was ordered to a halt for miles around so it would not disturb her.

Such indulgences are part and parcel of the life of the highest caste. Leonid Brezhnev drove his collection of foreign cars, which included a Rolls-Royce and a Cadillac; Yuri Andropov listened to his Western jazz records; and Mikhail Gorbachev's wife, Raisa, shops abroad with her American Express gold card. When the Gorbachevs dined with Prime Minister Margaret Thatcher on a state visit to Britain, one story goes, Raisa Gorbachev admired Mrs. Thatcher's diamond-and-sapphire earrings, a present from her husband, Denis. The Gorbachevs inquired where in London he bought them and Raisa ordered up an identical pair for herself.

Salaries have been a poor indication of privilege because they were kept low to avoid unfavorable comparisons with workingmen's wages. Lenin's April Theses, a platform drafted in 1917, six months before the Bolshevik Revolution, had included a proposal that official salaries not exceed those of an ordinary worker. Mikhail Gorbachev earns 1,500 rubles a month, or a little more than $2,100, while a Party secretary or factory manager might earn no more than a few hundred dollars a month. But this does not include extensive fringe benefits, like a free apartment in the city and dacha in the country, a car with driver, a free *putyovka* or holiday trip to a Black Sea resort, and access to special shops stocked with Western goods. The fact is that money makes relatively little difference in a Communist society, which reverts to a premonetary phase of economic development as it matures.

"In the best shops, there is some special *poyok*"—or section—"and they send the driver to the closed shop with a special ticket," said Veniamin Levich as he acquainted me one day with the labyrinth of privilege. Senior *apparatchiks* enjoyed the so-called "Kremlin ration," entitling them to fine cuisine in the Kremlin dining rooms, with a doggie bag of takeout delicacies thrown in. Those entitled to the Kremlin ration often spent their vouchers on subsidized gourmet food, liquor, and wine at restricted delicatessens to tote home to their families.

It has been this privilege that ordinary Russians seemed to resent most, possibly because it paralleled their most basic needs. A survey of 548 Moscow residents published in July 1989 by the weekly *Moscow News* found that 84 percent considered admission by the élite to closed stores and cafeterias unjust, while only 44 percent thought their use of government cars was unjust.

The Chinese admit to the existence of similar inequities. "Our present problem is not that our senior cadres are too highly paid but that they have too many privileges," Deng Xiaoping said back in November 1979. "This is liable to alienate them from the masses and lower-ranking cadres, and even to corrupt their family members, debase the general standard of social conduct, and make it impossible to overcome bureaucracy."[6] A document on "Some Regulations Concerning the Material Benefits for Senior Cadres" circulated by the Party and the State Council that year tried, unsuccessfully, to limit senior functionaries to single residences and to bill them for personal use of their official cars.

Delegations traveling abroad sometimes get packed with officials who have no business going along. Fang Lizhi, the outspoken astrophysicist, recalled that when a Chinese delegation went to the United States in 1985 for an international conference on cyclotrons, only ten of the twenty-five places were filled by scientists knowledgeable about the subject. The other fifteen delegates included a vice mayor of Beijing and assorted Party hacks.[7]

Whenever leading Party cadres rub elbows with the workers and peasants, it is as their betters, to approve or criticize what they have done. Fang Lizhi was devastating in his criticism of this long-standing Communist custom. "Does such a thing take place in a democracy?" Fang asked in a speech. "Representatives are selected by the people. They should represent their constituency, not inspect it."

When he spent a few months at Princeton University, Fang was intrigued to receive in his mail a form letter that a New Jersey legislator routinely sent out to constituents explaining his voting record. "In our genuine democracy, on the other hand, I have never received a report of my representative's activities or his voting record," Fang said. "My representative will be only too happy to cast my vote without having the vaguest idea of what I think."[8]

One of the more hopeful manifestations of reform is a willingness by top officials to appear more accessible. Mikhail Gorbachev gained popularity by plunging into crowds of surprised Russians or stopping to listen to factory workers. The irony is that the overwhelming majority of the élite in the Soviet Union and China came out of the working class, which they now disdain. In China, landlords and merchants escaped to Taiwan or Hong Kong, abandoning the country to the peasant guerrillas who overran it. In Russia, the aristocrats were shot or driven into Western exile, where some of them ended up as taxi drivers and waitresses. The educated intellectuals who remained to build the new societies were eventually killed or imprisoned. As a result, explained a Soviet academician, "all that was left after our revolution was telegraph operators and dentists." He thought it would take five generations to rebuild a new intelligentsia, although, he quipped, "I wouldn't know. I'm only in the third generation."

Chen Muhua, who rose to become China's Minister of Foreign Economic Relations and Trade and later head of the Bank of China, had a reputation for behaving as imperiously as a Qing Dynasty empress. I was told she once refused to bring home some sick Chinese students from Rumania because her jetliner was loaded with modern German furniture. In one of her rare news conferences, Chen announced some new foreign investment and then consented to take ten questions from the press. We seized the occasion to ask all kinds of economic questions. Chen delivered a few irrelevant platitudes and walked out. "The minister said she would take ten questions," her harried aide explained. "She didn't say she would answer them."

Unlike the original revolutionaries, who advanced themselves through dedication and hard work, the new caste perpetuates its bloodline in power. "The majority [of children] are reaping the achievements of their parents," a Soviet social scientist told me. Many of the first Chinese students permitted to go to study in the United States were the offspring of senior Party officials, including Deng Xiaoping's son. This practice became so widespread that the government in 1982 decreed that children of Chinese cadres above middle grade would not be permitted to study overseas, but some kept going. In Moscow, Leonid Brezhnev's son traveled abroad for the Ministry of Foreign Trade, and the son of Andrei Gromyko, the late Soviet President, headed a prestigious institute on African studies.

"The children of scientists become scientists, the children

of diplomats become diplomats," said Veniamin Levich, the physical chemist. "The same kind of stable class arises, constituting an élite, and each class has its own privileges. A stable society needs its élite class. It is the foundation of stability."

The arrogance of those born into the caste was satirized one December in the British Embassy's annual holiday revue for the foreign community in Beijing. A few years earlier, the British turned two Maoist revolutionary operas, *The Red Detachment of Women* and *Taking Tiger Mountain by Strategy*, into a wicked parody called *Taking the Red Detachment of Women by Strategy*, and the invited Chinese officials walked out. My favorite show had *Alice in Wonderland* tumbling into equally curious post-Maoist China and featured a catchy song, set to the old cockney tune of "My Old Man's a Dustman," in which a Party official's son confided his ambitions:

My old man's a cadre, he wears a cadre's hat,
He rides in a big black limousine with curtains on the back,
And when I am much older, I will be a cadre too.
And as for serving the people, I've got better things to do.

I enjoyed it because I had met such a young man a few months earlier when I joined a team of American mountaineers attempting a new ascent of Mount Everest through Tibet. The Chinese Mountaineering Association made us take along as our translator a plump fellow named Wang, who had been studying at a prestigious language institute packed with the children of Party and government officials. Wang was so conspicuously out of his element that he became a joke among the hardened American climbers. He had never slept outside before, he got so sick from the altitude that sometimes he wouldn't leave his sleeping bag, and he had no interest in venturing beyond base camp. Wang spoke no Tibetan and once refused to stroll with us through a Tibetan village for fear the natives would harm him. I ended up doing most of the translating when we negotiated for our pack yaks, but we couldn't get Wang to go back to Beijing, though we were charged extravagantly for his minimal services, because he wanted the official record of contact with foreigners to qualify to go abroad.

Wang proved amiable enough when he wasn't being ill. He told me his father and mother, both prominent officials and Party members, arranged his passage to Europe as a deck-hand on a Chinese freighter during the Cultural Revolution while other Beijing youth were drafted for menial labor in the countryside. Wang's proudest possession was an expensive camera with assorted lenses that his father had brought him from West Germany. I expect by now he has been assigned overseas, hopefully near sea level. Yet I was indebted to Wang because in an unguarded moment he made a boast so revealing that I wrote it down. "In China, money means nothing," he said. "Power means everything, because with power you have *guanxi.*" He used a Chinese word best translated as "connections" or "pull." If he had been the equally privileged son of Soviet officials, he could have spoken of *blat,* its Russian equivalent. These arrangements, which grease the wheels of a society afflicted with material shortages, are not confined to the top; they run clear down into the grass roots of both the Soviet Union and China.[9]

The Chinese speak of their *guanxi wang,* literally "connection nets," in which what a person can do for others determines how much they will do for him. After years of waiting, one couple I knew in Beijing finally got their own two-room apartment in a new building. When I last saw the husband, he said they were still waiting to move in because the utility companies refused to hook up the electricity and water until some of the new apartments were allocated to their employees. A new nursery school in Beijing offered another graphic illustration of *guanxi wang.* With most women working and day-care facilities in short supply (most children are left with grandparents), a place for a child in a good nursery school can be a necessity as well as a status symbol. And everyone on whom this nursery depended demanded favors in return for their services. Utility servicemen insisted that their children be enrolled before the electricity, gas, and water were turned on. A butcher's shop promised better cuts of meat if the butcher's children were accepted. Clerks selling vegetables and fruit at the local grocery wanted places for their kids. By the time the nursery school had acceded to their requests, little room was left for other neighborhood children. The stakes run much higher for officials who want to arrange apartments, trips abroad, or places in university for their children.

Those without *guanxi* included a lanky young taxi driver I rode with in Harbin. When I asked him how he liked his job, he replied bitterly, "I lost the eleven best years of my life to the Cultural Revolution." When he was ordered out of the city to the countryside, he said, "I couldn't get out of it because I didn't have connections and I wasn't an only son." Because he had driven a tractor, he was made a taxi driver once he was allowed to return.

Unlike after the Revolution, upward mobility into the new caste has become nearly impossible. Children of Party and government officials are disproportionately represented in the limited university enrollments, often because they squeeze in through the *hou men*, or back door. An American teaching English at one Beijing institute told me that over half of her students had been admitted through this *hou men* after failing their entrance examinations, because their parents exerted influence. The reopening of college in Beijing every autumn has been heralded by articles in the local press complaining that some students were chauffeured to class in limousines while their classmates rode bicycles. The children of Party functionaries also get preference in job assignments, which can last for life. In Sichuan, one work-assignment bureau filled job vacancies at state-owned enterprises with 136 children of Party members and only three workers' children.

The situation is hardly different in the Soviet Union. In 1987, the newspaper *Moskovskaya Pravda* looked into the Soviet capital's "special schools," which ostensibly emphasize foreign-language study for gifted children, and found them saturated with privilege and snobbery. "For some time," the newspaper reported, "it has been a matter of honor for a high-ranking comrade to place his offspring not in some ordinary school, even if it is right next door, but in some faraway but extremely respected educational institution where the children of prominent people are enrolled." Only 6 percent of first graders in Moscow's ninety special schools came from blue-collar families, and this modest percentage steadily declined until by graduation "it often declines to zero." Some pupils were chauffeured in official cars, had private tutors, and showed off cassette players and other imported playthings. The subject was so sensitive that when parents learned of *Moskovskaya Pravda*'s forthcoming article, they tried to pressure the editors and finally the Moscow Party Committee to kill it.

In both the Soviet Union and China, well-connected parents pull strings to spare their sons the hazards of military duty. The old Soviet and Chinese Communists were blooded in their civil wars and World War Two. Defending the motherland is still hailed as so glorious a task that neither country recognizes conscientious objection. But in 1987 *Pravda* published excerpts from a letter written by a worker in Moscow who charged that some officials were keeping their sons out of service in Afghanistan. The war would have ended, he argued, if the children of the Soviet leadership had been sent to fight it.

In China, where the Red Army veterans who fought their way across the country in the Long March of the 1930s are heroes of the Revolution, I saw a play that showed how times had changed. The play, titled *Wreaths at the Foot of the Mountain*, was set during China's brief border war with Vietnam in 1979 and featured a callow junior officer who listened to disco music and walked around with his tunic unbuttoned. His mother, a prominent official, asked his general to spare her son from the looming conflict.

The young man was sent off to fight the Vietnamese, predictably shaped up under fire, and won a medal for valor. "It's only natural to show concern for my son," the mother told the general in the final scene. "Where was your son when there was a war to fight?" The general led her to a military cemetery at the foot of the mountain to show her the black-wreathed grave of his own son, who had concealed his connections by enlisting under an assumed name. "So many people died for the country that we cannot think of our personal interests," the general declared. For all the deliberate melodrama, the Chinese in the audience around me applauded, because it was an open secret that many cadres had scrambled to keep their sons out of combat.

Perquisites are closely guarded at all levels of the new caste. Mikhail Gorbachev complained to the Central Committee, which is made up of Soviet Party élite, that "nothing is exploited as much as official position." A scandal that contributed to the fall of Grigory Romanov, the former Party chief of Leningrad, emerged from his daughter's wedding reception, for which he requisitioned the imperial dinner service of Catherine the Great from the reluctant Hermitage Museum. Some of the exquisite antique pieces were smashed when drunken guests threw them on the floor.

In China, a railway official named Zhang in Hebei province laid on a special train to fetch his son's new bride from a neighboring province. He impressed her by holding up all the other trains while she traveled uninterrupted on a single-track line under his control. Unfortunately, he chose the day before the Chinese New Year, a travel period as hectic as Christmas Eve is in the West. Ten stations were thrown into chaos and several thousand tons of coal got sidetracked along with the passengers. Zhang got sacked, but such high-handedness was not discouraged, judging by another report I read in 1987 from Manchuria, where the Party secretary at one factory celebrated his son's wedding with a reception for nine hundred guests that lasted thirteen days. The magnitude of such abuses, reported here in the *China Daily*, suggests that they were the tip of an iceberg.

The instinct for survival is particularly strong among Communist Party members who joined the Party to advance themselves. The members of one Party unit whose credentials were being reexamined in northern China scored an average of 98.5 percent on a crucial written test; they cheated by pooling their answers. Li Ximing, the Party chief in Beijing, reported that some of his members "lack any basic Marxist theory. Some are incapable of carrying out Party policies." Li said their behavior "has obstructed reform, damaged the interests of the masses, and seriously affected the reputation of the Party in the people's eyes."

Examples abounded in the official press through the 1980s. In Sichuan province, a Party member named Liu Xingdong used his connections as a township official to grab nearly one thousand pounds of scarce fertilizer before it could reach the local farmers, who occupied the local supply cooperative in protest. In Guizhou province, one of the poorest regions in China, nine Party cadres, fearful that they would be replaced in an upcoming local election, sold off the county's only tractor and spent the money on themselves.[10] In Beijing, a Railway Ministry official responsible for foreign visitors used 10,000 yuan from his ministry's budget to cover the travel expenses of some Western businessmen, who reimbursed him by paying the hard-currency expenses of his daughter studying overseas.

Such abuses become most common in areas of shortage, like housing. I read about a district housing-bureau chief in Beijing named Gao Zongding, who expected presents, from wristwatches and porcelain vases to rare medicinal herbs, paintings, and a color television set, before he allocated apartments. Gao once refused to return a private house confiscated during the Cultural Revolution until its owner sent him French wine and expensive sweaters, and took him and his wife to dine at one of the capital's better restaurants. At his eventual trial, where he was sentenced to seven years in jail, Gao explained that he was only providing for his retirement. When I visited Tianjin to write a story about the city's reconstruction from an earlier earthquake, a crusty newspaper editor confirmed that Party cadres had moved into new apartments built for the earthquake's homeless but moved out after his newspaper exposed them. "Our policy should be the masses first, and then the cadres," he explained. But a factory manager in Beijing predicted that housing reform would never work because so many Party officials were preempting apartments for their children.

Editorials inveighing against abuse of power allude circumspectly to "some individuals" or "a small number of comrades," when everybody knows the miscreants number a lot more than the Party can afford to tolerate. They are unlikely to be attacked by name unless their crimes are egregious or they have lost some internal power struggle. When the aging Politburo member Ye Jianying took a new young wife a fraction of his age, he billed the government 100,000 yuan (then about $50,000) for his wedding celebration. A conscientious official who balked at approving the payment from state funds got transferred out to the provinces, though he later worked his way back under Zhao Ziyang.

At about the time I arrived in China, a poet named Ye Wenfu, who was serving with a cultural unit of the People's Liberation Army, had caused a stir with a new poem titled "General, You Really Should Wash Up."[7] It told of a general who had a military construction unit build him a splendid residence complete with a modern bathtub. Everyone knew that it was not unusual for officers to use their soldiers as laborers or servants. But the poem was attacked for its "erroneous tendencies and undesirable social impact." Ye admitted the incident was fictional, but based on the special privileges he witnessed:

Yes, general, you really should wash yourself.
If you were to die you shouldn't leave too dried-out a corpse.
But don't use this kind of bathtub.
All these bathtubs are the height of modernization,
And how can you look upon modernization as a young girl whom
    you can rape at will?

I suspect that Ye was alluding to Mao Zedong's injunction that "cadres of all levels must wash their hands and feet clean and travel light." But the outrage triggered when a literary magazine published Ye's poem showed what a nerve he had hit. The poet was accused of lacking respect for the Party and the armed forces. According to a report reaching Hong Kong, twenty-five generals jointly petitioned Beijing that Ye be dishonorably discharged. Some detractors told his wife, who was working in another province, that Ye planned to divorce her because she wasn't pretty enough.

Ye Wenfu survived the calumny and remained in the army, I was told, but not without swallowing plenty of gratuitous advice. A critic named Lu Yu, writing in the army's literary monthly, urged that Ye "conscientiously learn some Marxism and cleanse thoroughly the mental dirt that has temporarily contaminated him, so that he will sing healthy and novel songs in the future."[12]

In theory, it should be easy to clean up a centrally controlled bureaucracy; in practice, entrenched interests have made it nearly impossible. Mao Zedong launched his Cultural Revolution in 1966 to "bombard the headquarters," but the casualties included more upright officials than corrupt ones, who hopped onto the new radical bandwagon. Party membership swelled with what were later called the "beaters, smashers, and looters," who perpetuated the chaos. Deng Xiaoping's own "rectification" campaign, launched in 1983 to rid the Party of the radical, corrupt, and merely incompetent, set a target of weeding out 400,000 "degenerates and lawbreakers"—barely 1 percent of the Party membership. Four years later, Bo Yibo, an aging revolutionary who supervised the drive, reported that fewer than 34,000 had been expelled, while another 90,000 were not allowed to reregister. Bo called the drive a success but conceded that power and connections were still being misused for personal gain.

The late Nikita Khrushchev was undone more by his efforts to bring the Soviet bureaucracy to heel than by his clumsy attempts at economic reform. Khrushchev tried to shuffle about his Party officials by ordering that one-third be replaced in each local Party election, which threatened to strip them of not only tenure but also the *blat* or influence they wielded. He later decided to dilute their authority by splitting Party committees into industrial and agricultural sectors. In October 1964, the *apparatchiks*, faced with a loss of power, united behind Leonid Brezhnev to dump Khrushchev. Brezhnev subsequently made an anemic show of cleaning up the Party by instituting an "exchange" of Party documents in 1972 to cull troublemakers from the ranks. It fizzled out over the next few years, and institutionalized corruption, which reached up to Brezhnev's relatives and cronies, worsened.

The officials know how quickly they can forfeit their accumulated privileges, which is reason enough for the widespread resistance that meets almost any serious attempt at reform in the Soviet Union and China. The assurance of life-long employment—what the Chinese call the *tie fanwan*, or iron rice bowl—does not guarantee tenure for the ruling caste. A Soviet or Chinese official who loses his post may forfeit his apartment, chauffeured car, and servants too and find himself hardly better off than the masses.

"When foreigners say the Soviet élite has everything, it is not true," one of my Moscow friends explained. "They are afraid of everything and they are very afraid, because they can lose everything at once. So everybody is dependent on the system." He might have been speaking as well about China's *gaoji ganbu*, or senior cadres (the Chinese nickname them *gao gan*, a pun that translates as "high and dry," or above the swirling tides of everyday life).

"Cadres, comrades, decide everything," Stalin once declared; even today an individual's worth in a collective society ultimately is defined by the authority he exerts over others at whatever level. An extreme example involved Wang Jingyou, an electrician who was also a deputy secretary of his Partry organization in Huayang, a small town in Anhui province. Wang had been drinking with a couple of young women and, at the last minute, offered to take them to see a new film. They arrived at the movie theater to find that the performance was sold out. The manager suggested they stand in the rear. "I'll shut off your electricity," threatened Wang, humiliated at losing face in front of his girlfriends. And when the seats were not forthcoming, he marched to his electric power station, pulled the switches, and blacked out the offending movie theater—along with one thousand households in the neighborhood. Other officials tried to restore the power, but Wang switched it off again. His drunken petulance coincided with a campaign to tidy up the Party's image, and he lost his Party card as well as his job.

Many of the incidents of rape I read about in China involved officials who assumed they had license to sexually harass women under their supervision. The director of an ammonia factory in Yunnan raped at least five employees, leaving the Party secretary to cover up for him until investigators looked into the mismanagement of the plant, where workers were gambling on the job. According to the investigation, one woman was fined three months' wages when she protested after being raped.[13]

Such cases, while hardly rampant, illustrate how far some officials feel they can go. At the 13th Chinese Party Congress in 1987, then Party leader Zhao Ziyang pointed in a speech to "frequent cases among certain Party members of tax evasion, smuggling and trafficking in smuggled goods, bribery, extortion, embezzlement and theft, moral degradation, breaking the law while in charge of executing it . . . appointing people by favoritism and vindictively attacking others." Everyone understood that "certain Party members" meant far too many. Mikhail Gorbachev raised a similar complaint to his Central Committee that same year when he said that "there was no strong barrier put up in the way of dishonest, pushing, greedy people who were intent on benefiting from their Party membership."

More often than not, when a venal official gets into trouble, his network closes around to protect him. In China's Hebei province, a bureaucrat entrusted with buying provisions for a coal-mining operation embezzled tens of thousands of dollars because, the *People's Daily* later reported, "some Party members and cadres forgot Party discipline and the law when confronted with personal interests. Some smoothed his path and some got involved." When I was in Beijing, the Party secretary at the city's Machinery Bureau persecuted three workers who tried to expose his corrupt actions. The tenacious workers hung on until eventually they got the attention of Party investigators.

The extent of a cover-up was illustrated in Latvia, where

Janis Sebrinis, a paralegal in the republic's administrative judicial department, hit a cyclist while driving drunk with a policeman friend and two young women. A passing taxi driver overtook the fleeing Sebrinis and made him return to the scene of the crime. Drunk drivers are usually severely punished in the Soviet Union. But when the police arrived, the cyclist's body was gone—Sebrinis and his friend had driven the victim not to the hospital, fifteen minutes away, but to a more distant morgue—and the hit-and-run charges were dismissed for lack of evidence. Though the dead man's family appealed to the Soviet Prosecutor General to reopen the case, charges against Sebrinis were dismissed a second time. Eventually, Sebrinis had to stand trial for vehicular homicide. He was given a suspended four-year prison sentence, ordered to pay the victim's widow a regular sum until her children reached the age of sixteen, and was transferred to mandatory labor at a construction site in Riga, where, thanks to his friends, he became the foreman.[14]

Deng Xiaoping once identified privilege seeking by cadres as one of the three problems most worrying the Chinese people, after rising prices and before the housing shortage. "In Shanghai, when I was going to work, the whole bus was full of people cursing the Communist Party," recalled the writer Ni Yuxian, whom I met later in New York. He told me about a friend, an economist once imprisoned for his views, who defended the need for price adjustments during a chat on another crowded bus. "People thought he was a mouthpiece of the Party and they wanted to beat him up," Ni recalled. "He said to me, 'First I was in jail, accused of being too hostile to the Party, and now people want to beat me up for being too sympathetic to the Party."

In 1979, Liu Binyan became China's most popular journalist when he exposed a Party secretary of a coal enterprise named Wang Shouxin who amassed a half million yuan through extortion and embezzlement in Heilongjiang province. Liu's investigation produced a best-selling book, *Between Men and Monsters*, and he acquired a reputation as the conscience of the Communist Party, for which his readers loved him and his enemies never forgave him. In January 1987, the Party expelled Liu in one of its campaigns against "bourgeois liberalization" and a few months later the *People's Daily* fired him. Liu's problem, his friend Ni Yuxian explained, was that he had taken Marxism seriously since joining the Communist underground in 1943. "He asks, 'If the Party can run everything, why can't it run itself?' " Ni said. "Party members are afraid of offending this or that person. They are unafraid only of offending the people."

But honesty does not translate into competence, whether in the Soviet Union or China. "The stereotype of a 'good cadre' is a person who is not corrupted, but who is also incapable of doing anything but while away the time drinking tea," said China's *Economic Daily* newspaper. I was struck by the lack of education and polish among lower-level cadres I encountered, until someone leaked me details of a confidential Party report from Shandong province that disclosed that fully a fifth of the agricultural cadres entrusted with instituting reforms in one key district were illiterate.

Such people play it safe by following orders, even when they don't make sense. Mu Qing, a writer from Manchuria known for his epic civil war novel, *The World of Banditry,* was among the intellectuals sent to the countryside to do stoop labor in the Anti-Rightist Campaign in 1957 and later the Cultural Revolution in 1966. When he was working in Liaoning province in 1958, Mu told an interviewer, the order came down that all fields had to be ploughed though the autumn harvest was not truly gathered. The local cadres ordered the remaining corn crop ploughed under to meet the arbitrary deadline. This happened on the eve of Mao's Great Leap Forward, in which fourteen million to thirty million Chinese were estimated to have died from starvation and famine-related illness.

The opponents of change—the Russian playwright Aleksandr Gelman called them "the newly discontented" because reform was jeopardizing their power and privileges—include those who live comfortably in the lap of the Communist Party and fear that more creative newcomers will expose their own mediocrity. When I was in Moscow, no one denounced the dissident artists who struggled to expand the parameters of acceptable art more than the paint-by-slogans illustrators at the Artists Union. And the powerful Writers Union, which the novelist Vladimir Maksimov disparaged as a "witches' sabbath of rank political hacks," earned international notoriety by expelling such literary giants as Boris Pasternak and Aleksandr Solzhenitsyn. When the Writers Union voted to expel Lydia Chukovskaya, a writer of charming children's books, for having defended Solzhenitsyn, the old lady, ailing and nearly blind, retorted in a feisty statement that reached our Moscow bureau: "What will those you expel occupy themselves with? They will write books. After all, even prisoners have written and are writing books. And what will you be doing? You will write resolutions. Write on!"[15]

Under the new era of Gorbachev, Pasternak and Chukovskaya were posthumously readmitted to the Writers Union, whose privileged writers, invariably Party members, thereupon vied in saying how much they admired the victims, secretly of course. A respected Soviet literary critic, Natalya Ilina, wrote in the magazine *Ogonyok* that talent had very little to do with success in Soviet literature and that those established writers whose books were published in the millions, even though no one wanted to buy them, were not eager to see things change. Official statistics show that over 70 percent of the 700 million new books stocked by Soviet libraries from 1976 to 1980 failed to attract a single reader, even as dog-eared typewritten carbons of banned works by Solzhenitsyn or Vladimir Voinovich circulated in *samizdat* and sold briskly on the black market.

The leadership in both the Soviet Union and China has cast about for ways to overhaul the tattered image of the Communist Party. They have replaced old revolutionaries with younger, better-educated technocrats, experimented with new elections and alternative structures that outflank the existing apparatus. But virtually everyone in authority is expected to belong to the Party, though Gorbachev moved to diminish its Leninist vanguard role.

To be fair, even the rejuvenation of Party and government ranks has been no small feat. The Soviet Union had a formal retirement policy, which never applied to the people at the top, but retirement in China was long resisted, perhaps also because of traditional reverence for age. I watched the late Ye Jianying, at the time China's de facto President, totter into the Great Hall of the People on the strong arms of two nurses to open a new session of the National People's Congress, the nominal parliament. The confused octogenarian declared the session closed before he was guided offstage. But no legislator dared suggest that Ye was too senile to preside, even when he fell asleep and drooled on the dais. At the 12th Party Congress in 1982, Deng Xiaoping made a dramatic show of retiring to a newly created Advisory Committee in an attempt to persuade other old men to follow. Yet no one doubted who ran China, even before Deng bounded back in 1989 to crush the student-led democracy movement, which had become the biggest threat to the Party in its forty years of power.

Elaborate plans were laid in China to induce cadres to retire, often on full salary. They were allowed to keep their apartments, cars, servants, and other trappings of power, including access to their former offices and files. To discourage them from hanging around their offices and bothering their successors, the old Communists were exhorted to write their memoirs for future generations. A friend, the daughter of Party cadres, said her parents asked her to help some of their retiring colleagues with the task . What they wrote, she confided, was ungrammatical and altogether tedious. Those in the uppermost echelons were assured of publication by the state, even if no one was interested in what they had to say. As for the rest, their memoirs piled up and gathered dust in Party archives, with no other prospects than to become the grist from which a doctoral thesis might be fashioned someday.

The vulnerability of a one-party state to mediocrity and the damage it can wreak was illustrated by Leonid Ilyich Brezhnev, who ruled the Soviet Union for eighteen of its dreariest and least distinguished years.

As a young Party functionary, Brezhnev survived the Stalinist purges while more charismatic Communists were dispatched to execution or labor camps. He arrived at the Kremlin as a non-voting member of the government's Presidium before Stalin's death in 1953 and then switched his fealty to Khrushchev, the man he was to overthrow in October 1964. Brezhnev was selected by his fellow *apparatchiks* to head the coup against the capricious Khrushchev because he promised a tranquillity that the Party craved. One trait helped Brezhnev dominate the cabal that ousted Khrushchev. He had the organization man's ability to involve his Politburo colleagues in decisions for which they would share blame if things went wrong, yet for which they never quite got credit when things went right.

Collective leadership has never worked in the Soviet Union or China. The Marxist-Leninist vessel seems to demand a single helmsman and the lack of any tradition under Communism of true participatory democracy leaves no grounds for trust among leading comrades, who, like salmon in spawning season, sense that they will perish if they do not advance. It was just a matter of time before Brezhnev nudged Prime Minister Aleksei Kosygin and the other rivals aside and assumed the trappings of the personality cult for which Khrushchev had excoriated Stalin at the 20th Party Congress in 1956.

The Soviet Foreign Ministry let me cover an official visit that Brezhnev was making to Mongolia in late 1974. When he departed in Ulan Bator, I ventured as close as I could at the airport to the man who ran the world's largest country. The Mongolian security men must have mistaken me for one of his numerous aides with my muskrat fur hat, sheepskin coat, and white face, for they parted to let me through and I found myself walking with him to the plane. Brezhnev kept pausing to catch his breath—"smoking is one of my faults," he once confessed—and he gasped as he slowly pulled his way up the steps onto his Aeroflot jetliner. The only remarkable thing I could detect about the man was his conspicuously bad health.

But this was easy enough to conceal, even when Brezhnev eventually looked to the quackery of a faith healer. His official portrait was years old, and subsequent photographs in the press were airbrushed to hide the graying hair and pouches under his beetle-browed eyes. As illness and age sapped his strength, Brezhnev dropped from sight for long periods, usually to his palatial Crimean villa near the Black Sea, which is not hard to do when leaders never have to account for their whereabouts.

During these disappearances, we correspondents would pour through the newspapers, buttonhole diplomats at receptions, and even stand outside the Kremlin's main entrance watching the limousines come and go, all in hope of grasping what was going on. The Soviet press kept publishing little homilies purportedly written by Brezhnev to various Soviet organizations and citizens, accompanied by old photographs to keep his face before the public.

One of Brezhnev's absences, caused by flu that was complicated by his chronic respiratory condition, lasted seven weeks, prompting rumors that he was dead. This was dispelled by an exchange of letters on *Pravda*'s front page between the missing Soviet leader and Leida Peips, a young dairy worker in Estonia.[16] She wrote him in bubbling prose that her "cherished dream had come true" when the Party accepted her as a member. In gratitude, she promised to squeeze more milk from her cows at the Viljandi state farm. In reply, *Pravda* quoted Brezhnev, who was nothing if not avuncular, as expressing his "deep satisfaction" that Miss Peips had fulfilled her five-year plan for milk output in three and a half years, and wishing her and her fellow dairy workers "good health, personal happiness and further labor successes for the good of our motherland." At a time when diplomats and correspondents in Moscow were desperately seeking Brezhnev, an Estonian milkmaid had no trouble enlisting the Soviet leader as her pen pal.

Brezhnev was so racked by illness, including heart attacks and strokes, that twice he hovered near clinical death. After he recovered, emergency medical teams tailed him with an ambulance. The press never mentioned his failing health, which nonetheless became such common knowledge that this

Russian joke circulated in Moscow about Brezhnev's fictitious
daily schedule:

8A.M.—Reanimation.
9A.M.—Breakfast.
10A.M.—Awards medals.
11A.M.—Receives medals.
Noon—Lunch.
2P.M.—Meets foreign delegations.
3P.M.—Nap.
6P.M.—Hosts official banquet.
8P.M.—Retires to bed.
9P.M.—Clinically dead.
8A.M.—Reanimation. . . .

When he did resurface in improved health, Brezhnev was
accorded such exposure that a popular riddle asked: What has
two long ears, four legs, and Brezhnev in the middle? The
answer was a television set. When he spoke, invariably from
notes, Soviet television showed the other Politburo members
furiously copying down everything he said. By now, his speech
had grown so slurred, whether from a stroke or jaw ailment,
that he was nearly impossible to understand. But everyone
nodded and pretended that Brezhnev was making perfect sense.

At the windup of the thirty-five nation Conference on
Security and Cooperation in Europe in 1975, I was part of a
small pool of reporters allowed into the Soviet Embassy in
Helsinki to cover bilateral discussions between Brezhnev and
President Gerald Ford. I assured Tom Brokaw, who was the
White House correspondent for NBC-TV, that I would translate
any remarks by Brezhnev when he emerged. Eventually, we
were summoned upstairs and Brezhnev stumbled out like a
bear emerging from hibernation. He pointed to Ann Compton
of ABC-TV and gurgled something. "What did he say?" Tom
whispered as Brezhnev, who had an eye for the ladies, chuckled
over his unintelligible quip. "I don't know," I said with much
embarrassment. Brezhnev repeated the remark to Viktor Sukhodrev, his interpreter, who had grown accustomed to his
speech defects. "He asks, 'Is it a little boy?' " Sukhodrev ex-

plained, nodding toward Ann Compton's pantsuit and short-cropped brown hair. Only then did I figure out what Brezhnev said by translating it back into Russian.

As Brezhnev consolidated power, pushing aside Nikolai Podgorny to make himself President as well as the Party's General Secretary, sycophants piled on the paeans. At the 25th Party Congress in 1976, they called him "a passionate fighter for Communism," "a son of the people," and "a bright and inspiring example of selfless service." Eduard Shevardnadze, who later became Foreign Minister under Gorbachev but was then the Party chief in Soviet Georgia, marveled at Brezhnev's "art of penetrating into the soul of a man" and said the Soviet leader helped create "a blue and cloudless sky above us." And Brezhnev turned tearful when a contingent of Soviet children in red Pioneer scarves traipsed down the aisle of the Palace of Congresses to recite "a big Pioneer thank you to dear Leonid Ilyich . . . for your fatherly concern about us."

When Brezhnev celebrated his seventieth birthday, I asked Vsevolod Sofinsky, chief of the Foreign Ministry's Information Department, whether the Soviet leader would consent to be interviewed by *The New York Times*. "I think not," Sofinsky sniffed. "Comrade Brezhnev is not a Hollywood movie star." Indeed, he was more than a celebrity, for his birthday was marked with a new outburst of adulation and the most glittering honors extended anyone since Stalin, all calculated to prove that political life did not end at seventy. At a grand ceremony in the Kremlin, Brezhnev collected his fifth Order of Lenin, his second Gold Medal of Hero of the Soviet Union, and a ceremonial sword for his "outstanding service in strengthening the defenses of the USSR."[17]

I think Brezhnev, a man of slushy sentimentality, came to believe what they were saying about him. His portrait borne in parades was made larger than those of his Politburo colleagues. When Brezhnev cobbled together some memoirs about serving as a Red Army political commissar at Malaya Zemlya on the Black Sea in 1943, the minor battle that occurred there was compared to the epic defense of Stalingrad and Kursk. Brezhnev was all but credited with having stopped the Nazis himself. He was proclaimed a Marshal of the Soviet Union, with more medals pinned to his dress uniform than Marshal Georgi Zhukov had earned leading the Red Army through World War Two. In 1979, his memoirs, expanded into three volumes by a team of ghostwriters, were awarded the Lenin Prize for Literature.

Party subordinates vied to acclaim the book, which was made compulsory reading for Soviet schoolchildren. "In terms of the profundity of its ideological content, the breadth of its generalization and the opinions expressed by the author, *Malaya Zemlya* has become a major event in public life," exclaimed the Party secretary of Stavropol in 1978. "Communists and all the workers of Stavropol express boundless gratitude to Leonid Ilyich Brezhnev for this literary work." This effusiveness, the price of political survival, came from Mikhail Gorbachev, who was to puncture Brezhnev's overblown image nine years later.

Brezhnev's friends, whom he favored over more capable outsiders, had him awarded the Lenin Peace Prize as well as the Gold Medal of Karl Marx for his "outstanding contribution to the development of the theory of Marxism-Leninism," though he never said anything original about the ideology. By the time Brezhnev died at the age of seventy-six in November 1982, he had amassed over 220 prizes, awards, orders, and medals, mostly undeserved, including four silver stars of Hero of the USSR.

In fact, much less happened under Brezhnev than met the eye on *Pravda*'s printed page. He achieved a couple of arms agreements with the United States, thanks to Andrei Gromyko, then his Foreign Minister. But Brezhnev's policy of détente fizzled when he invaded Afghanistan in 1979. His agricultural policy, for all the millions of rubles thrown at it, produced one lousy harvest after another. Brezhnev's preoccupation with order over innovation left Soviet society mired in stasis. Even as Brezhnev declared that "the development of recent years forcefully confirm that capitalism is a society without a future," infant mortality rose in the Soviet Union and life expectancy declined.

A Soviet political scientist I knew related an experience that captured the listless mood of disenchantment under Brezhnev. A few weeks before the festive celebrations of the Bolshevik Revolution in November 1977, my friend encountered some peasants selling watermelons in Mayakovsky Square and joined the queue, as Muscovites instinctively do. A passing drunk stopped to stare. "Fools," he berated them. "Sixty years of Soviet power and you're waiting for a watermelon." I asked what happened to the drunk. "Nothing," my friend replied. "Everyone turned away. We couldn't even look each other in the eye."

The failure of Brezhnev's rule was not admitted until January 1987, when Mikhail Gorbachev disclosed in a major speech the lamentable condition into which the Soviet Union had fallen. "At some point, the country began to lose momentum, difficulties and unresolved problems started to pile up, and there appeared elements of stagnation and other phenomena alien to Socialism. All this badly affected the economy and the social and cultural life," said Gorbachev, who had joined the Party's Central Committee under Brezhnev in 1971. Gorbachev spoke of the "serious discrepancies" in the economic planning he had inherited, "serious shortcomings . . . disguised with ostentatious activities," "social corrosion," and "the mass distribution of awards, titles and prizes." He recalled that "the world of day-to-day realities and make-believe well-being were increasingly parting ways."[18] He did not mention Brezhnev nor did he need to; everyone knew who was running the Kremlin in those years.

With the first disclosures of Brezhnev's fallibility, ardent old supporters scrambled for firmer ground. Gaidar Aliyev, a Party secretary and KGB chief from Azerbaijan whom Brezhnev had brought into his Politburo, was on record as fawning over Brezhnev's "wisdom and principle, boundless energy and organizing talent, modesty and simplicity and selfless struggle for the triumph of Communist ideals." Aliyev singled out Brezhnev by name for effusive homage nine times in a speech at the 25th Party Congress and thirteen times at the 26th Party Congress. At the 27th Party Congress in 1987, reporters asked Aliyev what he thought of his patron now. "Well, this really isn't the subject of this press conference, is it?" Aliyev sputtered. "We're here to talk about social policy." On October 21, 1987, the faithful old Azerbaijani secret policeman was dumped from the Politburo, ostensibly for poor health.

Sharif Rashidov, the Party chief of Uzbekistan, had publicly admired Brezhnev's "excessive modesty and brilliant talent" as well as his "spiritual beauty and personal charm." After Rashidov died, the Party turned on Brezhnev's man and posthumously stripped away his honors for having presided over endemic corruption in Uzbekistan. Other Brezhnev supporters were knocked off in turn.

Once Gorbachev, like the child who cried that the emperor had no clothes, had stated the obvious, Brezhnev's posthumous slide began. The truck-manufacturing town of Brezhnev on the Kama River became Naberezhniye Chelny again, at the request of its inhabitants. The Brezhnev district of Moscow reverted to being Cheryemushki, and other town squares and neighborhoods reclaimed their old familiar names.[19] The weekly magazine Ogonyok in early 1988 published a letter from a war veteran named Snegirev who asserted that Brezhnev's prize-winning book of memoirs "is not worth keeping in public libraries and the war museum since, as everyone knows, Brezhnev never wrote it . . ."[20]

The most damaging developments involved the corruption of his era, which Brezhnev was now accused of having tolerated, if not abetted. A Soviet legal specialist, Arkady Vaksberg, charged that some of Brezhnev's old cronies had become "a huge clan of bribe-takers and embezzlers, who turned their high offices into festering ulcers, into market places where everything, absolutely everything was for sale: duties, titles and awards, diplomas and country houses."[21] Brezhnev's daughter Galina had been implicated in a corruption scandal when Yuri Andropov, Brezhnev's successor, first cracked down on corruption and abuse of authority. Now Brezhnev's son-in-law, Yuri Churbanov, was dismissed as the country's First Deputy Interior Minister, convicted of pocketing nearly a million dollars in bribes and sent to prison.

Though I speak ill of the dead, I am being no harsher on Brezhnev than the Russians I knew whose lives were scarred by his rule, including some jailed or exiled for saying things about their country that became tolerated under Gorbachev's policy of *glasnost*. Brezhnev was recognized for what he had been, a Party hack without a vision who eschewed boldness for caution and succumbed to the flattery of his comrades. The Party that had embraced him as "the most outstanding political figure of our epoch" tried to forget him. Leonid Ilyich Brezhnev, naked in all his frailties, was left to the cold judgment of history.

4

NOT A THIEF UNTIL YOU ARE CAUGHT: THE INEVITABILITY OF CORRUPTION

▬ ▬ ▬ ▬ ▬ ▬ ▬ ▬ ▬ ▬ ▬ ▬ ▬ ▬ ▬

Disregard for laws, report padding, bribe taking and encouragement of toadyism and adulation had a deleterious influence on the moral atmosphere in society.

—MIKHAIL S. GORBACHEV
January 1987[1]

At home and abroad lawless people began taking advantage of China's opening to the outside and used every means possible to make profits. . . . Some customs officers were bribed by smugglers with money and beautiful women.

—*BEIJING REVIEW*
May 1988[2]

DESPITE ITS NAME, which means "rainbow" in Chinese, Hengkou is a dreary industrial district of northeast Shanghai. I was there to attend an embezzlement trial at the Hengkou District People's Court, whose austere mood was unrelieved by the bars on the window and the unconvincing wooden paneling. The defendant, Luo Yuansheng, was a middle-aged man in baggy blue jacket and brown pants who hardly looked like a criminal.

The people's judge, Xing Wenhua, wearing a severe black Mao jacket, swept into the courtroom followed by the two lay assessors chosen to hear the case with him. I anticipated some spirited inquiry, but I soon discovered that a Chinese courtroom is not the place for spontaneous drama. The police had already wrung a confession from Luo during his pre-trial detention. It remained only for him to submit to the humiliation of public exposure and throw himself on the mercy of the court.

Luo stood accused of falsifying a bill of lading in order to embezzle steel plates worth 2,200 yuan—then about $600. In collusion with a confederate, Hou Tanxing, Luo had sold the steel to a small rural enterprise at Changli in neighboring Jiangsu province. His payoff was a black-and-white television set, worth about $110, and $200 in cash.

"The above-mentioned facts have been proven by documented evidence and the accused has confessed his crime," the clerk reported. Nonetheless, Luo was instructed to "tell the true story," which he recited in a dispirited voice.

"Speak loudly," Judge Xing ordered.

"Hou Tanxing, my accomplice, asked me to bring the steel plate from my factory. He said the steel plate was badly needed in the Changli agricultural machine plant. So I tricked the leader of my work unit to obtain a bill of lading that should have sent the steel plate to the Huaqiao agricultural machine plant. The Changli factory needed steel plating badly but could not get it from us, because it was not making any processing machines for us."

Though everyone agreed on what had happened—Hou had been convicted at a previous trial—Judge Xing nevertheless called in the witnesses. Yu Yongsun, Luo's boss, identified the fake bill of lading and testified that Luo had indeed diverted the steel.

"Because he made use of the gaps in our management, the state and our enterprise suffered the loss of 2,200 yuan," Yu said. "I shall draw lessons from these mistakes."

Judge Xing turned to ask Luo why he altered the document. "If I said Changli wanted the steel plate, I couldn't have gotten the bill of lading," said Luo, groping for a more accommodating way to repeat what he had already said.

"But why cheat to obtain three tons of steel?" Judge Xing pressed.

"Because my friend Hou Tanxing asked me to help him obtain the three tons of steel plate. I could not refuse him. The Changli plant is situated in my hometown and we have had close relations in the past. At the beginning, I only wanted to help Changli, and my daughter was working in the plant. That is why I wrongfully obtained the three tons of steel plate and transferred it to the Changli plant.

"Afterward, I hinted that I wanted something in return, so I got a television set valued at four hundred yuan from my partner. In addition to that TV set, I later asked for help in buying a color television set, so he gave me seven hundred and fifty yuan."

"Was it a used TV set?" The question seemed irrelevant, but Judge Xing browbeat the frightened defendant as aggressively as any prosecutor.

"I got it for my wife's sister. She gave me four hundred yuan and I sent the television set to her." The defendant pointed to a clumsy-looking set placed on the table as evidence.

Sounds of children's laughter and recorded music drifted into the courtroom from a nearby school. But Luo gave no sign of hearing it as he related how he turned himself in.

"I was very afraid the accounts of the factory would be checked," he said. "So I wrote a letter to my boss. I told him I supplied the Changli plant with three tons of steel consigned to Huaqiao. . . . And yes, I returned the seven hundred and fifty yuan to the Changli plant. I took a train out there and went to the Party secretary's office to confess my offense and to admit I had acted wrongly in cheating my factory and the other factory.

"The commune leader called a meeting and I told the members I borrowed seven hundred and fifty yuan from Hou. And the leaders said, 'It's good that you returned the money to our factory.' Now I understand that by doing this I was just trying to cover up my crime from the leaders of my own factory. I returned the seven hundred and fifty yuan and a receipt was given to me."

"What do you think of your offense?" Judge Xing asked.

"My act can be regarded as taking state property illegally without paying the state. I received over one thousand yuan, so my crime constitutes one of embezzlement. I admit the crime of embezzlement."

At last Luo's defense attorney, Ni Xiding, rose to his feet, and I anticipated a spirited objection to this badgering of his client. But Ni only pointed out some extenuating circumstances.

"How many times did Hou ask you for help in getting steel plate?" Ni inquired.

"He came to me three times for help, because his plant needed the steel badly," Luo said, grateful for a more sympathetic line of questioning.

"And what was your purpose in providing the help?"

"At the beginning, I wanted to help him because he was my old friend and because my daughter was working in his plant. And if my relationship with him was good, the leaders of his plant would look after my daughter better."

When the interrogation finally ended, the prosecutor began reading his summary. "In our criminal law, the defendant has encroached upon the property of the state so the defendant must be duly punished. We must understand not only that the defendant obtained more than one thousand yuan but also that the real value of the steel amounts to an entire year's salary for one worker.

"The defendant's attitude was bad. He did not want to confess," the prosecutor continued. "One of the purposes in punishing an offender is to reform him. His attitude is one of the main features. . . . He appeared to be making restitution, but actually he was covering up his crime."

"Do you have anything to say to the prosecutor's statement?" Judge Xing snapped at the defendant.

"Yes, when my case was first discovered, I wanted to shift

responsibility and cover up the crime, so as to escape punishment. I was afraid if I confessed completely I would get a heavy punishment."

When the defense attorney's turn came, he never suggested that his client might be innocent. "My duty is to speak for the accused, to help the court render a more suitable punishment," Ni said. "I think this case should be dealt with leniently. The defendant's attitude is good. He tried to correct his ways before the investigation really started. The defendant repeatedly confessed his embezzlement to his leaders."

Ni echoed the theme central to China's concept of justice. "One purpose of handing down criminal punishment is to reform the offender," Ni argued. "This defendant has already shown signs of repentance and the effect of his crime on the state has been minimized. This should be considered."

The lawyer then launched into a defense used throughout China to excuse errant behavior: that the radicals surrounding Mao Zedong had so confused notions of right and wrong in the Cultural Revolution that misconduct became inevitable.

"During the ten years of the Gang of Four, the social and legal system was seriously undermined," Ni said. "After the Gang of Four was smashed, some people poisoned by their pernicious ideas didn't pay attention to observing the rules. These people must draw lessons from their past mistakes. We must use this overall method in analyzing what caused this crime. I have interviewed the defendant three times and he regretted committing the crime. He has not lived up to the aspirations of the Party and people.

"Let's review his economic status," Ni said, as Luo stood hanging his head. "Five family members are working and one child is attending university. So the defendant's family life is reasonable enough. With the help of his family, he said that he will bid farewell to his past behavior and mend his ways and do more for the Party, state, and country."

Ni never raised Luo's best defense. The rural enterprise where his daughter worked could not get enough steel to make machinery except through what the Chinese called the *hou men* or back door. It was a problem endemic in China and the

Soviet Union. To boost his daughter's standing with her employers, Luo diverted some surplus steel. But his lawyer did not dare indict the country's clumsy economic system, though everyone in the courtroom knew its defects. It was far safer to blame the Gang of Four.

"Since my case was investigated, I have gradually come to understand that what I did caused serious consequences for society," Luo replied. "With the education by the prosecutors and my work-unit leaders, I have gradually turned good. I understand the facts speak louder than my confession did. My act constituted embezzlement and what I have done is a crime against the state and the people. I thank the prosecutors and my unit leaders for this. Without their help, I would have committed even more serious crimes. I'm determined to mend my ways completely and to contribute more to the state and the people to repay my crime."

After the judge and his two lay assessors briefly recessed, the defendant was brought before the bench. The judge pronounced his sentence: one year's imprisonment reduced to probation conditional on the embezzler's good behavior. As the policemen led Luo from the courtroom, I could see no relief in his grief-stricken face.

The trial said a great deal about law and order in a Communist state. When the authorities bend the regulations for their needs, such as in suppressing dissent, they send out a signal for ordinary people to do the same. Notwithstanding Marx's contention that crime is caused by flaws inherent in bourgeois society, the Soviet Union and China have created a brave new world of lawbreakers who reap illegal profits by making the economy work.

Overt criminal violence was not as apparent as in the West. My wife and I went about Moscow and Beijing at night without the uneasiness that we have sometimes felt in New York. Large Soviet and Chinese cities have relatively stable populations. People get about on trains or airplanes, for which reservations, and sometimes permission to buy a ticket, are needed. Controls like internal passports and residence permits make it hard to move undetected. But where the population is transient or unstable, crime soars. "In Vladivostok, which is the worst, you can't go out on the streets at night," said a Moscow acquaintance, speaking of the boisterous Pacific port in the Soviet Far East.

Stiff gun-control laws have also kept down violent crime. Possession of an unauthorized firearm is punishable by up to two years in prison under Soviet law. The prohibition extends to so-called "cold weapons," as knives and daggers are called. I returned from Helsinki with a hunting knife given me by a Finnish friend, only to have it confiscated at the border because the Soviet customs officer insisted it fit the definition of a "cold weapon." Still, Russians manage to kill and maim each other with smaller knives, axes, and hunting shotguns, which are legal. Sawed-off shotguns, nicknamed *obrezki*, are a preferred weapon among Russian criminals.

A handwritten sign I read at the airport on Hainan island suggested a similar problem for China. "Illegally made weapons are to be handed in to the relevant authorities," it said. "Those who have knives and other weapons may be detained in camps and fined up to 500 yuan." Hainan, it seemed, had rivalries among its rural clans, who were inclined to settle disputes with guns when they had them, spears and knives when they didn't.

But I suspect that an authoritarian police state discourages violence just as it inhibits free will. Soviet police call themselves the *militsiya*, or militia, and Chinese police the Public Security Bureau, as if policemen are unnecessary under Communism, but neither follow Miranda-like procedures, which constrain American cops. Chinese police have not been hesitant to thrash the truth, as they want to hear it, out of suspects. A Chinese legal publication acknowledged in May 1985 that police brutality was "giving the erroneous impression to the masses that if one enters the Public Security Bureau one will inevitably be beaten." My dissident friends in Moscow who had been through the Soviet penal system described it as no more benign. The magazine *Ogonyok* reported in 1988 how the Soviet police battered confessions out of several citizens in Petrozavodsk who were later found to be innocent.

While I was living in Beijing, Deng Xiaoping launched an anti-crime campaign for reasons that were never officially explained. According to one rumor, Deng cracked down after a favorite subordinate's child was mugged. Another rumor had his motorcade ambushed by bandits near the seaside resort of Beidaihe. Whatever the reason, the criminals, real and imagined, were rounded up and tried, sometimes at public rallies. Those sentenced to death were taken out to a field, made to kneel, and killed with a bullet in the back of the head. Though I never witnessed an execution, the truck convoys carrying shaven-headed prisoners to their death became a familiar sight one summer. The condemned men stood in the flatbeds facing the street, with placards hung around their necks announcing their names and offenses: murder, rape, incorrigible theft. If a man being carted off for execution did not hold his head high for passersby to see, I was told, police guards would jab him with a knife. Sometimes a cord was tied around his neck to throttle him if he tried to shout. The Chinese called the spectacle "killing the chicken to scare the monkey," sending a chilling reminder that crime does not pay.

China's death penalty, which punished twenty-nine offenses, also seemed a deterrent, whatever the human cost, because retribution was shown to be swift. Recorded crime dropped nearly 47 percent in one of the first months of the anti-crime campaign. Although the law allows a condemned criminal ten days to appeal, one rapist in central China was caught, tried, convicted, and shot in six days, and another criminal in Canton in eight days. Posters appeared in cities and towns listing every local condemned criminal with his crime and punishment. After the man was shot, the police put a large red check by his name.

The Chinese authorities denied that every province, region, and municipality had been assigned a quota, though we suspected otherwise. As the executions climbed to five thousand or more, protests were raised by Amnesty International (which increased its estimate to thirty thousand by 1989),[3] but not by the Chinese themselves. The brutal summary justice enjoyed some popularity among people I knew. Yes, they conceded, mistakes happened. But the alternative, they insisted, was *luan,* a scare word that can mean chaos, upheaval, disorder, even sexual promiscuity. A young intellectual with dissident sympathies was appalled when I told him that many American states had abolished the death penalty. "But if you don't kill someone who committed murder, other criminals will take a negative lesson from him," he protested.

China's legal system was patterned after that of the Soviet Union, which repealed the death penalty in 1947 only to restore it in the 1950s for treason, espionage, homicide, and serious economic crimes.[4] But Chinese justice seemed more disposed to remold the offender, once his surrender was total. Judges could impose a death sentence that would be lifted if the criminal reformed. Few legal devices—this one was left over from the Qing Dynasty—so stimulated an offender's eagerness to contribute to society.

Russian and Chinese convicts are expected to earn their keep and are sent as forced labor to inhospitable places like Siberia or Qinghai on the Tibetan plateau. Georgi N. Mikhailov, a physicist from Leningrad who told me he was jailed for dealing in dissident art, served three years logging timber at a "light regime" camp in northeast Siberia. So remote was his forest camp, Mikhailov said, that escape made no sense. Mikhailov was released and emigrated to the United States with a remarkable collection of his photographs, which showed prisoners, many of them recovering alcoholics, wrestling with logs in sub-zero temperatures or supplementing their diet of porridge and bread with fish poached from a nearby river.[5]

The Soviet categories of punishment ranged from prison and labor-camp sentences to heavy fines. The Chinese themselves distinguished between *laogai* (reform through labor for hardened criminals) and *laojiao* (reeducation through labor for less serious offenders). "Whoever commits a crime should not be considered innocent," the *People's Daily* explained, "however the treatment may vary in accordance with different concrete conditions." Some of us foreign correspondents were offered a look at *laojiao* when we were invited to the Tuanhe

Reformatory, a penal farm for minor offenders southeast of Beijing.

"Reeducation through labor is a kind of compulsory educational measure, but also a method of handling contradictions among the people," explained Liu Shili, the deputy director of Tuanhe. "The ultimate aim of this system is to educate offenders in technical and ideological ways so they will become people who love the motherland, who love work and obey discipline and the laws. We ask all our personnel to treat the offenders here just as doctors treat patients with infectious diseases, as mothers teach their children, as teachers instruct pupils."

Deputy Director Liu, a tough man in a policeman's white tunic with red collar tabs, said that the majority of his farm's 2,410 inmates were under twenty-five years old. They were required to work in the surrounding orchards, vineyards, and vegetable fields by day and study in the evening. "Discipline and regulations are very strict," Liu admitted. "But corporal punishment is strictly forbidden. And we are not allowed to use swear words." He looked as though he did not need them.

None of Tuanhe's inmates, it turned out, had been convicted in court. The police had the right to sweep potential troublemakers off the streets and into detention until they proved they could behave. This detention normally lasted two to three years but was extended if the inmate did not shape up. "All those people who have been educated here—and their families—are very grateful to us. They write us letters and praise the work done by our personnel," Liu said. "Of course, there are also cases of people who leave here and commit new crimes. As far as we know, they are a very small number." He reckoned the recidivism was only 8 percent.

The penal farm was divided into three brigades and fifteen production teams. "Enter and become new again," promised the Orwellian sign at the gate of a walled compound. We looked into a one-room barracks whose brick floor had been scoured clean. Two dozen prisoners squeezed onto the communal sleeping platform at night. For now, their padded winter jackets were stowed on a rack overhead. Small striped washcloths flapped on the clothesline outside.

The young prisoners in their baggy white shirts and black pants were marched out to perform military drills for us in the dirt courtyard. Then several young men sang folksongs to a guitar and accordion while the other inmates sat stiffly on small camp stools they had carried in with them. The entertainment staged for us seemed joyless and overrehearsed.

After the performance, we were permitted to talk briefly to some of the inmates. A young worker serving a three-year sentence for injuring someone in a fight parried questions with the response, "I will do whatever I'm assigned to do." A coal miner who had spent nearly two years at Tuanhe for assault and battery was skittish of one American reporter's wife who had tagged along wearing a skimpy tank top and was pumping him for his opinions. "If we continue to make mistakes, our sentences will be extended," he blurted, trying to keep from staring at her bare shoulders. I drifted outside to the adjacent vineyard, where an amiable twenty-one-year-old pickpocket in a floppy straw hat was pruning grapevines. He was serving two years for lifting someone's wallet, he said, "and I am looking forward to getting out."

The camp director, Sun Yibin, said over half of the inmates were there for stealing and another third for hooliganism, a catchall offense that he defined as fighting, disturbing the peace, or taking liberties with women. "No one here has gone through any criminal prosecution," Sun confirmed. "These inmates formed some kind of bad habits in society. They may have been detained by the police and when they decide they can't handle them, they send them here." The offender benefited, Sun said, because once he was released he had no formal prison record to hold him back in life. This also meant that he didn't show up in China's statistics of convicted criminals. It was an ingenious way of handling the "contradictions among the people" that crime creates for a socialist society.

China and the Soviet Union have confronted the problem of defending what is legal and what is not at a time of economic retreat from the clumsy precepts of central planning in a command economy. What was prohibited yesterday has become permissible today and perhaps will be desirable tomorrow.

This became apparent in a scandal that broke a few years ago on Hainan, which is officially described as China's second-largest island (the first is errant Taiwan, which has shown little desire to return to the bosom of the motherland). The minor billing slights Hainan, with its lush mountains, white sand beaches, coconut palms, coral reefs, and quaint wooden junks. Some of us reporters who flew down to escape the polluted winter of Beijing were disenchanted when Hainan's officials called us together to promote their interest in foreign investment. Hainan had been closed to foreigners because of its strategic location as China's heavily fortified outpost near the coast of Vietnam. I could imagine the pristine beaches overrun by topless hedonists from Club Med and the fishing hamlets crafting tacky souvenirs from the indigenous pink coral and coconuts. But the islands' leaders wanted to copy the special economic zones in Guangdong province that offered tax incentives and cheap land and labor to foreign businessmen. "We are going to have very flexible policies here," said Lei Yu, Hainan's commissioner, in what proved quite an understatement.

To develop Hainan's primitive infrastructure, the banks in Beijing lent the island the equivalent of $1.5 billion. Hainanese officials swapped this at black market rates for precious foreign currency. Over the next fourteen months, the island used this nest egg to import duty-free 89,000 vehicles, 122,000 motorcycles, nearly 3 million television sets, and a quarter million videocassette recorders—and resold them to eager buyers on the Chinese mainland for up to three times the cost. Everyone seemed to join in, from local banks to kindergartens. Even Hainan's daily newspaper sold off four hundred Japanese mini-vans. The island, no bigger than New Jersey, filled up with more Toyotas, Sonys, and Panasonics as fast as the Hainanese could sell them. When Beijing got wind of the fiddle, government investigators descended on Hainan, but about $700 million of the original bank loans were never recovered.

No one was executed, but officials, including our erstwhile host, Lei Yu, were transferred back to the mainland and punished. A plan was subsequently drawn up to develop Hainan under more careful scrutiny.[6]

The scam on Hainan was notable for its size, not its occurrence. Judging by all the articles in the official press, similar abuses happen daily, if on a less conspicuous scale, in the Soviet Union and China. In the aftermath of a two-year crackdown on fraud, economic crime in China dropped 40 percent in 1987 over the previous year. But China's Supreme People's Procuratorate reported that the reduced total still amounted to 26,000 cases nationwide, three-quarters of which involved major corruption and bribery.

When demand in a centrally planned economic system, whether for steel plating, consumer goods, or theater tickets, continually exceeds supply, it invites corruption. And corruption usually begins with a bribe—*vzyatka* in Russian or *hùilù* in Chinese. "Bribery—it's gone back to the time of Peter the Great," lamented a Russian friend. "It's an Oriental tradition that has always been with us." It also became a Communist tradition.

To get prompt service in Moscow, we slipped bottles of Stolichnaya vodka to repairmen or delivered fancy boxes of chocolates to Aeroflot or Intourist agents to expedite flight and hotel reservations. An American commercial attaché, who, after a trade exhibit, found himself left with a rackful of cheap suits, doled them out to Russian workmen at his exhibits and got the smartest service Moscow had seen since the Czar's abdication. Russian friends told me of bribing salesclerks to get a better cut of stewing meat or a pair of shoes from East Germany. They talked of sending "birthday presents" to teachers to guarantee their children attention at school.

These ordinary people took their cue from the top. Soviet bureaucrats in the Kremlin were given *pakyeti*—discreet packets of cash or foreign-currency certificates—to augment their officially modest salaries. The practice caught on in Soviet sports, where an "amateur" hockey player, who earns 100 rubles a month for work he never does as a plumber, gets much more in a *pakyet* from the Sports Federation. "You give a *pakyet* to a surgeon to get better care, rather than go to the district polyclinic, where three minutes are allotted to each patient," explained a middle-aged Muscovite with a heart condition.

In China, I did not encounter such blatant bribery, not because it didn't exist but because it was harder for me to get inside the fabric of society. "Nowadays, every work unit does the same, as I do with everyone I deal with," wrote a Sichuan businessman to his local oil wholesaler, in offering a bribe for a discount on state fuel. "If you and I just rely on our wages, how can our families ever get rich?" To his credit, the wholesaler mailed the letter to the *Economic Daily* (*Jingji Ribao*) newspaper in Beijing, which printed it on the front page.

In 1987, the 27th Soviet Party Congress included in its future targets the elimination from Soviet life of the "negative phenomena" of embezzlement and bribery. At a rare news conference, Gaidar Aliyev, a former KGB chief from Azerbaijan who enjoyed a brief tenure on the Politburo, conceded that such corruption occurred "unfortunately even among Communists and the leadership," but, he said, "it's impossible to know how much."

Aliyev was probably being as candid as he knew how. Bribery can mean not just cash but also a barter arrangement advantageous to everyone except the state. In the Voronezh region of southern Russian, a railway station manager named Kashkin overlooked fines charged to local enterprises that failed to collect their cargo. In return, the local granary gave him animal fodder. Another customer filled his car with free gasoline, and a bakery sent him meat pies. The deal, hardly unusual in the Soviet economy, was only uncovered when state investigators looked into an accident at the railyard. In Azerbaijan, state sales of gasoline reported one month dwindled to a cupful per registered car; the rest was sold or bartered on the side.

Crimes against the state outnumber those committed against its citizens, so much so that the Soviet government maintains a separate police apparatus, known by its Russian initials, OBKhSS, to investigate economic offenses. In theory, everyone in a Communist society owns the means of production, which makes state enterprises fair game for pilferage. "I'm afraid it's an irreversible process, because everyone wants to live," explained a college-educated woman in Moscow. "We have two economies, state and private; the state produces it and the private sector uses it. It's natural, because you can't exist otherwise. Who steals lives better."

In 1987, *Pravda* reported, over ten thousand Russian workers were arrested in Moscow alone for stealing from their factories, and the city's security chief conceded that such thievery was widespread. Boris Yeltsin, the former Moscow Party chief, said that over a two-year period eighty-six factory and institute directors in the capital were expelled from the Communist Party, a punishment that precedes criminal prosecution, and that in many cases this was for corruption.

When I lived in Moscow, it was estimated that more than half of the one million fir trees put up in homes for the New Year's holiday were illicit; the majority were poached or bought from poachers. An acquaintance captured the mood by citing an old Russian proverb: "You are not a thief until you are caught."

The Soviet press complained that even honest bosses and workers found it easier to turn a blind eye. A senior police investigator named Oleinik who uncovered endemic corruption in Moscow's retail distribution network described to *Izvestia* how store managers unwilling to bribe suppliers were penalized. "Deliveries of scarce goods are few and far between, unmarketable goods are supplied in abundance," he said. "Nothing is provided throughout the month and then, toward the end of the month, they overload you with perishables."[7]

Oleinik, who had to appeal to high Party officials to beat back efforts to derail his investigation, exposed Moscow's most elegant grocery, the Gastronom on downtown Gorky Street. Its director, Yuri Sokolov, was arrested for massive bribery in 1982. He was found to have pocketed nearly 300,000 rubles— over $400,000—in bribes and to have spent 200,000 more rubles to pay off various officials. In 1984, Sokolov was convicted and shot. Two years later, another Moscow retail-trade official, Nikolai Tregubov, was given a fifteen-year prison sentence for corruption. And in early 1988, the press reported that the director of all the state-owned restaurants in Moscow, a man named Busarev, went to jail for corruption. Oleinik's office exposed at least sixty similar thefts known to have totaled at least 3 million rubles, or more than $4 million. In one day, his investigators posed as ordinary customers and found themselves overcharged or given short measure in 156 of 193 purchases at stores whose managers had received awards for efficient operation.

The most flagrant abuse I found in both the Soviet Union and China was probably the unique crime of feeding livestock bread, which, because of price subsidies, costs less than fodder. Although farmers who carried out the practice risked up to three years in a labor camp, *Izvestia* disclosed in June 1986 that 2.5 million tons of bread a year were fed to cattle in the Russian Federation alone. One peasant fed her forty-five cows and pigs on bread for a year before she was caught.

The late Russian dissident Andrei Amalrik told me of a scam popular among farmers in Kaluga, a town south of Moscow to which he was banished. To spur egg production, he said, peasants who delivered eggs to the state were given coupons good for cheap fodder grain, which was in short supply. The eggs were shipped to Moscow and sold at subsidized prices in state stores. The farmers he knew took the train to Moscow, bought eggs, and swapped them in Kaluga for more grain coupons. The eggs circulated until they were too rotten to sell. When Amalrik related the story, he chuckled that the authorities had yet to catch on.

The geographical prevalence of corruption suggested one significant difference between China and the Soviet Union. China's Guangdong and Fujian provinces, and particularly their Special Economic Zones set up to attract foreign investment, were particularly vulnerable because of their proximity to Hong Kong. Haifeng, a county in Guangdong, gained such notoriety that most of its officials got sacked and one, as I recall, was executed. Yet Loufeng, the county next door, was relatively honest. "In Haifeng, things were very bad because the cadres were very weak. They could not resist bad influences and they took bribes," explained an official in Canton. "But in Loufeng, almost nothing happened because the political consciousness of the cadres was high and they could resist."

Without such proximity to temptation, corruption in the Soviet Union seemed to increase in proportion to its distance from Moscow. It ran highest in the southern non-Slavic republics, whose people hew to an entrepreneurial rhythm that flourished before the Communists took over. The Soviet republic of Georgia in the Caucasus was known in Moscow as much for its wheeling and dealing as for its full-bodied wines. Whatever was unavailable in Moscow could be procured somewhere in the Georgian capital of Tbilisi. Veniamin Levich once went to a conference in Tbilisi, where a taxi driver inquired how much he charged to tutor his students on the side. When he replied he didn't do it, Levich told me, "The driver thought I was either a liar or a very poor teacher."

Eduard Shevardnadze, whom most Westerners know as the Soviet Foreign Minister, made his reputation cleaning up blatant corruption when he became Georgia's Party secretary in the 1970s. Presiding over one meeting, he asked subordinates for a show of left hands and then took note of the imported wristwatches inadvertently exposed. A Russian friend who visited Georgia related how Shevardnadze ordered the state-run trolleys to stay in the garage one morning. Then he had his policemen grab the private trams operating illicitly on the same tracks. For this incorruptibility, Gorbachev elevated the tough Shevardnadze to the Politburo.

But the most spectacular rip-off of the Soviet state emerged from Uzbekistan.[8] This Central Asian republic, with its sun-baked cotton fields and adobe villages, was praised for having vaulted from feudalism into socialism after the Red Army expelled the khans and emirs in the 1920s. It pretended to be more Soviet than the rest of the Soviet Union. During my tour in Moscow, Sharif Rashidov, the Party chief of Uzbekistan, got along so well with his Russian big brothers that a non-voting seat was found for him on the Soviet Politburo. His swarthy face looked down from portraits across the country: here was the man for all Soviet nationalities to emulate.

The effect of the blank check that the Kremlin gave Rashidov in return for his fealty became apparent after his death in 1983, when the Communist Party stopped erecting bronze busts of Rashidov around his homeland. Uzbekistan's own Communist Party disclosed that Rashidov had been guilty of "flagrant deviations from Leninist norms of Party life, widespread bribe taking, fraud, and report padding and serious violation of socialist legality."

Almost everyone in authority was implicated in Rashidov's "flagrant deviations." About 5 billion rubles, or $8 billion, were siphoned from Uzbekistan's cotton industry, which is so important to the economy that hundreds of thousands of schoolchildren leave school to pick cotton at harvest time. Massive shortfalls in cotton production were concealed. In the five years leading up to 1983, when Rashidov died, investigators found that 4.5 million tons of raw cotton sold to the state existed only on paper. Even when there was no cotton to pick, workers, including schoolchildren, were kept in the empty fields to create the illusion of a harvest.[9]

In the ensuing investigation, Uzbekistan's Minister of Cotton Industry, Vakhbozhan Usmanov, was tried and shot for "organizing the padding of reports on cotton-fiber production, protecting thieves, and accepting large bribes" to the tune of several hundred thousand rubles. Ten of the republic's thirteen district Party secretaries were removed and hundreds of other Party officials purged for the corruption that Rashidov had institutionalized.

"Not one question was decided without bribes," *Pravda* quoted a police investigator as saying. So entrenched was Uzbekistan's mafia, the Party newspaper said, that policemen were sent from Moscow to arrest the Party secretary of Bukhara, Abduvakhid Karimov, and had to change license plates on their car to avoid tipping off the local police, who protected Karimov's palatial home.

The most sordid disclosure, later published in the *Literary Gazette (Literaturnaya Gazeta)*, told of a fifteen-year reign of

terror in eastern Uzbekistan by Akhmadzhan Adylov, a Rashidov crony appointed to run a large agricultural operation in
the fertile Fergana Valley. Adylov set up his own court to
impose long hours of unpaid labor on his farm workers for
purported infractions. About one thousand of the workers, un-
convicted in a proper Soviet court, were forced to dig their own
underground dungeons under a statue of Lenin, made of silver,
that Adylov erected. He tortured some opponents, eliminated
others through "accidents," and compiled blackmail material
on Uzbek politicians.[10]

Four years after the scandal broke, *Pravda* admitted that
corruption remained rampant in Uzbekistan. And in June 1989,
Ogonyok's editor Vitaly Korotich shocked a Communist Party
conference when he rose to accuse four Uzbek delegates in
attendance of being known bribe takers.

The system of reporting up the line to an impersonal centralized bureaucracy makes the cheating easier. In 1975, when
I was living in Moscow, up to half of the embezzlements uncovered were committed by falsifying audits and other records.
At one plant in the Central Asian republic of Kirghizia, embezzlers carted off 12,000 rubles' worth of goods before they
were caught; the only irregularity that an internal audit had
reported was a salary overpayment of 3 rubles. Some thievery
is concealed as permissible losses. A friend of mine knew a
bookkeeper in Moscow who made 1,000 rubles writing off good
bottles as broken. Investigators found 35 tons of cheese and
4.5 tons of poultry in Moscow refrigerators dropped from the
inventory as inedible though it was fresh enough to sell.

The official press has devoted so much attention to economic misdeeds that one would expect surveillance to get
stricter. But in June 1987 the Soviet Politburo noted that such
oversight had been declining. The introduction of new technology could make matters worse. "The days of computer
fraud may be just over the horizon," a Soviet lawyer said. "It's
hard here because of the lack of credit cards and so forth.
Purchases are usually in cash. But a planned economy has a
strong potential for abuse."

The Soviet Union and China eventually took steps to undercut the opportunities for corruption by decriminalizing some economic activities that flourish legally as private enterprise in Western countries. In a major speech on economic restructuring in June 1987, Gorbachev revealed that Soviet citizens were paying out more than $2 billion a year to a "shadow economy" for goods and services that the state had shown itself incapable of providing in realistic quantity.

In Moscow, I drove a gray Volga sedan, a boxy Soviet car that was indistinguishable at night from the state-owned taxis. Late one evening, I was returning home from visiting friends when a woman jumped out from behind a snowbank and frantically flagged me down. I stopped, assuming there was some emergency. But instead she arranged herself across the back seat, shook the melting snowflakes from her cashmere knit cap, and gave the address of her apartment. She had taken me for a taxi driver and not necessarily a legal one.

Having found this new window into Russian life, I took to stopping when my Volga was waved down. My passengers invariably remarked on my accent; after I explained I was an American journalist, a few nervously asked to get out. But more of my passengers, who had never met an American before, engaged me in animated conversation and occasionally invited me up for a cup of tea. I once moved a couple of young newlyweds to their first apartment, my Volga stuffed with boxes and a mattress tied to the roof. Because I declined to take money for my services a passenger sometimes pressed a small enameled lapel pin or other souvenir into my hand. And they told me how the system worked and how, if you were desperate, you must hold out three fingers to tell the cabbie that you are prepared to pay three times the official fare.

This sporadic moonlighting ended abruptly one night after I stopped for what turned out to be four mean drunks, one of whom vomited himself into unconsciousness while his friends quarreled over how to get him into my car. I left them and abandoned the game as too risky. But I learned that it was not hard to make money *na levo*, literally "on the left," in the

Soviet Union. Under Gorbachev, these gypsy taxi operations have been made legal, as long as the car owners pay taxes on their earnings.

Though the current reforms in both the Soviet Union and China have improved delivery of goods and services, they have also led to new problems with corruption. When it comes to things un-Marxist, many officials have had trouble distinguishing between what is illicit and what is not. Deng Xiaoping was quoted as saying that China's war on serious economic crime would continue until the day that the Four Modernizations, of agriculture, industry, science and technology, and defense, were realized, which meant into the twenty-first century.

With officials reluctant to step in for fear of disturbing a new prosperity that they barely understood, the Special Economic Zones along the Chinese coast became venues for black marketing, smuggling, theft, and fraud. A customs official in Canton told me that the police in Guangdong province had intercepted over a thousand boats, with more than twenty thousand cases of contraband, in the last year. "Without the open-door policy, our economy won't grow so fast, but with it, problems come in," he worried. "If we are not careful, our socialist system will be threatened and China's sovereignty will be threatened too."

I discovered what he meant on a visit to the Special Economic Zone of Shenzhen, which borders Hong Kong. Amid the construction of new factories, high-rise office buildings, and hotels, I noticed a proliferation of white posters on walls and fences. They were signed by the local Public Security Bureau, or police, but many of the Chinese characters were unfamiliar, so I copied them down to look up later in my dictionary. The posters, it turned out, warned the "triads," or old secret criminal societies, to stay out of Shenzhen and threatened stiff penalties for Chinese citizens who collaborated with them. I requested an interview about the triads with the Public Security Bureau in Shenzhen, which first agreed and then reneged. So I took the train to Hong Kong and talked with police detectives who watched organized crime there. They confirmed that the Wu Shing, the Shui Fong, the 14-K Gang, and other notorious societies from Hong Kong's underworld were trying to penetrate Shenzhen. As far as I could tell, the triads were kept out, but by the end of 1987 Shenzhen was the target of sixty-six separate investigations into corruption and bribery.

Communist Party members, because of their positions, seem to figure prominently in corruption cases in both China and the Soviet Union. Roughly one in twenty-three Chinese belongs to the Party; but over a third of fourteen thousand Chinese bureaucrats under investigation for bribery and embezzlement in late 1988 held Party membership, according to Liu Fuzhi, the nation's senior prosecutor.[11]

But most economic criminals are ordinary people who find themselves abruptly in a position to make money. As the reforms created new wealth, the demand for quality consumer goods—and smuggling—increased. On the main street winding down to the harbor of Xiamen, formerly called Amoy, peddlers approached me hawking shirts and jackets with made-in-Taiwan labels, Hong Kong jeans, even Japanese wristwatches. In Shanghai, a black market developed in Marlboros and other American cigarettes. Television sets, cassette recorders, and cameras were smuggled in by fishermen and swapped for antiques, family heirlooms, or traditional-medicine ingredients, since the local renminbi was worthless outside China. Xiang Nan, then Fujian's Party secretary, startled me in an interview by saying bluntly that the rampant smuggling into his province would not stop until Hong Kong and Taiwan were reabsorbed by the motherland.

Yet some of this was quite legal by the standards of Western capitalism. In the Latvian capital of Riga, a group of young entrepreneurs set up an underground factory that stenciled Western slogans and sewed Western labels on Soviet-made tee-shirts, then peddled them to other youths longing for Western-style clothing. For a while, they paid the local police not to interfere. But after they outsold a state-run concern struggling to cater to youthful tastes, the young Latvians were arrested and sent to jail. This was in 1986.[12] Less than a year later, Gorbachev gave a cautious green light to such collective enterprise. And in 1988 at the Viru Hotel in Tallinn, I bought a tee-shirt produced by an Estonian collective, emblazoned with the English word "Rock." These young Balts knew better than the planners in Moscow what the public wanted. The Estonians by accident of timing got away with it; the Latvians didn't.

The evidence is that in groping for a way out of the stasis paralyzing a Communist society, the line between what is proper and what is not has been blurred, dissipating the prosecution of real economic crime. In China, an artist told me over dinner about a young man he knew in Hunan province who offered to buy up sunglasses that a local factory couldn't sell (the Hunanese preferred sunglasses smuggled from Hong Kong with a prestigious foreign label pasted on one lens). The factory gratefully unloaded 2,000 pairs of its unwanted sunglasses for 2 yuan, then about 50 cents, apiece. He hired a truck and drove his wares over the mountains to Tibet, where he had heard the snow glare made any sunglasses desirable. The state had failed to ship enough to Tibet, and the young businessman sold his 2,000 pairs for 37 yuan each, making a profit of 1,750 percent. However, his return home coincided with a new ideological campaign in Hunan against "spiritual pollution." The factory was upset to learn how well the young man had done and he was arrested for economic crime. He protested that there was nothing illegal about selling sunglasses made in Hunan to another part of the motherland. The officials couldn't come up with an answer to that, so in the end they slapped a hefty tax on his profits and let him go.

5

WATCHDOGS OF REFORM: GETTING TO KNOW YOUR NEIGHBORHOOD SECRET POLICE

▪ ▪ ▪ ▪ ▪ ▪ ▪ ▪ ▪ ▪ ▪ ▪ ▪ ▪

> We are not utopians, and do not in the least deny the possibility and inevitability of excesses on the part of individual persons, or the need to stop such excesses. . . . However, no special machine, no special apparatus of suppression is needed for this.
>
> —VLADIMIR ILYICH LENIN
> September 1917[1]

> The Commission [to Fight Counter-Revolution] is to watch the press, saboteurs, strikers, and Social Revolutionaries of the right.
>
> —Lenin's decree creating the Soviet
> secret police, December 1917[2]

THE ONLY TIME I have ever been mugged it happened under police supervision. I had driven out to southwestern Moscow on a quiet Sunday afternoon to view an art exhibit that some unofficial artists were holding in a vacant lot near the Belyayevo subway station. I was chatting with an artist from Leningrad when several dozen husky young men in civilian clothes showed up. They may have known nothing about art, but they did know what they didn't like.

First, they knocked over the exhibits. Then they made a bonfire of some of the paintings, ignoring pleas from the incredulous artists and spectators. An artist attempting to put out the flames was knocked down. When a bulldozer drove up and began grinding modern canvases into the ground, I found myself in the middle of a major story.

The troublemakers seemed in such an ugly mood that we Western correspondents on hand retreated. But when a city water truck mounted the curb and began spraying down the onlookers, I had to take a photograph. Before I could focus my Nikon, someone shoved it hard into my face, chipping a front tooth, and several other men grabbed me from behind. Lynn Olson, a spunky reporter for the Associated Press, tried to stop them, but their leader flattened her with a powerful punch. Then he turned calmly and began slugging me in the stomach while my arms were pinioned. I gasped out to a uniformed policeman who was watching, but he only smiled and turned away. Fortunately, my muggers released me and went off in search of someone else to beat.

Moscow's official version was that some workers devoting their Sunday to turning the vacant lot into a neighborhood park had been attacked by hooligan artists. The artists predictably disputed this account; several of them had been hauled off to a local police station, where they had seen some of the assailants change back into uniform. But the police had been luckless enough to flex their muscle on a very slow news day. Their destruction of the art show became such a major story for Western newspapers and radio that the Soviet authorities were embarrassed into lending Moscow's Ismailovo Park to the dissident artists for a grander exhibit two weekends later. Thousands of Russians who learned of the original incident from Western radio broadcasts attended. I missed it because *The New York Times* sent me off to Helsinki to have my teeth fixed.

A few months after the art-show débacle had gained world renown, a *Pravda* commentator who had seldom deigned to speak to me before drew me aside after a news conference. In a hushed voice, he explained that "higher circles" had authorized him to state that my beating was not intentional. The affair, he was informed, had gotten out of hand.

I could have reminded him that Soviet history is filled
with affairs that have gotten out of hand, on a vaster scale and
with more disastrous human consequences than a chipped
tooth. When the Party relies on the watchdogs of the police,
and not its own moral authority, to counter dissent, abuses
seem inevitable, and the kind of belated apology that I received
is more likely to take the form of posthumous rehabilitation.
Repression was so much part of the Soviet Union and China
for so long that their secret policemen grew used to unbridled
power for its own sake; as a result, they became identified with
the problems, not the solutions of Communism. One of the
ironies of reform is that leaders like Gorbachev and Deng still
find this apparatus indispensable to ensure social stability for
changes that would logically render the secret police irrelevant.

Everyone in the West seems to have heard about the Soviet
Union's Committee for State Security (*Komitet Gosudarstven-
noy Bezopasnosti*), known for short as the KGB. Its 100,000 or
so secret policemen are ordinarily recruited from the *komsomol*, or Young Communist League, and join the Party later as
a condition of employment. Their revolutionary example was
set by Felix Dzerzhinsky and his Cheka—the popular acronym
came from the Russian initials of the all-Russian Extraordinary
Commission that Lenin created in December 1917 "to make
war on counterrevolution and sabotage." As with the rest of
Communist society, this has deteriorated over the years into
blatant careerism. Being in the KGB had its own rewards. Secret policemen qualify for special privileges, and for those
clever enough, the opportunity to travel abroad. Never mind
that, aside from a vague phrase that Leonid Brezhnev inserted
about national security being a citizen's duty, the Soviet Constitution makes no provision for the KGB or its predecessors
to exist.

The KGB types I met abroad were hardly the sinister vil-
lains of the James Bond films. They went into their work for
the money and travel, not for the ideology. They tended to be
well-educated and fluent in the local language and sometimes
possessed an amusing cynicism. Often, they performed col-

lateral duties in order to work abroad (the Federal Bureau of Investigation estimated that a third of the Soviet citizens working in the United States have intelligence responsibilities).

This has not worked entirely to the disadvantage of reform. The KGB's foreign agents are more at home than most Soviet dissidents with the dynamism of an open democratic society, where information is freely available. The extent to which Soviet diplomacy and espionage are interrelated is apparent in what we know about Vladimir A. Kryuchkov, whom Gorbachev appointed to head the KGB. Kryuchkov graduated from the Soviet Foreign Ministry's higher diplomatic school, was assigned as a third secretary to the Soviet Embassy in Budapest, and rose in time to head the KGB's First Directorate, which conducts foreign espionage.

In Moscow, I made the acquaintance of Vsevolod N. Sofinsky, a dapper, silver-haired diplomat who invariably reeked of cologne. As chief of the Foreign Ministry's Information Department, Sofinsky supervised the foreign press corps, for whom he barely concealed his contempt. Our suspicion that Sofinsky had other loyalties seemed borne out a few years after I left Moscow. Sofinsky was sent to New Zealand as Soviet ambassador, where he got caught bribing some trade-union leaders and was ordered to leave by the outraged government in Wellington. I assumed that this bungled attempt to undermine the institutions of the nation to which he was diplomatically accredited would have finished Sofinsky, but not so. In 1985, I covered an international conference in Ottawa reviewing the progress made in human rights under a thirty-five-nation agreement reached ten years earlier in Helsinki. Sitting at the conference table as head of the Soviet Union's delegation on human rights was a smiling Vsevolod Sofinsky.

China has its own secret-police apparatus in the Ministry of State Security, which ironically was created in the Orwellian year of 1984 "to protect the security of the state and strengthen China's counter-espionage work." It superseded the old Ministry of Public Security and assumed additional responsibility for foreign espionage just like the KGB. Domestic surveillance is still conducted through the Public Security Bureau (Gong

An Ju), or local police force, which maintains a less ambitious profile than its Soviet counterpart. Chinese society has been so thoroughly structured, with its watchdog neighborhood and street committees and network of informers in factories and offices, that Chinese authorities don't need to work as hard to target potential troublemakers.

One incident in the Xinjiang Autonomous Region of westernmost China illustrated a difference between Soviet and Chinese secret policemen. When the Chinese authorities let the first handful of Western journalists into the desert town of Kashgar, the scene of serious riots by the Uighur ethnic population a few years earlier, we were followed by a couple of athletic young men, one of whom we nicknamed Boris after an imagined KGB cousin. He was tall for a Han Chinese and wore shiny aviator sunglasses, but he was also shy and would vanish behind a tree or building whenever one of us raised a camera in his direction.

It did not take us long to drift to the old downtown bazaar near the Id Kah mosque, where hand-loomed antique Oriental carpets could be bought for a fraction of their value in the West. In theory, the private sale of these antiques to foreigners was illegal, though they were available at much higher prices in the Friendship Stores. On one back street of Kashgar, I acquired an old carpet from the Taklamakan desert settlement of Khotan for the equivalent of a few hundred dollars and a half hour of bargaining. A fellow reporter in an adjacent alley was trying to decide between two rugs when he saw the Uighur merchant's eyes widen, and he realized that Boris, sunglasses and all, was standing behind him. My friend was wondering how to extract himself from this awkward situation when Boris leaned forward to whisper in his ear. "The one on the left," he said, "is a better bargain." Boris helped him roll up the carpet, tie it with thick twine, and carry it back to our minibus. Our minder from the PSB, it turned out, was a nice guy, and after we stopped trying to take his photograph, he consented to demonstrate his formidable skill in kung fu.

Yet we were watched closely enough so that if Boris didn't report on our shopping someone else did. After we flew back to Xinjiang's capital of Urumqi, a team from the local Gong An Ju materialized at our hotel and proceeded to confiscate carpets, but only from those correspondents who had skipped out of a folklore performance in Kashgar to meet secretly with some dissident Uighurs. This must have caused the secret police to lose face. I was not on the hit list of the "rug squad" because I sat through three hours of folk dances and songs that evening, trying to chat up the Party secretary sitting beside me, and was never challenged about my Taklamakan carpet.

The Soviet secret police seemed more sinister, with its succession of menacing initials from the VChK to the OGPU, NKVD, MGB, and finally KGB, successive tenants of the yellow stone building of Lubyanka in downtown Moscow ("the highest building in the country because from there you can see Siberia," says one hoary Soviet joke). It expanded its authority and influence through what Solzhenitsyn called the "Gulag Archipelago" of prison camps and used its own informers, called *stukachi* in Russian.

Because the secret police was created to defend the status quo of the Bolshevik Revolution, it would seem one of the elements most resistant to change. Yet some of its more sophisticated officials, who enjoyed privileged knowledge of the true extent of the Soviet Union's stagnation as well as the real vitality of the West, plotted ways to reconstruct the country even before Brezhnev's death. It was the power base from which Yuri Andropov rose to lead the Party and hatch the Soviet Union's first recent reforms. Gorbachev himself has promoted allies in the KGB to protect his restructuring policies.

The KGB has made a show of adjusting to the realities of *perestroika*. Its former chairman, Viktor M. Chebrikov, complained back in 1981 that socialism's enemies were disseminating "slanderous fabrications alleging that the Communists of the old generation are doing a bad job of building a new society or, at best, adopting the wrong approach." These slanderous fabrications became guiding verities four years later, once Gorbachev expressed them as the new Party leader. By late 1987, Chebrikov himself was singing about "the positive changes" in the Soviet Union, and promising that "this rev- olutionary process will be reliably protected against any sub- versive intrigues"—an implied threat to human-rights activists not to press too far. Gorbachev evidently was not impressed, because in 1988 Chebrikov was replaced by the more urbane Vladimir A. Khryuchkov, and in 1989 was ejected from the seat reserved for the KGB on the Soviet Politburo.[3]

Gorbachev, a protégé of Andropov, needed to recruit the KGB just as Deng Xiaoping got the Gong An Ju to support his reforms. Both organizations have resources to ferret out po- tential opponents, to deter dissidents from taking too many liberties when discipline is relaxed, and to uncover economic malfeasance. As Andrei Sakharov once noted, the KGB is the agency least riddled with corruption, a virtue shared by the Ministry of State Security in China. That Gorbachev, the prophet of *glasnost*, and the KGB would become bedfellows is not surprising, now that the reformers in the Kremlin have some real opponents to worry about. Deng employed his own secret police to hunt down the student leaders of China's de- mocracy demonstrations.

Perestroika and *glasnost* are mixed blessings for someone paid to worry about the proliferation of videocassettes and photocopying machines, which the KGB and Gong An Ju are supposed to control. The KGB has tried to polish up an image tarnished by years of repression. Accustomed since the 1920s to never apologizing or explaining, the secret police initiated a small column in a weekly propaganda newspaper, "Argu- ments and Facts" (*Argumenty i Facty*), to describe some of its more palatable successes.[4] Between 1987 and 1988, 10 full- length movies, 40 short films, and 235 books were released to put a more benign spin on the KGB.[5] Its generals began sub- mitting themselves to unaccustomed interviews, in which they talked about their war on corruption or organized crime, if not on dissent. In early 1989, the weekly *Nedelya* published an article, with lots of photos, on an ostensible workday at the KGB.

Long before the KGB launched its own *glasnost*, the secret police had become a foil for political jokes told among Russians, if only in a whisper. The extent to which the security apparatus was tucked in bed with the Party was mocked in a well-worn bit of blasphemy circulating when I arrived in Moscow:

An apocryphal contest was held for Soviet artists on the theme of "Lenin in Poland." Most paintings showed the predictable: Lenin clutching his lapel as he spoke to adulatory crowds, striding among workers or children, or poring over some crucial edict. But in one pastoral country scene, Lenin was nowhere to be seen. The only human presence consisted of two pair of legs, one shod in heavy leather boots and the other bare, protruding from under a bush.

"Comrade, who is that?" asked one of the puzzled judges, pointing to the upper set of legs.

"Comrade, that is Felix Dzerzhinsky, our selfless guardian and protector of the achievements of the Great October Revolution," the artist replied.

"And that?" asked the judge, pointing at the naked legs.

"Those, comrade, belong to our beloved Nadezhda Krupskaya, wife and helpmate of the great Vladimir Ilyich Lenin, who inspired him to revolutionary triumphs after his long years in exile."

"But where's Lenin, comrade?" the baffled judge asked.

"Look at the picture, comrade," the artist replied. "Lenin is in Poland."

There is no evidence Iron Felix ever coveted Lenin's wife, who by all accounts was neither glamorous nor witty. But the joke was so familiar that a mere allusion to "Lenin in Poland" was enough to elicit laughter at some Moscow parties I attended.

As fear of the KGB has subsided, it has been replaced by a groundswell among Russians for making the secret police as accountable as a factory or collective farm. On my last trip to Moscow, I visited *Izvestia*'s office, where one of its editors, Vladimir Nadein, read me some of the letters the government newspaper was receiving in an age of *glasnost*. "We don't need our spies in other countries," one man from Belgorod wrote.

"Let's just fight spies here at home." Another reader went further. "You may talk about everything, but it is impossible to speak about *perestroika* in the Party or government until you speak about *perestroika* in the KGB. What has happened inside the KGB?" In July 1989, General Kryuchkov was subjected to the kind of grilling from the once docile Supreme Soviet that a nominee for CIA director undergoes before the American Senate committee. "There is an army of thousands who inform on what is going on in the workplace," charged the former Moscow Party secretary Boris Yeltsin, and called it unacceptable.

There are signs that the Soviet leadership has reined in the KGB. In 1987, Chebrikov was forced to apologize on *Pravda*'s front page for the misbehavior of KGB officers in the Ukrainian city of Voroshilovgrad. They had persecuted and jailed Viktor Berkhin, a reporter for a mining newspaper, when he tried to write about the local corruption he had uncovered. A medical newspaper disclosed that Berkhin died a few months after his ordeal.[6]

The Kremlin also moved to halt the KGB's perversion of psychiatry, in which dissenters were diagnosed as suffering from "sluggish schizophrenia" or "delusions of reform making," then locked away indefinitely and pumped with mind-altering drugs. "Do you see how easy it is? You don't need to have a trial. You can just put him away," said Anatoly Koryagin, a Siberian psychiatrist who spent time in prison for exposing the abuse. During Yuri Andropov's tenure at the KGB, every fifth Soviet political prisoner was confined at some point in a mental hospital.

It is not difficult for a foreign correspondent to come in contact with the KGB in many of its guises. Before I was given my visa to go to Moscow as a correspondent, I was vetted over lunch by an urbane Soviet official at the United Nations whose KGB links were common knowledge. He let me pick up the check, which was unusual. Russians employed abroad by the KGB or its military equivalent, the GRU, are given enough foreign currency to entertain Westerners. Lesser Russians working overseas don't have sufficient access to dollars or hoard them to buy consumer luxuries to take home at the end of their tours.

Visitors to the Soviet Union first encounter the KGB in the person of the uniformed border guards who check their passports and visas at the airports or other control points. When we lived in Moscow, my family and I were scrutinized every time we flew in and out of Sheremetyevo Airport, though it did not take long to know who we were. The guards, nervous young men wearing green service caps and shiny Komsomol badges on their brown tunics, treated every arrival like a potential spy and each departing traveler as a potential defector, sometimes holding a passport to eye level to check every feature of a person's face with the passport photograph.

The KGB enjoyed an advantage in monitoring Western correspondents in the Soviet Union, because our journalistic forays invariably started from the foreigners-only compounds. Our eight-story apartment building at 12/24 Sadovo Samotechnaya in northern Moscow was built by German POWs after World War Two. It had a single entrance that was watched around the clock by a pair of KGB men wearing the gray uniforms of ordinary Soviet cops. Whenever I left, one of the sentinels would step into his sentry booth, pick up a phone, and log my departure. Sometimes a black Volga or Zhiguli sedan parked down at the corner of Yermolaya Street would start tailing me.

While they were uncompromising with me, the guards seemed to soften when my children came out to play—my son Chris used to trade his Doublemint chewing gum for Russian souvenir badges they brought—and they ignored our family cat when she wandered in and out to inspect the garbage cans along Yermolaya Street. One of my lingering images of Moscow was of one boyish KGB guard in his heavy greatcoat and felt boots standing in the lamplight during a December snowfall and playfully pelting the sagging tree branches with snowballs, unaware that I was spying on him for a change from our kitchen window.

We could not hire our own office staff or maid; they were

assigned to us by a government agency—UPDK in Moscow and the Diplomatic Services Bureau in Beijing—with known security links. We were lucky in both countries; our employees seemed such loyal, decent people that it was hard to believe they would be called upon to talk about us in their weekly sessions. I used to leave papers out on my desk to give them something to report because I was afraid that if they couldn't deliver they might be replaced by others neither as competent nor as nice.

Still, we were left with the feeling that we were never alone, and one bizarre episode I experienced in Moscow only fed my paranoia. One evening, the phone in my office was inundated with calls from Russians inquiring if I was the *pult*, a Russian word for switchboard. With increasing irritation, I said no and hung up. The callers continued, their voices sometimes shrill with urgency. When I complained to the telephone company, a bored supervisor replied that it would take a month or longer to trace the problem. So when the next caller asked for the *pult*, I told her to start talking, and she poured out a confusing complaint about neighborhood crime. I inferred that the wiretap had been bungled so that the calls of some law-enforcement agency were feeding into my phone instead of the other way around. I told the telephone company that my callers seemed to want the police. Within a couple of minutes, the supervisor cheerily assured me the problem was fixed and urged me to call if it happened again.

When I arrived in Moscow, I had no sense of being followed, until I realized that my companions were not suspicious men in trenchcoats but plump middle-aged ladies toting shopping bags. Some dissident friends explained that women were assigned to the more menial stakeouts. The KGB tried to remain out of sight, but never very far. Once I visited Aleksandr Lerner, a Jewish scientist who ran a seminar for other scientists who had lost their jobs after applying to emigrate to Israel. I was struck by the number of young men reading newspapers at the bus stop near where I parked my car. Bus after bus pulled up, but they never climbed aboard.

We took what precautions we could, like parking our cars

several blocks from whomever we were visiting to make it a little harder for the KGB to follow us. In Moscow's south-western suburbs, I emerged about 2 A.M. from a late dinner in the apartment of Valentin Turchin, who set up the first Soviet chapter of Amnesty International. I had parked well around the corner, but when I reached my car at that late hour, a white ambulance of the kind used for emergency first aid was drawn up behind. As I fumbled in the dark to fit the key into my door lock, the ambulance flashed on its bright headbeams and transfixed me for a few seconds before driving off.

On my travels in the Soviet Union and China, the security authorities usually assigned a watcher, ostensibly to help me, but in fact to see that I kept to my approved itinerary. When I first went skiing in China's Heilongjiang province, someone ran up and down the hill to make sure I did not schuss out of sight. Jim Laurie, the bureau chief for ABC-TV in Beijing, got more companionship than he bargained for on an assignment at the Manchurian oilfield in Daqing. Jim set out with two Chinese assigned to his project and picked up four more officials in the provincial capital of Harbin. Three other officials attached themselves in Daqing and Jim had to hire a bus to carry everyone. By the time he was ready to start filming the oilfield, Jim told me later, "there were five of us and nine of them."

If foreigners slip through the quarantine, the authorities can depend upon some public-spirited busybody to blow the whistle. I traveled to Siberia on a trip organized for Western correspondents by the Soviet Foreign Ministry. One morning in the chilly little city of Yakutsk, we discovered that Peter Gall, our colleague from *Business Week*, was missing. Our handlers grew more and more nervous until Peter walked into the hotel at last and reported that he had been delayed at the local KGB office.

It seemed that Peter went out for an early-morning stroll and came across a quaint log cabin amid the snowdrifts, the last of a row of shacks being razed to make way for an apartment block. Some chunky new buildings were already rising in the background and Peter thought the contrast would make a good picture to illustrate his story on Siberia's development. Foreigners find such huts charming, with their carved window frames and fairytale snugness, though anyone who had entered one knows they are dark, stuffy, and without running water or toilets, in short the kind of housing the Russians do not equate with progress. No sooner had Peter focused his camera than an elderly pensioner walked up and made a citizen's arrest. The old man marched Peter down to the KGB office and bragged to the embarrassed officers on duty that he had caught a foreign spy.

The KGB men, who knew everything about our presence as guests in Yakutsk, found themselves in a dilemma. To tell the old man that he had arrested an accredited Western correspondent traveling under the protection of the Foreign Ministry would have sent the message that the KGB's incessant calls for ideological vigilance counted for little. So they took the Soviet bureaucratic way out. The pensioner was congratulated, escorted to the next room, and directed to fill out a lengthy report on his triumph. Then the KGB told Peter to get out.

The surveillance was more conspicuous in the outlying Soviet republics. When some of us reporters took a trip to Frunze, the capital of Kirghizia, the hotel clerk would not let us stay on the same floor; instead we were stacked one upon another, in Rooms 201, 301, 401, and so forth. I suppose they couldn't afford to bug an entire floor. Bob Toth of the *Los Angeles Times* and I got permission to visit the Latvian port of Ventspils, where an unmarked van with an antenna protruding from its roof tailed us. If we ducked down some narrow side street, the van turned and followed. When we headed back to the hotel, it reversed. We never saw its occupants.

On such occasions, our watchers avoided a confrontation, but there were also times when they used their presence for intimidation. One autumn evening, Andrei Sakharov and his wife, Yelena Bonner, came to dinner at our home. I drove them into our compound past the police guards. Sakharov was charming, squatting on the floor and using the children's Tinker Toys to construct a model of an atom for them. We had just finished dinner when Hal Piper from the *Baltimore Sun* knocked on our door to warn us that several men were sitting in an unlit Zhiguli sedan outside our apartment entrance. When we emerged, the men, burly but otherwise unidentifiable in the darkness, started popping camera flashbulbs in our faces. Sakharov raised his arms as if momentarily blinded. The men ran back to their car. I tried to copy down the license plate, but there was none. The headlights flashed and the car accelerated at me, barely swerving as I jumped aside. I was probably more shaken than the Sakharovs, and when I returned from driving them home, I asked the KGB guard at our entrance what an unmarked car was doing inside our compound. "I thought they were friends of yours," he replied and hopped back into his sentry booth.

The modern folklore of the Soviet Union includes tales of sultry young women, nicknamed "swallows" in Russian, assigned by the KGB to ensnare foreigners. My only experience, if it was even that, was banal. A woman with a velvet voice telephoned my office one night and asked for me in passable English. She introduced herself as Ludmilla or some such common name. She had enjoyed meeting me, she said, and wanted to know me better. When might we rendezvous? Our bureau number was unavailable to ordinary Russians and I didn't recall any Ludmilla. I asked where we had met.

"Don't you remember?" she said with mock disappointment.

I took a chance. "Was it the hockey match between Moscow Dynamo and Finland?" I asked. "You were sitting behind me with your friends?"

She complimented my memory. "I don't go to hockey matches," I told her. There was silence as the phone clicked. Ludmilla never called back.

The unofficial art exhibit notwithstanding, the police did not make a habit of assaulting correspondents, though I knew of two cases where a Western reporter was drugged and then accused of drunkenness. This is not to say that the *gebeshniki*, as the KGB types are nicknamed from the latter two initials, were as scrupulous with Soviet citizens. The goons I met in

Moscow were different from the sophisticated travelers I encountered abroad. I suspect the locals were not smart enough to be entrusted with an overseas assignment and were left the dirty work at home. I had seen their malevolent faces before. With long sideburns and low foreheads, they looked at lot like some Ku Klux Klansmen I ran afoul of when I covered civil rights in Mississippi as a young reporter. These Russian cousins tried to blend in, but the cut of their clothes—usually black jackets and shoes with thick rubber soles—often gave them away. At one demonstration in Moscow, the *gebeshniki* turned up wearing identical Finnish ski parkas with red and white rings around the sleeves. Imported clothing was hard to find in Moscow, but the special store at which they were entitled to shop must have received a shipment.

At the human-rights demonstrations in Moscow, I learned to hang back just behind the KGB cameramen who photographed the demonstrators for identification afterward. Because they homed in on any confrontation, it was easier to pick out the instigators of violence. One December evening in Pushkin Square, when Moscow's dissidents gathered silently around the poet's statue to observe the anniversary of the Soviet Constitution that in theory protected their rights, I watched some KGB thugs start shoving to give the regular police a pretext to make some arrests. One of the troublemakers was slapping around a scrawny mathematician I knew slightly when a uniformed policeman grabbed them both and frog-stepped them toward the waiting paddy wagon. The assailant jerked away and indignantly flashed some credentials. The policeman let go and saluted. The mathematician was flung inside the van while the KGB man plunged back into the crowd and roughed up another demonstrator.

By comparison, China's Public Security Bureau, which like the KGB has a separate department to watch foreigners, is more subtle. It could afford to be, for in a crowd of Chinese we *yang guizi*, or foreign devils, invariably stood out. One Monday, I ran into an American diplomat who had spotted me waiting alone that Sunday at the gateway to the Summer Palace. He warned me that the Gong An Ju had the site under heavy surveillance because it knew diplomats and journalists were using it to meet Chinese who were afraid to invite a Westerner home.

The Chinese police were suspicious enough of foreigners for the European manager of a hotel in Beijing to tell me that the trash it accumulated was divided into three categories— wet, dry, and security. The last, which included letters and notes discarded by foreign guests, was carted off to the Public Security Bureau for examination (I heard that the KGB was fascinated enough to perform the same messy inspection of our garbage in Moscow). The PSB, the manager said, also tried to increase the number of plainclothesmen stationed inside the hotel, ostensibly for the security of the guests. He went back after midnight with a flashlight and flushed six security agents out of vacant guest rooms, where they had been asleep. The next day, he proposed that the Public Security Bureau increase its vigilance by keeping the assigned plainclothesmen awake, and the demand for reinforcements was dropped.

With few exceptions, I never felt the kind of heavy-handedness in China I had experienced in the Soviet Union. My mail occasionally arrived slit open, but my telephone in Beijing didn't have the hollow echo that characterized a wiretap in Moscow. My Chinese staff seemed indifferent to my activities, though a translator working for another news agency confided that he had been criticized for not disclosing enough about his boss's habits to the Diplomatic Services Bureau. Another Chinese whose spouse worked at a Western embassy in Beijing estimated that one-third of its employees reported directly to the Public Security Bureau.

A Chinese friend once tried to teach me how to recognize those who he said were assigned to follow me. Unlike the modishly attired KGB, he said, the cops from the Gong An Ju wore cast-off clothes confiscated off the backs of criminals and issued to the bureau's own plainclothesmen to save money. Many Chinese around me dressed so shabbily that I never could tell the difference.

While I never grew used to being watched, a Russian intellectual cautioned me not to overrate the power of the secret police. "Too many are trying to justify their salaries," he said. "After all, it is not the KGB that determines things, but the apparatus of the Central Committee. Too many dissidents overestimate the KGB, but they only carry out the orders. They are rather influential, and sometimes they can control what to do, but the decisions are made at the top."

Never having undergone one of their interrogations in the windowless rooms of Lubyanka or Lefortovo prisons, as some acquaintances have, I am hardly an expert in the matter. Perhaps some secret policemen have not embraced the latest enlightenment as gracefully as I implied earlier. When two friends, Tiziano Terzani of *Der Spiegel* and John Burns, my successor in Beijing, were separately detained and expelled from China for ostensible illegalities, there was speculation that it happened because hard-liners in the State Security Ministry wanted to show that they still carried weight.

The safest inference to draw from this is that the secret police is loath to consider itself superfluous in an age of reform. Roland Silaraups, a young machinist from Latvia who was jailed and then expelled from the Soviet Union for his nationalist activities, told me of a conversation he had in a basement cell of the KGB building at the corner of Lenin and Engels streets in downtown Riga: "My interrogator, KGB Major Andres Strautmanis, told me this: 'For you [ordinary citizens], the Stalinist era was the worst of times, but for us [secret police], it was the best of times.' The major said he wanted to make me rot in prison. And he said this in 1986!"

A personal experience in Moscow gave me an unsolicited insight into how closely the KGB worked with ostensibly more benign institutions. One Tuesday evening I returned from an embassy dinner party to get a phone call from a friend at the French news agency, Agence France Presse, who told me that I was among three Western reporters facing insinuations of espionage in a long article appearing the next day in the *Literary Gazette (Literaturnaya Gazeta)*.[7] In the pre-Gorbachev years, this official weekly newspaper of the Writers Union performed periodic character assassinations of dissident and

Western critics, among them foreign journalists. The chore revealed the extent of KGB influence over Soviet life. In the preparations for the seventieth anniversary of the founding of the Soviet secret police in 1987, the secretary of the Writers Union, Vladimir Karpov, publicly praised the tradition of "creative friendship between Soviet writers and Cheka agents."

On this occasion, the *Literary Gazette* devoted a full page to attacking the American news media in general and hinted at nefarious activities by George Krimsky of the Associated Press, Al Friendly of *Newsweek*, and me in particular. Though it never specifically accused us of working for the CIA, the article concluded with a snide assertion that "we know who their true masters are." As far as I could tell, all that the three of us had in common was longevity in Moscow (I had been there nearly three years), some fluency in Russian, and a cross-section of Russian friends that went beyond the dissident movement. The timing of the article had followed an American television documentary identifying some Soviet journalists in the United States as KGB agents.

I was upset by the innuendoes, since I had never worked for the CIA, and even avoided the information swapping that some reporters engage in with CIA station chiefs at American embassies. I doubt that any correspondent for a reputable American news organization would work for the CIA in Moscow, not only because the assignment is a journalistic plum and CIA links, once exposed, would scuttle anyone's rising career, but also because none of us had the time. After wading through the Russian-language press, running around Moscow to visit sources because our phones were tapped, and then filing a story, I rarely got to bed before 2 A.M.

As soon as I had read the offending article, I called up the *Literary Gazette* and demanded a retraction. I was told I could talk to the newspaper's foreign editor, Oleg Bitov, the next day. When I marched into his office, Bitov, a plump man with unctuous manners, invited me to sit in front of his desk and asked what he could do for me. I told him that he could begin by showing me the evidence to back up what his weekly had published.

He sighed, leaned back in his chair and thoughtfully regarded the ceiling as I began taking notes. "The information that exists belongs to our editorial board," he replied after a while. "I have no right to put it at your disposal."

I asked where his material came from.

"Our readers write many letters and I have ten letters about you," he said. "I cannot make them available to you but I can acquaint you with them."

He rummaged among some coarse manila folders cluttering his desk, finally extracted one, and began reading it in Russian. The letter came from Frunze in the Central Asian republic of Kirghizia. "In the restaurant, we met Wren, who introduced himself as an accredited correspondent in Moscow," it said. "This man was sitting with another man at another table. He introduced himself and wanted to know where I worked. The American said he was glad to meet me and invited me to drink a bottle of champagne."

I had stayed overnight in Frunze a few months earlier with Bob Toth of the *Los Angeles Times*. There had been a party at the next table in the hotel dining room to celebrate the birth of someone's son, and they had insisted we have a glass of their champagne. A taciturn local man who had been seated at our table, ostensibly because the hotel dining room was full, strolled out after them when the restaurant closed. I later decided he must have been KGB.

The letter writer said he worked at a secret military factory and claimed I had asked what it manufactured. "He was interested in certain types of products at my plant," said the letter Bitov read to me. "His questions expressed interest in the life of the workers. He wanted to know the profile of basic orders, the volume of production, the supplies of raw materials, and the living conditions of the staff. It seemed like a joke to me. It was like a movie," the letter concluded. I had asked none of those questions, but I could imagine the new father wriggling under interrogation at the local KGB office about why he had invited a couple of American journalists to join his party.

Bitov extracted another letter. "In Ust Ilimsk, you took a

picture of a bridge over the Angara River, which is forbidden,''
he said. I told him that I had been traveling on an escorted
Foreign Ministry tour of Siberia, and never photographed any
bridges. "But you were in Ust Ilimsk," Bitov interrupted to
prove his point.

A third letter put me at a party in Moscow, where I was
alleged to have asked the wife of a Soviet Army draftee in what
unit her husband served, and to have pressed for more details
when told he was in the missile forces. The fourth contended
that I asked a Komsomol official, "How does the Komsomol
select fellows for the special operations troops?" I wasn't permitted to read the letters indicting me. Bitov had mentioned
ten letters, so I asked about the other six.

He sighed with the exasperation of a schoolmaster trying
to reason with a thick pupil. "I cannot get them because there
is a definite procedure of working with letters. But in a few
days it might be possible." His voice took on a sharper edge.
"We might work further with these letters. We have no definite
intentions of doing so but the possibility remains because your
reaction is very sharp.

"And may I say that other organizations have very serious
information that proves what is written in our newspaper," he
added. What organizations? I asked. "If you don't understand,
I ask you to think about it and then you will understand it
better," Bitov said. His smile had disappeared, and I knew he
was talking about the KGB.

Bitov professed astonishment that I would challenge his
newspaper's article, which he said proved I was guilty. "If I
was sure I was innocent, I wouldn't ask for the evidence,"
he explained. "It happens that your information organs make
accusations against our correspondents who work in the
United States," he said. But Soviet journalists accused of
spying didn't make a fuss over evidence, he said. They simply
went home.

"From my point of view, we are making these accusations
in a soft, tactful manner, and if we return to this subject, it
will become considerably more serious," he said. "Another

article is not excluded." I told him to get his facts right the next time.

He stood up and ushered me toward the door. "I think, Mr. Wren, that I have said everything. As I see it, I do not have a right to give you any of the letters. The letters are addressed to the editorial board. I am showing you the letters only from the point of journalistic solidarity.

"If we return to the letters again, we will do it through this newspaper." And they did, but never as convincingly.

It struck me afterward that the KGB hadn't really put its heart, or at least its resources, into the charges. I had been in every place they had put me, but every alleged act was invented. There was no mention of the numerous attempts I made to pry into the Party and other sensitive areas of Soviet life for stories. There was not even a reference to my stint sixteen years earlier as a paratrooper in the U.S. Army Special Forces, which would have made better grist for the disinformation mill. I decided that the KGB was not watching me as closely as I thought.

The initial article in the *Literary Gazette* managed to frighten off some of my Soviet sources even as it prompted unexpected reactions from others. "The article was not directed against you but against us. It is a warning to us to stay away from you," said a university student who said he thought the charges preposterous. He was right, for many Russians I knew now thought twice about seeing me. A couple of Jewish refuseniks told my colleague David Shipler that I should be proud to be identified with the CIA, because it was fighting for democracy. Dave tried to explain to them that no American journalist considered it an honor.

I still wonder whether the Soviet authorities really assumed that, because their journalists had to perform collateral intelligence duties as a condition of working abroad, American journalists were under the same obligation to the United States. One of the best Soviet journalists I knew later in the Middle East was rumored to hold the KGB rank of colonel. And in China, a Tass correspondent was among a group of journalists taken on a tour of a major new petrochemical complex under construction. While the rest of us tucked our notebooks away and admired the view from the top, our Tass colleague opened his large black notebook and deftly sketched a detailed overview of the complex.

I think the attack on my colleagues and me was also calculated to emasculate our coverage of the Soviet Union by sowing psychological doubts. I found myself asking whether what I was doing or asking could be construed as intelligence gathering rather than honest journalism. Had I been behaving suspiciously? Yet reporting from the Soviet Union and China involved, like a vacuum cleaner, sucking up all information available and then selecting what was appropriate for an article. In reading my notes after an interview with one Soviet official in the wake of the *Literary Gazette* article, I was appalled to find my cautious questions spongier than his answers. This self-censorship was what the Soviet authorities wanted, so I tried to put the incident behind me.

Americans remain naïve about the technique, developed under Hitler but shared by Stalin, of making a lie outrageous enough to sound plausible. When I was in New York on a scheduled home leave, a local television station called to invite me to join a panel discussion about the CIA. I told the program coordinator I didn't know anything about it. "But the Russians accused you of being a spy," she coaxed. "You can go on our program and defend yourself." I thanked her for the offer and hung up.

As for my colleagues smeared by the *Literary Gazette*, Al Friendly left a few weeks later when his tour concluded. George Krimsky, one of the most enterprising correspondents in Moscow, was expelled on a fabricated charge of currency speculation; he had given his maid some foreign-currency certificates to buy groceries at the hard-currency store, a practice universal among Moscow's foreign residents. The American government responded by ordering out one of the few Tass correspondents in Washington known not to moonlight for the KGB. The Soviet ambassador was also informed that if I was tossed out of Moscow *Pravda*'s man in Washington would follow me.

Bob Toth was set up by the KGB days before his scheduled departure. After an acquaintance handed him an envelope on the street, goons jumped out of a car and hustled Bob off for thirteen hours of interrogation at Lefortovo Prison before he was permitted to leave the country. The same thing happened in 1986 to Nick Daniloff of *U.S. News & World Report*, when the KGB arrested him in order to get the FBI to release a compromised Soviet agent at the United Nations.

After I let the Foreign Ministry know that I planned to stay a fourth year, and a fifth or sixth if the calumny continued, the harassment stopped. The attacks resumed for a while after I left the Soviet Union. One television documentary featured clandestine KGB footage of my daily road run in bright blue track suit and orange running shoes; the narrator explained that I was conveying secret messages between the U.S. Embassy and Soviet dissidents.

There were more postscripts. In 1985, I met a former Soviet journalist who had emigrated to Canada. When he had worked for the Novosti Press Agency, he said, the KGB sent down files on eleven Western correspondents in Moscow and directed the Novosti staff to prepare articles attacking them. One of the KGB files bore my name. So close were Novosti's ties to the KGB, that a colonel at the KGB headquarters in Lubyanka had two telephones, a black one to the security apparatus and a white one to Novosti.

Oleg Bitov, the foreign editor for the *Literary Gazette*, defected to the West while on a trip to Italy. I had hoped to look him up and learn what really happened. But then Bitov defected back home—he was reportedly worried about a teenage daughter—and announced at a Soviet press conference that the CIA had abducted him and pumped him full of drugs to make him cooperate. Bitov is back working for the *Literary Gazette* as a special correspondent.

When I got a Soviet visa and went back to the Soviet Union in 1988 to write a magazine article on *perestroika*, the rump charges against me never came up. I stopped at Novosti for help with some official appointments, and one of the senior editors remarked over tea that he remembered me. After some thought, he recalled the occasion; we had worked together covering some Soviet-American summit talks years earlier. Unlike Bitov, the Novosti editor seemed happy to see me.

6

SEEK TRUTH FROM FACTOIDS: RED TAPE, COVER-UPS, STATISTICS, CONTRADICTIONS

▬ ▬ ▬ ▬ ▬ ▬ ▬ ▬ ▬ ▬ ▬ ▬ ▬

> The solution of a simple problem
> can be delayed for six months or
> a year or even indefinitely,
> vanishing without a trace in red
> tape.
>
> —DENG XIAOPING, 1980[1]

> The greatest mistake is the fear
> to err. If someone, fearing the
> complexities of the current stage,
> sits it out cowardly in his office,
> without reacting to the fact that
> life is knocking ever louder at
> the doors and windows, this will
> become the biggest mistake.
>
> —MIKHAIL S. GORBACHEV, 1987[2]

ON A CRISP SUNDAY MORNING in November, I was visited at my hotel in the Chinese coastal city of Fuzhou by two officials from Fujian's provincial planning commission. I was winding up a weeklong visit to the province, which winds along the rocky coast of the Strait of Taiwan, and had requested a briefing on the impact of Beijing's new reforms. The older man in the high-buttoned blue tunic, whose name was Qiu, was accompanied by a subordinate named Sun, whose task was to copy down all the questions I asked. It happened in all my interviews with officials in China, and I often wondered where my questions were filed.

Though they were too polite to say so, I sensed that my

two visitors didn't want to be sitting in my hotel room. It was a delightfully sunny day, balmy for November, with a soft wind blowing the scent of salt air in from the ocean. Putting myself in their corduroy shoes, I would not have wanted to leave my family and spend my day humoring a foreign journalist. They seemed relieved when, after the usual formal exchanges, in which they pretended that my spoken Chinese was much better than we all knew it was, I proposed that we get down to business.

For more than two hours, Qiu recited the economic facts of Fujian province from his small notebook. I might better describe them as "factoids"—the kind of impressive-sounding statistics that don't really mean much but are trotted out at almost every briefing in the Soviet Union and China. Qiu informed me that the province had increased its production by 39.9 percent over the last four years, which averaged 8.6 percent higher annually than in the previous twenty-eight years. Production of coal was up 5.7 percent, electricity up 9 percent, steel up 7.7 percent, cement up 17.8 percent, bicycles up 40 percent, and sewing machines up 150 percent. Qiu warmed to his task: peasant income in the province now averaged 268 yuan a year, up 15.8 percent from the previous year, and that of government and factory workers was 765 yuan, up 11.9 percent—here Qiu lowered his notebook to deliver an impromptu aside that this was roughly equivalent to the national average. And workers' salaries, he said, were up 7.6 percent.

Here I interrupted Qiu's monologue. If workers' salaries were up 7.6 percent and their incomes up 11.9 percent, I asked, what accounted for the 4.3 percent discrepancy? Qiu looked up with some astonishment. I suspected that he had never before been waylaid in mid-briefing. His companion Sun furiously scribbled down my question in a row of cursive characters. They exchanged whispers in the rapid-fire Fujianese dialect.

Qiu flipped back and forth through the notebook, running a slim finger up and down the margins. "Probably they contribute articles to newspapers," he explained at last. "Or they may write books. Or invent scientific things. It doesn't mean just salaries."

And he was off again, ploughing through the province's foreign-trade turnover ("975 million yuan, of which 263 million yuan are imports and 712 million yuan are exports"), but he had lost my attention. I couldn't help but think of Fujian's proletarians spending that sunny Sunday toiling over their novels or researching articles for the *People's Daily*, or perhaps devising a better mousetrap on their kitchen tables—anything to account for that not inconsequential 4.3 percent statistical gap between salaries and incomes. Doubtless there was a logical explanation, though I never heard it.

I should not fault Qiu, who was sitting in my hotel room because his superiors ordered him to come. The briefing was only part of the larger Chinese, and Soviet, habit of trying to impress a visitor by overwhelming him with irrevelant information. On a press trip to the Guangxi Zhuang Autonomous Region in southern China, we were briefed on the latest border clashes with Vietnam. "In February, there were fifty-eight occasions when the Vietnamese shot 1,896 bullets at our side, and ten occasions when they shot 194 propaganda shells," a regional official named Zhang told us. "In March, there were sixty-eight occasions where they shot 2,761 bullets." Someone asked who had done the counting when the bullets were flying. "Of course, this is not an absolutely correct figure." Zhang shrugged. What was more important, he told us, was that "they killed our people in haughty arrogance. They flagrantly occupied our land by force, built military fortifications and fired and shelled our side." That made more sense, though I don't recall that we learned how many Chinese were killed.

Statistics that illustrate a point provide the bread and butter of a working journalist; they are abundant enough in this book. But in Communist societies, they exist for their own sake, as if to prove by themselves the superiority of the Marxist ideology. Soviet statistics were no less mind-numbing, particularly when they got into heavy industrial output of rolled steel and such. I never visited a Soviet collective farm without being bombarded by figures on what it had achieved, down to the number of sewing machines in farm homes. The late Soviet comedian Arkady Raikin spoofed this chest thumping when he quipped in one of his skits. "I hear we're doing better than in 1913. That's pretty good."

The manipulation of statistics extended to suppressing those that might reflect unfavorably on the system or its representatives.[3] We knew that the grain harvest was bad or infant mortality was up when the pertinent statistics disappeared from the Soviet press, as they did for about five years in the 1980s.[4] The Maoists circulated wildly inflated harvest output for the model commune of Dazhai in order to make peasants across China believe they were not working hard enough. This misuse has produced a backlash against statistical overkill under the new reforms. In 1984, when I asked an official in the Manchurian city of Harbin for some minor economic indicator, he laughed and replied, "We don't have the total figure for the city but you can find it in various enterprises. We are trying to decrease the use of statistics. We don't use so many useless ones."

Yet statistics seemed to take precedence over people in most of the Communist bureaucracy. It is a swollen behemoth, displaying the attentive solicitude of an office of the New York State Department of Motor Vehicles on a Friday afternoon in August. In his study *Oriental Despotism*, Karl A. Wittfogel defined bureaucrats as those who "rule through bureaus," though, Wittfogel said, "in a specific sense, the term is also applied to any official who uses secretarial devices (red tape) to delay action, to make himself important, to idle on the job"—a definition more pertinent.

The Communists did not invent bureaucracy in China or Russia, though it had adapted easily to Lenin's view of a centralized command administration of leading comrades. According to Wittfogel, in the last period of China's Qing Dynasty, which collapsed in 1911, "about 40,000 ranking officials had at their disposal over 1,200,000 clerks and over 500,000 runners." In 1903, which was fourteen years before the Bolshevik Revolution, Lenin wrote that "just as peasants

THE END OF THE LINE 171

were the slaves of the landlords, so the Russian people are still the slaves of the officials."

In 1865, an English visitor to China named J. Doolittle described the deference he saw shown to Qing Dynasty administrators: "When high officials appear in the street, it is accounted a misdemeanor for the common people to mix up in procession. . . . The sign-boards of stores and shops must be removed from the street when the high mandarins pass by, as a mark of respect on the part of the shopkeepers."[5] Gogol's satirical play *The Inspector General* poked fun at Czarist provincial officials who indulged an impecunious young impostor, believing him to have been sent from Moscow to rate their performance. Andrei Zdravomyslov, a Soviet scholar, implied in the *Moscow News* that Soviet bureaucrats were worse than their Czarist antecedents because ideology had polluted their thinking.

Such a mentality remains a brake on change. That may be why Deng Xiaoping continually urged Chinese to "seek truth from facts," to "make practice the sole criterion of truth," and not to listen just to the production statistics. Mikhail Gorbachev criticized "output for the sake of output and the plan for the sake of the plan." They were hardly the first Communists to inveigh against this prominent defect of their system. Lenin described the young Soviet regime as a "workers' state with bureaucratic distortions" and Stalin talked of "incorrigible bureaucrats and chair-warmers" in his totalitarian ranks. In a famous essay "On the Ten Great Relationships," Mao Zedong complained of "dozens of hands meddling in regional affairs, making them difficult to manage," and of "statistics and reports . . . rushing in like a torrent."[6] Zhou Enlai, when he was Prime Minister, called bureaucracy a "political illness" afflicting the country at all levels.

There was more than a little dissembling in such complaints, which sometimes were intended to convince ordinary Russians and Chinese that their burdens would lighten if only Stalin or Mao could bring the bureaucrats to heel, when in fact these civil servants were carrying out orders from the Kremlin or Zhongnanhai. Similarly, Deng and Gorbachev attacked the bureaucracies for inhibiting their reforms, while stopping short of thorough purges. Instead, they adopted similar remedies in leaving their bureaucracies in place and turning to more responsive think tanks and Party secretariats for new ideas, much as Mao Zedong bypassed the well-defended cities and captured the countryside in his guerrilla war against the Nationalists.

Breaking the stranglehold of the bureaucracy has yet to be achieved in either the Soviet Union or China because the bureaucrats are the ones who carry out, or ignore, the policies promulgated at the top. "The biggest obstacle to reform is the bureaucratic state, the monopolization of power, and the abuses of privilege that go with it," an American diplomat in Beijing told me. "The rationale for the Cultural Revolution was to break through this bureaucratic structure, but the cure was worse than the disease."

Vladimir P. Kabaidze, the manager of a Soviet machine-tool factory, drew applause and chuckles of recognition at the Soviet Party conference when he wryly ridiculed the red tape that he said was strangling his industry. "It's useless to fight the forms. You've got to kill the people producing them," he said. Kabaidze had a few words too for the central planners: "I'd set them all [to work] catching mice. And if they didn't catch any, then they wouldn't get paid.'"[7]

Gorbachev promised to thin out the ranks of 18 million Soviet bureaucrats by eliminating up to a third of them in the central ministries and half down at the republics' level.[8] China, which is estimated to have about 20 million bureaucrats at all levels, announced the creation of a professional civil service with admission by examinations open to all, reviving the corps of mandarins devised thirteen centuries earlier during the Sui Dynasty. The problem is that, because unemployment officially cannot exist, discharged bureaucrats have to be found jobs somewhere else. The futility of streamlining was apparent in Beijing's 1982 effort to trim the number of state ministries and agencies from 98 to 52. By late 1987 the number of employees in government offices and affiliated bodies in Beijing was estimated at 7.43 million, or double their number in 1978.

Between 1984 and 1987, the newspaper *Capital Information* said, the central government kept adding 560,000 new employees a year.

A frequent complaint leveled at the Communist bureaucracy is not just that it is unresponsive, but that it is often incompetent. In 1985, *Pravda* reported that a freight train with twenty-eight gondola cars filled with crushed rock left a quarry at Tomashgorod two years earlier and never reached its destination. An attempt to find the vanished tons of rock mired down in recriminations within the government. The Ministry of Railways couldn't help because all its records were destroyed after one year.[9] In China, I learned of another railway shipment of two incompatible chemicals that were poured together in loading and consequently damaged the production line of the recipient factory, causing losses totaling over a million yuan. The officials who knew about the blunder never bothered to warn the plant.[10] It was not an isolated incident, for the national losses suffered through economic mismanagement the year before had run 1.6 billion yuan, at the time about $687 million.

Andrei Amalrik, a Soviet dissident friend, observed that obedience, not independent thought, became the key to survival in the postwar Soviet Union, creating a bureaucratic élite that grew increasingly ineffectual. A similar suffocation of talent occurred in Maoist China. "Accustomed to obey unconditionally and without thought in order to attain power, bureaucrats, once they have attained that power, are very good at holding on to it but have no idea how to use it," Amalrik wrote. "Not only are they incapable of conceiving new ideas; they regard any novel thought as an assault on their own prerogatives."[11]

The inanity into which the bureaucracy can descend was illustrated during my tour in Beijing when the *China Daily* reprinted this letter circulated by one village committee in central China: "To all villagers—We are hereby sending you the urgent notices issued by the provincial government, prefectural administration, the county and the town leaderships. It is hoped that they will immediately be carried out." At-

174 CHRISTOPHER S. WREN

tached to it was a second covering letter from the township, a third from the county, and a fourth from the prefecture, all saying precisely the same thing. The final letter from the provincial government, for anybody who read that far, asked everyone to behave nicely during the forthcoming Chinese New Year holiday.[12]

I was afforded my own glimpse into the thinking of the Chinese bureaucracy, or at least of the Ministry of Forestry, when I went on a trip laid on for the foreign press to the Wolong Nature Preserve, a stunning panorama of mountains, waterfalls, and forest in Sichuan province. Wolong, which the Ministry of Foresty administered, was at the center of efforts to save the giant pandas that were dying off because of a dearth of their favorite bamboo. By letting us see the famine on the ground, the Chinese government hoped to generate financial support abroad for its conservation effort. The only pandas we saw were in cages, though we wandered their mountain habitat for the better part of a day. There were luxuriant groves of edible bamboo down in the valley, but the Forest Ministry's logging trucks thundering along the dirt roads made the shy animals afraid to descend. From time to time, the nature preserve was also shaken by dynamite exploding at the site of a new hydroelectric station being built along the preserve's boundary. A Ministry official named Lai was philosophical about the explosions. "The pandas will be frightened if they hear the blasting," he assured us. "But they won't be frightened if they don't hear it."

When we asked Sichuan's wildlife specialists how they were spending the $13,000 in "pennies for pandas" donated by American children and ceremoniously turned over to the Chinese government by no less a celebrity than Nancy Reagan, these hard-working Chinese reacted with surprise. No one had told them about the highly publicized donation. The "pennies for pandas" turned out to be in the Forestry Ministry's hard-currency account at the Bank of China. Back in Beijing, I asked to interview officials from the Forestry Minister Yang Zhong on down, all of whom made themselves unavailable. I never learned whether the American children's pennies reached the panda-rescue effort or whether they were spent on imported chain saws. China's plea for international help to save the pandas seemed sincere enough. The crime here seemed to be bureaucratic indifference rather than embezzlement.

Bureaucratic indifference, however, does prepare the ground for corruption in China and the USSR. When I lived in China, a devious purchasing agent for a coal mine in Hebei province siphoned off a half ton of grain, among other foodstuffs, because the mine's managers did not bother to examine the recurring discrepencies between purchases and deliveries. But corruption alone is not to blame for all the losses that pile up. Nearly 1,600 tons of spoiled potatoes bound for Hong Kong were dumped into the sea, at a loss of over 600,000 yuan, because they sat rotting on the dock while two rival offices argued by phone over who was responsible for inspecting them.[13] And an export company in Zhejiang province ignored four urgent warnings from Beijing and continued to ship goods to a customer who was not paying his bills, causing 430,000 yuan to be written off in uncollected debts.

No less damaging has been the bureaucracy's willingness to carry out higher instructions mindlessly. I once went to Xian to find out why the local authorities had demolished a marvelous medieval tower gate, dating from the Ming Dynasty, to build some workers' dormitories. Officials in Shanxi said the provincial government told the city to stop, but the word didn't filter down to the bulldozers until after the old tower was reduced to rubble. Xian's chief engineer seemed appalled by the demolition and told me the city had been ordered to restore the tower, but he admitted that he didn't know how to do it because, as he said, "Nothing is left." A few months earlier in Hunan province, the city government of Changsha knocked down a palace built during the Qing Dynasty after officials at the cultural bureau twice gave erroneous assurances that the palace, Changsha's oldest building, was not worth preserving.

Ironically, such thoughtlessness results from a fear of assuming responsibility. The late Marshal Chen Yi, when he headed the Foreign Ministry in the early 1960s, recalled how one of his deputies kept asking for instructions. "Today, you want me to give you instructions," Chen said he told the subordinate. "Another day when I commit some error, you will be the first one to be against me and expose to others what I said on such and such a day."

The Western businessmen I knew invariably talked about the reluctance of the officials they encountered to decide anything. "In this bureaucratic system, where there are very few rewards for doing things right and very many penalties for doing things wrong, there is very little incentive for getting things done," explained an American oilman who had been negotiating offshore drilling rights in China. Another trader I met tried to buy a large quantity of corduroy cloth for the American market; the factory readily agreed, but the Party secretary at the enterprise never got around to putting his "chop," or seal, on the contract.

Steve Markscheid, a Chinese-speaking American who worked for several American firms in Beijing, found that there was seldom pressure on Chinese officials to wrap up a deal. "A lot of businesspeople think they're getting the runaround, but the Chinese are trying to cover their flanks," Markscheid said. "For all their talk about economics being in command, politics isn't far behind. Any Chinese industrialist who makes the terms so tough that the foreigner says, 'Forget it,' can portray himself as protecting China. Everybody is scared to make a decision, because no matter how right you are at the time, it could look wrong later on. So they want to get as many people in on the decision as possible and it takes a long time."

This caution has extended to the underuse of expensive imported technology. An American physicist told me that he made a habit of checking the power controls on the imported laboratory equipment in the universities and institutes he visited in China. He usually found them covered with dust. "Apparently, the penalties for breaking it were much stricter than the rewards for using it," the physicist concluded. A West German technician who inspected a sophisticated printing press his company had sold the Chinese two years earlier began by reading a dial that recorded the hours of use; the press had been used for forty-five minutes. This stemmed in part from an unwillingness to admit ignorance. Another West German businessman who kept being asked the same questions by ministerial and provincial delegations complained to the *Beijing Review:* "They never read the printed materials we provided them. At first, I thought they perhaps didn't know any foreign language, but I later found they did not even read the Chinese translations."[14]

The reluctance to take the most trivial responsibility inevitably permeates down into the farthest reaches of Communist society. One evening I pulled into the Tibetan town of Xigatse after a bone-jarring ride of several hundred miles over mountain road in a battered Soviet four-wheel-drive vehicle. I asked for a beer to cut the dust of the open road, and indeed the rest house where we spent the night had some bottles in the larder. But the clerk on duty said that he could not sell me any beer without the manager's authorization. Someone went off to look for the manager, but I never did get my bottle of beer, though I offered to pay in scarce dollars.

The bureaucrats have moved more briskly when it comes to covering up mistakes. In February 1988, a fire that raged for nineteen hours through the Library of the Soviet Academy of Sciences in Leningrad destroyed an estimated 400,000 books, many of them irreplaceable. An additional 2.7 million books and manuscripts were damaged by the smoke and water sprayed by two dozen fire engines. Library officials had disregarded warnings in the press that the library was in dangerous condition. But after the fire occurred, they tried to conceal the extent of damage, initially forbidding subordinates to try to salvage some waterlogged editions and even bringing in a bulldozer to bury thousands of books. The estimate of minor loss by the library's director, V. A. Filov, turned out to be about one percent of the disaster's actual cost.[15]

Aeroflot, the Soviet state airline, and CAAC, the Chinese state airline, became celebrated for their rudeness and incompetence as well as their delays and inedible food. I remember one scheduling mixup in which Aeroflot's entire fleet of long-distance TU-134 jetliners wound up sitting on the runway in faraway Khabarovsk in the Soviet Far East, while thousands of passengers waited in Moscow, 4,375 miles to the west.

Airlines in Communist countries, because of their monopolies, are notorious for service with a snarl rather than a smile. Jaqueline and I were bumped from an Aeroflot flight in Baku and left standing on the airport tarmac with our boarding passes in hand because the pilot decided at the last minute to give his local soccer team a lift to Yerevan. And at the CAAC office in Xian, when I tried to book a flight back to Beijing, the ticket agent would not give me the available seat until I filled out a reservation form costing two fen, less than a penny. But the clerk selling this flimsy piece of paper had already gone home—it was a quarter hour before closing time. A few minutes later, the service window slammed down and the rest of the staff left too, but not before a departing clerk taunted, "You look rich enough; why don't you buy yourself a plane?" His co-workers thought his insult terribly funny. In both cases, I settled for a much later flight. Yet both these state airlines were accustomed to treating foreigners far better than most of their own citizens, so my frustrations gave me some taste of what ordinary Russians and Chinese endure. CAAC has since been humbled by the introduction of competing new regional airlines. And Aeroflot has promised to improve service and to recompense passengers kept waiting hours for scheduled flights.

The battle against bureaucracy has become the stern stuff of which Soviet and Chinese novels, plays, and films are fashioned. In a Chinese magazine I read this scenario of an otherwise forgettable movie, titled *Blood Is Always Hot*, released by the Beijing Film Studio:

"China's economic system, just recovering from serious illness, is like a gigantic machine with rusty and biting cogs, unable to operate normally. Sober-minded reformers are searching for ways of improvement. At that time Luo Xingang takes up the post of the director of Fenghuang Silk Printing and Dyeing Factory. In order to carve out a way in the international market for his products, he tries to change the existing production process in a down-to-earth manner. But the brambly road of progress is riddled with difficulties. With ardor and sincerity, Luo Xingang wages relentless struggle against bureaucrats and their conservatism, breaking through one barrier after another. Beset with difficulties, he nearly gets discharged from his post. Undaunted, however, he calls for all staff and workers of the factory 'to use our blood as lubricant to put the rusty and unworkable machine in motion . . . for our blood is always hot.' "

There was more drama in incidents that surfaced in real life, because the bureaucrats did not always lose. In 1986, Mikhail Gorbachev told an audience about a Soviet engineer named Chabanov who had developed new technology for machine tooling and consequently was given temporary charge of an old factory in the Ukrainian city of Cherkassy. When he tried to introduce his new technology, some old-timers denounced him for overstepping his authority and accused him of faking records. Chabanov was fired as director and subjected to a criminal investigation that eventually cleared him. Even so, his ill-wishers got him expelled from the Party. Gorbachev himself had to intercede to restore Chabanov's job and reputation.

A similar incident occurred at a factory I visited in the Yangtze River city of Wuhan, a joint venture with the Parker-Hannifin Corporation of Cleveland, Ohio, making rubber industrial seals. Chen Weizhen, the new general manager, described to me how he had recruited his eighty workers by examination and hired them on renewable work contracts, which was a break from the "iron rice bowl" of lifetime tenure tolerated at most state enterprises. All his employees were high school graduates younger than thirty-five, he said, which meant that he had skimmed the cream of Wuhan's labor force. Chen, himself an engineer rather than a bureaucrat, hoped that by meeting world quality standards, two-thirds of his rubber seals could be exported for hard currency that would pay for imported rubber and American molds. The rest would be used domestically for everything from oil-drilling machinery to truck engines. His factory walls had none of the usual bombastic Party slogans, only a tidy blue-and-white sign proclaiming the new work ethic: "A reputation for quality is the life of an enterprise."

The rubber-seal plant was the most promising joint venture I visited in China, so I was surprised to learn that two years later the province's Bureau of the Machine-Building Industry forced Chen and his deputy Cai Guoning to resign. The Chinese partner in the joint venture, the Hubei Automotive Industry Corporation, was state-owned, and the bureaucrats in charge did not approve of joint ventures with capitalist countries. They accused Chen and Cai of being lackeys for the foreigners and sent investigators into the plant to look for flaws that provided the pretexts for sacking Chen and Cai.

Parker-Hannifin only learned what happened when its American representative came to Wuhan three months later to meet the board of directors and found Chen and Cai absent. The Cleveland corporation threatened to stop transferring technology unless the two executives were reinstated. Under pressure, the Bureau of the Machine-Building Industry relented, but Chen and Cai then had to reorganize the factory anew to impose their old standards of quality and reverse declining profits.[16]

This almost daily interference by the bureaucracy has scuttled repeated efforts to make industry and agriculture in China and the Soviet Union more responsive to the demands of the modern marketplace. In 1988, Mikhail Gorbachev told the Soviet Party's Central Committee that "there are people who are in essence against the reforms, who sabotage the introduction of economic methods of management and try to discredit them in every way." At virtually every layer of the Soviet and Chinese economies, partisan factions, each one armed with its own ideological ammunition and beholden to political warlords at or near the pinnacles of power, have waged guerrilla wars behind the smokescreen of upbeat economic forecasts and statistics.

An attempt by Gorbachev to impose tougher quality-control standards on Soviet industry was obscured in a blizzard of shuffled papers, while some new inspectors were denied office space and other facilities at the factories to which they were assigned, prompting *Izvestia* to write in despair that "we are seeing the effects here of stereotyped thinking, the custom of surrounding any and all endeavors with necessary and unnecessary paperwork, the habit of 'playing it safe,' and the lack of proper initiative, independence, and competence." During another highly publicized drive to curb bureaucratic excesses in China, I read a letter in the *China Daily* from a reader who cautioned that the bureacracy "has plenty of battle experience, for it endured the 1952 and 1957 anti-bureaucracy campaigns."

Gorbachev and Deng had difficulty trying to boost labor productivity by getting workers to perform better. Gorbachev described the Soviet version of China's "iron rice bowl" this way: "It is no secret that even now many people get their pay only for reporting to work and hold positions regardless of their actual labor contribution. And the most surprising thing is that this hardly worries anyone." Nor should it, at least while the penalties for foot dragging are so diluted as to be practically harmless.

The Chinese, to their credit, have devised a way of creating flexibility out of rigidity, of bending certain bureaucratisms to their advantage while leaving the behemoth undisturbed. The word for this circumnavigation is *banfa,* which literally means a way of doing things. When I asked a prominent Chinese writer to define *banfa* for me, he ventured that it was a synonym for resourcefulness in the face of a system choked with petty or conflicting regulations.

Short of outright graft, the Soviet Union seemed to have no such way of end-running the bureaucracy. In 1967, I drove about 1,200 miles from Leningrad to Tbilisi. My trip took a couple of weeks, in part because every day I had to stop to have my Volga sedan washed, for it was illegal to drive a dirty car in the Soviet Union. When I asked why, Dima Biryukov, my companion from Novosti, explained, "Because it is forbidden." But why was that, I pressed. "Because it is against the law," Dima replied patiently. So was hanging baby booties from the rearview mirror, painting the car in contrasting tones, or adding a cute bumper sticker like "Party secretary in trunk." When I moved to the Soviet Union in 1973, dirty cars were still illegal, as they were when I visited in 1988, and during those two decades, I never got a satisfactory explanation. The air pollution and seasonal mud and slush made it nigh impossible to drive a clean car in the Soviet Union. I suspect that the law remained on the books to collect the 30 ruble fine and give policemen license to do what they wanted, since grime exists legally in the eye of the beholder. When the police were ordered to clear Moscow's streets of traffic for the 1980 Summer Olympics, they picked up motorists for driving dirty cars.

I saw my first Chinese *banfa* on a hot July afternoon in Beijing. I had bicycled back to my apartment in the foreigners' compound at Jianguomenwai to find three Chinese fire engines parked outside the gate. The policeman on duty had retired to his sentry box and was conversing on the telephone as the firemen stood around in full firefighting regalia. The cop emerged to talk to the fire chief, who threw up his hands and ordered his men to drive off. Their animated Beijing dialect, furry-tongued at the calmest of times, went too fast for me to follow clearly, but it turned out that a fire had broken out in the kitchen of a diplomat living in the high-rise apartment next to mine. He telephoned the fire department, but the government does not permit Chinese to enter the foreigners-only ghettos without explicit permission. By the time the sentry had secured it through the chain of command of the People's Armed Police Force, the kitchen fire had fortunately burned itself out.

Another diplomat I knew was so unnerved by the bureaucratic delay over the fire that he asked a Chinese official what to do if his apartment caught fire. As the diplomat related it to me later, the official, who knew the rules, thought for a while and then replied that there was a *banfa*. If the diplomat ever had a fire in his apartment, he should not hesitate to call the fire department. But then he must walk out to the front gate and invite the firemen and their engines in as his personal guests. Once he made the nature of the firemen's visit clear to the sentry on duty and vouched for their behavior in his apartment, the official assured him, there need be no problem.

A young British diplomat with whom I had studied Chinese at Cambridge shared his own abrupt introduction to the *banfa*. Shortly after arriving in Beijing, he went down to the Capital Hospital to take the requisite physical examination for a Chinese driver's license. (The license, encased in a red plastic case embossed with gold characters surrounding the official government seal, looks impressive, rather like Party membership credentials.) My old classmate did well up until the final test, which consisted of covering one eye with a soup ladle and using the other eye to identify some letters on a chart. He proceeded to put on his spectacles, which upset the examining physician. The doctor pointed out that my friend was not wearing glasses in the photograph attached to his British driver's license. How could Tom be issued a Chinese driving license that didn't conform to his existing British one? Together they pondered this, until the doctor at last presented a *banfa*.

"You may drive in China," the doctor said, "but you must never wear your spectacles."

In the Soviet Union, I experienced the fatal insensitivity of the bureaucracy when I accompanied a team of American mountaineers on their first ascent of 23,400-foot-high Lenin Peak, the Soviet Union's third-tallest mountain.

I met Elvira Shatayeva in the Glade of the Edelweiss, an isolated alpine valley tucked high in the recesses of the Pamirs, a snow-covered range of mountains running north from the Himalayas along the Soviet-Chinese border. A striking blonde with high cheekbones and catlike blue eyes, she had come there to lead a team of the Soviet Union's best women climbers in an assault on Lenin Peak. That evening in camp, we chatted over strong tea in one of the mess tents, and I sensed a steel core beneath her lithe fashion-model exterior. Her husband, Vladimir Shatayev, told me later that Soviet mountaineers affectionately nicknamed her "the fairy of the mountains." Certainly, none of us had expected to encounter her beauty in so wild a place.

When I next saw Elvira Shataveya, little more than a week later, she lay dead, a victim of one of the worst tragedies in modern mountaineering.

The Soviet press, when it finally acknowledged the disaster, blamed the deaths of Elvira and her seven teammates on hurricane-force winds and bitter cold that froze the women on the uppermost slopes of Lenin Peak. Everyone lamented the worst weather in the Pamirs in a quarter century. No one said anything about the obstinacy of the Soviet bureaucracy.

The Soviet Mountaineering Federation had invited mountaineers from ten Western countries to an international mountaineering camp at twelve thousand feet in the Glade of the Edelweiss. A wind-protected amphitheater not far from the unmarked frontier with China, it was populated seasonally by semi-wild camels, yaks, sheep, and Kirghiz herdsmen.

The foreign climbers were assigned by nationality to their respective rows of tents in one encampment, while the Russians had their own campsite across a small creek on the far side of the grassy meadow. Our hosts encouraged us to fraternize with each other but not with the Soviet mountaineers in the area. We sometimes met them on the trail as we transported our heavy gear up the glacier, and we stopped to compare equipment and chat. But it was always understood that we were climbing separately. On other high mountains, climbing parties tend to keep in contact by radio, but the Soviet Mountaineering Federation calibrated the emergency radio of each nationality to a different frequency, so our messages to each other, even high on Lenin Peak, had to be relayed through the Soviet base camp.

For our own communications, the American expedition had seven powerful Motorola radios, which arrived in Moscow a day after the climbers. Soviet customs officers, nervous about the range and sophistication of the radios, impounded them. We were lent Soviet-made radios of poorer quality in place of our own.

Despite its formidable height, Lenin Peak was considered more of an endurance slog than a technically difficult ascent. But our climbing seemed doomed almost from the outset.

Seven of us Americans set out for a first ascent of a 22,500-foot satellite peak, from which we could traverse across to Lenin Peak, bagging both summits. A few inquiries disclosed that it had been called Moscow-Peking Peak back when Soviet-Chinese friendship was declared eternal. After relations soured, Soviet geographers unnamed the mountain.

To reach our target, we had to ferry our equipment and food over Krylenko Pass, a 19,000-foot snow-covered col linking Lenin Peak and 19th Party Congress Peak, so named after Stalin's last Party Congress in 1952. At 17,000 feet, we paused to rest under a tall serac of ice protruding from the steep face like a snag tooth. The silence was suddenly broken by two loud cracks. Snow, ton upon ton of it, slammed down on us. The avalanche roared as if a subway train were rolling over us. Crouched on hands and knees, I flailed to keep the flying snow from freezing around my face.

Fortunately, the full blast of the avalanche was taken by the serac, which saved our lives. We lost much of our gear but we salvaged what we could and retreated down the slippery slope, which had been scoured clean down to the glacial ice. Fresh falling snow touched off smaller powder avalanches and obscured our vision in the failing twilight.

Four teammates attempting the first ascent of the north face of 19th Party Congress Peak were not so lucky. Another massive avalanche hit them as they slept, killing Gary Ullin, a young airline pilot from Seattle. The three others lost most of their gear and one suffered snow-blindness because he was left without his goggles. They took shelter in a snow cave they dug with their hands.

The response of our Russian hosts at base camp was magnificent. Despite the appalling weather, they summoned a helicopter. Its burly bush pilot hovered dangerously close to the sheer face in high winds so that Peter Lev, an American climber, could drop new ice axes and sleeping bags to the survivors. The constraints against fraternization were ignored as Russians enlisted American, French, German, Swiss, and Dutch volunteers in two rescue parties that immediately set off up the mountain. Our comrades trapped on the north face retrieved the air-dropped gear, and after wrapping Gary in an American flag and burying him in the snow, they worked their way across to the northeast ridge in time to meet the ascending rescuers.

It was the kind of spontaneous international cooperation from which inspirational movies are fashioned. The Russians organized a memorial service for Gary, let us build a rock cairn in his memory, and lowered the camp's American flag to half mast. But when the drama had passed, the Russians in the rescue effort were sent back to climbing with other Russians, leaving the foreigners to each other. We heard that yet another avalanche had swept a party of Estonian climbers off the east face of Lenin Peak, killing at least three of them—we were never told how many, though I was told later that two more died in the hospital. The mountaineering officials were reluctant even to concede to foreigners that the Estonians were missing. We only realized something was amiss when the best Russian climbers left abruptly.

When the weather seemed to brighten, I went back up the mountain with two American teammates, Allen Steck and Jock Glidden, to try Lenin Peak by its northeast ridge. On the first try, we ran into unstable snow that seemed ready to avalanche and backed down. On the second try by a less hazardous route, we reached nearly 22,000 feet before the big storm hit us.

A passing team of descending Siberian climbers had told us that Elvira Shatayeva's party was ahead of us and pushing for the summit. When we had signed out with the Soviet authorities, we were not told the Russian women were on the mountain. Since they included the Soviet Union's best female mountaineers, we assumed they were already descending by another ridge. We had our own problems as we dug in to ride out the storm. The screaming wind reached such intensity that our aluminum tent pole snapped, and we burrowed for warmth in our sleeping bags, wearing all our clothes and boots in case the tent blew apart. We kept trying to radio base camp, which lay two vertical miles below us, but the Soviet-made walkie-talkie was too weak.

We spent two restless nights before the storm passed over. We had cached our rope lower down to cut down on weight, so we moved independently, gasping in the thin air. Six Japanese climbers emerged on their own ascent from behind a rock outcrop, and we took turns breaking a trail through knee-deep snow. In a few hours, we reached the last snow slope, at 23,000 feet, leading to the summit.

Someone seemed to be lying asleep in the bright sunshine. An odd time for a nap, I thought. Despite the snow goggles, I recognized Elvira. She was frozen. We contacted base camp over the Sony radio lying next to her body. But when we got through, the Russian on the other end only asked if we had seen the other seven women.

We began finding them as we climbed up the summit snowfield. Three sprawled across a cloth tent lacerated by the storm. Another was doubled over a climbing rope. Two more lay as if they had fallen down the snowfield. We seached for the eighth around the 23,400-foot summit and assumed she was blown off the mountain, though Elvira's husband told me later she lay tucked under one of her comrades. Some of the women had lost their mittens and pulled socks over their hands in a futile attempt to keep warm. They still wore metal crampons on their frozen boots. Their ice axes were strewn about as if mislaid. The only sound was a stiff flutter of parkas and torn tents in the wind. We marked the bodies with willow wands in case another storm deposited more snow and, too exhausted to do more, started down.

We reached the base camp two days later to learn the details of the tragedy. The women had bivouacked at the summit before descending the mountain's northwest ridge. Rather than retreat when the storm came in, they made a miscalculation to wait until the visibility improved. I suspect that they did not want foreigners to think Russians were quitters.

Once the whirling snow and wind of the storm took away the visibility, it was too late to go down and the women began dying. During those final hours, they talked with base camp over their Japanese radio. The Soviet officials never told them that we might be just below them; not having heard from us, they feared that we too had perished. Elvira reported that they were weak and the snow had frozen too hard to dig a cave to escape the icy blasts. The girls were beginning to go, she said. Because our radio was not tuned to their frequency, we could not hear the dialogue little more than a thousand feet above us. But our expedition's climbing leader, Robert Craig, was at base camp and overheard Elvira's last words: "And now we will all die. We are very sorry. We tried but we could not. . . . Please forgive us. We love you. Goodbye."

The Soviet press did not report the deaths of the country's best women climbers until after I had returned to Moscow and revealed the disaster in *The New York Times*. A government inquiry subsequently concluded that the eight had died "not from mismanagement or mistakes, but from a natural disaster."

Vladimir Shatayev, a fine mountaineer, went up to locate and bury his wife. "Something dreadful must have happened because they were all dressed warmly, especially Elvira," he told me when I visited the Federation in Moscow to offer my testimony on the accident. "It took only eighteen hours for them to die. I was troubled that the tragedy happened so fast, because we have had cases where people fight for their lives three or four days.

"It is very difficult to imagine how the girls behaved when we were not there. I kept thinking what I could have done if I had been there."

I did not tell the grieving Shatayev I had the same thought. What if a common radio frequency had been given to all parties climbing a major peak in such unpredictable weather? What if Soviet customs had let us keep our powerful American radios, so that we could have known enough to mount a rescue? What if the women surrendering to the storm had been assured that a well-equipped American team was only a thousand feet below them? What if we had not been kept segregated from the Russian climbers in the first place?

The Soviet Mountaineering Federation awarded me a flashy enamel badge attesting to my ascent of Lenin Peak, then thereafter found excuses to keep me from climbing anymore in the Soviet Union. A few months after I returned from the Pamirs, I heard that an Estonian filmmaker who visited the international climbing camp was going to screen his documentary before an audience of Soviet climbers in Moscow. I walked in uninvited that evening, but the surprised officials did not ask me to leave because I took the precaution of wearing my Lenin Peak badge.

The color film delved at length into the death of Gary Ullin and the heroic efforts of the Russians to help rescue our surviving comrades. It talked about the intensity of the storm. But there was nothing about the Estonians swept off Lenin Peak's east face or the eight Russian women who died on its summit. I was not the only one stunned at this selectivity. When the film ended, the filmmaker walked out on stage to discuss his work. The first question called out from the audience drew a vigorous murmur of angry assent: "What about Elvira Shatayeva?"

7

WHO WILL
WATCH MY DUCKS?
INDIVIDUAL INITIATIVE,
EGALITARIAN SOCIETY

▬ ▬ ▬ ▬ ▬ ▬ ▬ ▬ ▬ ▬ ▬ ▬ ▬ ▬ ▬

In themselves, money and
commodities are no more capital
than are the means of production
and of subsistence. They want
transforming into capital.

—KARL MARX, 1867[1]

To try to prohibit entirely, to put
the lock on, all development of
private, nonstate exchange, i.e.,
trade, i.e., capitalism, which is
inevitable among millions of
small producers . . . would be sui-
cidal and foolish for the party
that tried to apply it.

—VLADIMIR ILYICH LENIN 1921[2]

WINTERS ARE THE CRUELEST SEASON in the old
Chinese city of Harbin, when the Manchurian wind rearranges
the snowdrifts, rivers of ice flow down the treacherous sidewalks, and orange-and-tan streetcars, their windows fogged by
the passengers squeezed inside, slip and squeak on the steel
tracks. Even on bitter days, the entrepreneurs stand along Sofa
Street, resisting the cold by blowing on their mittened fingers
and stamping their boots lined with dog fur. This is where you
go to find not only a new sofa, but also a bed, wardrobe, or
coatrack, all made better than what the state-run stores offer.

The vinyl sofas were laid out end to end down the middle
of the street when I was there, as shiny and enticing as cars
fresh off a Detroit assembly line. Most were deep red and stud-

ded at the corners with bright brass tacks. At the approach of
a potential customer, the sellers, brushing back the earflaps
dangling from their pile caps, would whisk the snowflakes off
their handiwork with feather dusters. The buyers, equally bundled in padded cotton jackets, would be entreated to linger, sit
down, stretch out, bounce a little on the sturdy springs without
obligation.

"I wear a lot of clothes," said Zheng Lianzhou, a retired
transport worker. Zheng had risen long before dawn to pull
his wares to market in a small cart. The journey took him an
hour and a half. "I'm happy inside, so it doesn't make any
difference to me whether it is cold or hot."

As a youth, Zheng had been apprenticed to a carpenter,
and, once it was declared legal, he took up making furniture.
Zhang spent three days on a pair of small armchairs that he
had just sold for 90 yuan. He said he had sold four sofas to
satisfied customers in the past week, and he netted about 200
yuan a month, after paying out for materials and taxes. It made
a difference in his life.

"Before, we were not allowed to sell anything and I lived
in a mud house," Zheng said. His clipped words formed clouds
in the cold, dry air as they escaped his mouth. "Now I've built
two brick houses and we have a television set and two bicycles.
Our living standard is higher than before."

Business along Sofa Street did not strike me as bustling,
but Du Xiancai, the city-appointed manager of the market,
said that over fifty thousand pieces of privately made furniture
had been sold the previous year. "The market starts as early
as the sun rises and runs as late as the sun sets. It runs until
you can't see," Du said. There were usually four hundred to
five hundred sellers, who had to be Harbin residents, needed
licenses, and paid 5 percent of their earnings in taxes. As for
the prices, they were negotiable. "They will bargain, the buyer
and seller," said Du. "The better the quality of the merchan-
dise, the better it sells." A sofa cost about 150 yuan if it was
designed to double as a bed. A small armchair might go for 40
or 50 yuan.

"Some people have earned a lot of money," said Du as he

walked along the row of sofas, inspecting the paper licenses on display. Along Sofa Street, other vendors were peddling their own meat dumplings, candied cherries on sticks, ground spices, and hair curlers. "Some have even bought expensive sewing machines, color television sets, even motorcycles." That was what Adam Smith or Karl Marx would have called creating wealth. "It benefits the country to open this kind of market. Both the people and the state benefit," Du Xiancai said.

The reemergence of sofas seemed to me a marvelous confirmation of human ingenuity, which is sorely tested in a Communist society. Because it contained manifestations of capitalist exploitation, free enterprise has long been seen as incompatible with Communism. One of the greatest ironies of change in China and the Soviet Union has been the resurrection of private initiative as a salvation for socialism, and, like other reforms, its flaws, not least a growing prosperity gap, lie in not having gone far enough.

Initially, there was no room for capitalism in the Bolshevik Revolution. But to feed the new Soviet state after the devastation of the civil war and Allied intervention, Lenin instituted his New Economic Policy, which revived private trading, small-scale farming, and concessions to foreign businessmen, while leaving "the commanding heights in the sphere of production" to the state.[3] His policy bore a startling similarity to what has happened in China and the Soviet Union in more recent years. Some fellow Bolsheviks denounced this compromise as a betrayal of the proletariat. After Lenin's death in 1924, Stalin strangled the New Economic Policy, persecuted its petty tradesmen, and later shot some of those, like Nikolai Bukharin, who espoused the sort of experiments that Gorbachev embarked upon more than a half century later.

China likewise tolerated its private entrepreneurs for a few years after the Communist takeover in 1949. But as economic policies based on the Soviet model were introduced, their number plummeted from early 8.4 million businessmen in 1953 to barely 160,000 three years later. They continued to decline during the Cultural Revolution, when even itinerant peddlers were persecuted as "the tail of capitalism." When Deng Xiaoping junked the perception that private enterprise was evil, the number of private businessmen rebounded to 7.5 million by 1983.⁴ Deng, no closet capitalist, was compensating for the state's failure to meet consumer needs, from private tailors to noodle shops and bicycle-repair stands.

The resurrection of private enterprise may be the most controversial reform undertaken in the Soviet Union and China, prompting long debates about its propriety in a society where the means of production are publicly owned. The Chinese have done it better than the Russians, and with fewer ideological qualms, perhaps because the Chinese, as their immigrants proved overseas, take to commerce more instinctively, I haven't come across any Russian takeout restaurants in the West.

China's watershed was a directive issued in November 1981 by the government and Party telling the unemployed to get out and find their own jobs. The authorities realized that the state could not guarantee everyone a job for life. The Chinese nicknamed this tenure the *tie fanwan*, or "iron rice bowl," because it was almost impossible to get fired, no matter how badly you worked. Most young Chinese I met shied away from the call and waited to inherit jobs held by their parents. They were born too late to remember how private enterprise flourished before the Communists, but they did know what happened to it afterward, and there was not a little fear about their fate if the policy was canceled. But enough Chinese were dissatisfied with the low salaries and tedium of factory labor to take a risk; over four-fifths of the restaurants and shops opened since 1978 have been private. Of course, Beijing's crackdown on dissent could not help but dampen enthusiasm.

"I was afraid of setting up an individual enterprise at the beginning too," explained Bai Shimin, a self-employed photographer in Harbin. "But I decided to see if I could earn more money."

Bai, a young man with a shock of black hair, was grossing 80 to 100 yuan a day, more than most state employees were paid in a week, and he earned it. His studio, set up in his family's cramped home, was open from 8 A.M. to 8 P.M. Then he worked into the night processing the film. Bai didn't take weekends or holidays off because he said his customers depended on him. Some even knocked on his door at midnight for some photograph to affix to a legal document. He also did weddings. There was a state-owned photography studio down the small street, but Bai said, "My rates are slightly lower and I am faster. I also concentrate on quality because too many studios now are run by the state." He did not have to finish his thought: every Chinese knew what notoriously poor service the state offered.

I got in touch with Bai Shimin because a local newspaper had hailed him as a role model for other youths thinking of going into business. Bai said the article had brought him nearly three hundred letters, including offers of marriage from women interested in a young bachelor with a knack for making money. I asked why more youths had not followed his example. He said the egalitarian influence of the leftists surrounding Mao Zedong had made his peers timid. "We should not blame these people," he said. "Because of the Gang of Four, all they could do was wait for someone to give them a job. We must teach these people that it doesn't matter what work they do, whether it's state or collective or private. Whatever job one does can serve the people."

I found Bai's ethic of individualism and hard work curious because he had recently joined the Communist Party. I asked him if there wasn't what the Chinese call a *maodun*, or contradiction, here. The popular word *maodun*, which combines the Chinese characters for "spear" and "shield," has its origins in a folktale about private enterprise in ancient China. An arms seller in the market advertised that his spears were so sharp they would penetrate anything and his shields were so tough as to repel anything. A suspicious customer asked what would happen if his spears got used against his shields. The seller could not answer; hence, the contradiction, with which modern China seems no less rife.

When speaking to a foreigner, most Chinese deny that their life has any contradictions, and I was surprised to hear

Bai concede that he had given it some thought. "As a system, private enterprise is against the theory of Marxism," he said. "But in China, the situation is quite different, because we are at an early stage of socialist society. Whether private enterprise exists depends on our country's situation, not on myself or other people. People cannot control these things."

I pointed out that once China marched toward Communism, Bai could find himself out of a job. "Yes, that is the law of objective development," he agreed. "Individual enterprises will finally disappear. But now they have to exist. If your leather shoes break down, they have to be repaired. But if our life becomes richer, we won't have to repair our shoes. We'll just buy new ones."

The growth of private enterprise spread fast in the countryside, where, by one official estimate, 45,000 free markets proliferated. The most spectacular I ever saw was in Kashgar on the edge of the Taklamakan desert in westernmost China. Kashgar had been an old caravan stop on the legendary Silk Road and it still knew how to stage a bazaar. When Marco Polo had preceded me seven centuries earlier, he had taken note of Kashgar's prosperity and the stinginess of its Uighur population. The latter seemed unfair toward the Uighurs, an ethnic minority of Turkish descent, who had survived through the centuries by their wits.

In the cool of the early morning, carts laden with produce and people began to converge along the tree-lined dirt roads from the outlying desert and mountains. The wagons were mostly pulled by horses, donkeys, and even a couple of gangly camels, though I saw a small tractor hitched to one cart. Everyone seemed headed for the Sunday bazaar, and those who could not climb aboard the crowded carts walked. The outstretched arm on an eighty-foot-high white statue of Mao Zedong seemed to point the way. I was told that the crowd sometimes exceeded ten thousand people.

The bazaar sprawled as far as the eye could see. It swarmed with vendors of cartwheels, silk, leather riding boots, camel bells, horse saddles and bridles, hand-crafted daggers, door frames, farm tools, tentlike felt yurts, Japanese wristwatches and bars of American soap trucked over the treacherous mountain passes of the Karakorum, knitted shirts and sweaters smuggled in from Hong Kong. Tomatoes, carrots, and apples were sprinkled with water to make them look fresher. The fragrance of saffron, cinnamon, and other spices mingled with the smell of sweat and manure from camels, horses, sheep, goats, chickens, and their sellers. But there was not a single white-jacketed policeman in sight to control so vast a crowd. This was a people's market, beholden to naked mercantilism and serving the people to an extent unimagined by the economic planners back in Beijing.

I got lost amid this chaos and paused at one of the many food stalls to buy a skewer of barbecued mutton and a flat loaf of unleavened bread crisp from the earthen ovens. Many of the traders had blue eyes and Turkish features and they wore embroidered black-and-white skullcaps or floppy blue or olive Mao caps. Much of the commerce I saw was conducted in body language, as buyer and seller gestured in what I first mistook for argument over a shaggy horse or imperious camel, until a middleman pulled their hands together into a firm shake that stopped the haggling. An old man with a wispy beard was asking about 70 yuan for his tired old donkey. A little dark-eyed girl loudly demanded 120 yuan for one of her father's shaggy sheep. A rug vendor from whom I asked directions sold me a bright-colored felt carpet, though I could not understand a word he said in Uighur and had no idea how to carry my bulky purchase home to Beijing.

"During the Cultural Revolution, the bazaar was closed for more than ten years and all those in trade were labeled as speculators," said Eisa Shakir, a Uighur who was deputy commissioner of Kashgar prefecture. "Everything had to be bought through state stores, and many goods were not obtainable. But the trading still went on in the countryside outside Kashgar."

In 1981, the bazaar reopened and Shakir estimated that Kashgar prefecture had more than ten thousand traders, some of whom had acquired their own trucks. The only prohibitions applied to contraband, like weapons and narcotics, and speculation, which meant buying something to resell promptly at a much higher price. The traders paid a 5 percent tax on every sale and another 3 percent on their total business turnover, though I couldn't figure out how the authorities managed to collect it.

"If you enter into that sort of business, you can get rich every day," Shakir explained over dinner. "You have to find out which commodities turn over fastest. Peasants have to wait for a year to earn their income. Traders can earn theirs in one day."

Some merchants had hired agents in the eastern cities of Shanghai and Beijing, 2,500 miles away, to ship the best-selling goods off to Central Asia by train, which took about ten days. "If you went through the government bureaucracy," Shakir said, "it would take a year." His estimate struck me as optimistic.

By contrast, the Soviet authorities were schizophrenic about the return of private enterprise, as became apparent when I visited a Sunday market held by artists in Moscow's Ismailovo Park. The wares stretched for a mile along a walk bounded by birch trees. There were paintings, among them nudes more appropriate to a pin-up calendar, religious icons, and modernistic abstracts. Artisans squatted on the ground holding up handmade puppets, toy airplanes, lanterns fashioned from string, and jewelry crafted from wire, plastic, or semi-precious stones. One thin, bearded artist sold red badges hand-lettered with the word "Perestroika." Handsome wooden Russian *matryoshka* dolls looked far more animated than their counterparts in the state souvenir shops; artists had recycled the cheap ones and repainted them with charming delicacy.

My companions and I grew hungry and looked about for the food. Private food vendors would have been conspicuous in Harbin or Kashgar, but because the Moscow authorities had sanctioned the private sale of art, not food, I couldn't find one among the thousands of Russians browsing in Ismailovo Park. So we queued up at wooden tables for watery fruit juice and stale pastries offloaded from the truck of a state catering company and sold by brusque women in white smocks.

After seven decades under Communism, the Russians, un-

198 CHRISTOPHER S. WREN

like the Chinese, have no lingering memory of legal private enterprise. Although a new Soviet law authorizing cooperative ventures assured skeptics that such commerce was "honorable and prestigious and is encouraged in every possible way by the state," they approached it with caution.[5] Some citizens resented seeing a private entrepreneur make more money than they would ever be paid on the factory floor or down on the farm. "A lot of people work a little and earn a little," explained a writer I met in Moscow. "They cannot understand how some people who work more earn more. It is the result of egalitarianism. Some people think if others earn more, it means a step away from socialism."

This mentality affected even some members of the new cooperatives, in which people pooled resources and skills and divided the profits. One evening in Tallinn I hailed a taxi and was picked up by a brown Moskvich sedan, one of a stream of private cars with yellow roof tags designating them legally for hire. The driver, a former merchant seaman, worked for the state-owned taxi company, which paid him only 250 rubles a month. So he moonlighted on his off days for a taxi cooperative and earned five hundred more rubles a month. I asked why he didn't quit his poorer state job. He said he couldn't afford to because his cooperative had no health, sick leave, and pension benefits.

Under the New Economic Policy, by the late 1920s cooperatives were handling 50 to 70 percent of basic consumer products before Stalin closed them down. In resurrecting cooperatives in 1987, Mikhail Gorbachev cited as his motive "the slow progress in the solution of the food problem, the shortages in and narrow choice of many consumer goods, and the limited range of daily services."

The new ventures took two forms: production cooperatives, which made light industrial goods, and consumption cooperatives, which offered consumer goods and services. Some entrepreneurs are continuing what they did in the shadow economy, in which workers loafed in their poorly paid state jobs and moonlighted briskly on the side. The Kremlin's reluctance to yank the security blanket of state employment away from the Soviet worker left private enterprise filled largely by pensioners, housewives, and students, because working for oneself was still looked down upon. Despite higher earnings and job freedom, workers in cooperatives in 1987 accounted for hardly more than .15 percent of the Soviet Union's labor force of 131 million.[6]

A Soviet journalist blamed the lackluster response on lack of support or outright hostility within the government. "It's a new headache for the bureaucrats, because at the end of the day they don't earn anything," he said. "So they say, 'It's impossible because it's impossible, because it has never been done before.' " Officials charged stiff fees for registration, demanded excessive paperwork, levied taxes as high as 85 percent, refused to provide work space or raw materials, and engaged in outright suppression. In Volgograd, policemen smashed private greenhouses growing tomatoes and plugged the wells used to water them, despite the country's perennial shortage of fresh fruits and vegetables.[7] In Krasnoyarsk, a taxi cooperative was disbanded after the district council decided that its drivers were making too much money.[8] In Moscow, some officials refused to license private hairdressing salons, claiming the state had enough, despite evidence to the contrary.

Though the cooperatives were revived in 1987 to subject the existing underground economy to supervision and taxation, reports surfaced of criminals investing in private restaurants and other cooperative businesses as a means of laundering illegal gains. Some Russians complained that other cooperatives were speculating in scarce commodities. Gorbachev himself asserted that "some cooperatives, taking advantage of their small number, boost their profits by jacking up prices. This justifiably evokes the indignation of the working people."

The prices charged by the cooperatives were certainly higher than in state-run concerns, but their managers often had to buy raw materials and produce privately because they were denied access to the state's subsidized distribution system. On my last visit to Moscow in 1988, Phil Taubman, then *The Times*'s bureau chief, took me to dinner at a cooperative

Georgian restaurant in a converted stable overlooking Novo-devichy Monastery. We dined on spicy barbecued lamb, fresh goat cheese, and hot Georgian bread to a gypsy serenade by a strolling violinist and guitarist. My dinner must have cost four times as much as my lunch at the Intourist Hotel, where the soup was cold, the pork cutlet tough, the tablecloth soiled, and the waiter kept flicking off the lights to make his customers eat up and leave.

Cooperative and private entrepreneurs could also charge more because they didn't face enough competition from the state. A few days earlier in Tallinn, I bought an ice-cream cone at a state-run kiosk for about 45 kopeks, and bought another from a private vendor for 59 kopeks. The state sold only vanilla—the generic flavor of central planners—while the private vendor offered a creamy chocolate concoction poured into a crunchy waffle cone. With a monopoly on chocolate, she cornered the market.

Among people I met who strove to rise above mindless egalitarianism, Liu Si comes to mind, though not without his ducks. Liu, a husky Cantonese farmer who looked uncannily like the country musician Johnny Cash, was rich—if not by American standards, certainly by whatever standards were available to peasants throughout China's hard history. When I visited his old commune of Dali, now a township on the fringe of the waterlogged alluvial plain called the Pearl River Delta, Liu was earning 17,500 yuan a year. At the time this was equivalent to more than $8,000, though this figure needs to be multiplied tenfold to give an accurate picture of its purchasing power in rural China.

Liu Si made his money raising ducks for export to the dining tables of Hong Kong, a hundred miles across the border. Liu's father had kept ducks until the Maoists made him stop. Once the prohibition against owning livestock was dropped, Liu Si, who had been a farmhand, began raising his own ducks with a forced-feeding technique that he had devised. "Of course, I didn't have the freedom to do it before," he said. "But now you can do what you like, as long as you have the skill.

So I think it's my right to get more money." Indeed, the authorities of Nanhai county in Guangdong province had blessed his prosperity with a colorful certificate that proclaimed for all the neighbors to see: "Laodong Zhifu Fuyu Guanrong"— "Get rich through hard work. Getting rich is glorious."

We walked back to his new two-story cement house. Ducks lived everywhere, quacking in wire pens, foraging in the dirt for remnants of ground-up fish. Inside the house, ducklings, freshly hatched and downy, jostled each other inside wicker baskets on the bare cement floor or skittered under the beds. Liu Si reckoned he was down to about eight hundred ducks in his inventory when I dropped in, though there seemed a lot more underfoot.

Liu ticked off what prosperity had brought. He had finished building his house and given his old one to his three sons. Last year, he married off his daughter with a handsome dowry. He had purchased a wristwatch, three bicycles, and a walking tractor—it looked somewhat like a huge power lawnmower—to replace the family water buffalo.

"And a television set?" I prompted, for all along the dozen miles of road from Canton, I had seen the "fishtail" television antennas pointing toward Hong Kong. Every time the Party launched another drive against "spiritual pollution," the Cantonese were told to dismantle their ultra-high-frequency antennas, which pulled in Hong Kong's gaudy TV fare of game shows, disco dances, and aging American serials dubbed into Cantonese. Once the drive ended, the locals restored the fishtail antennas.

"I can't afford a television set," Liu sighed.

"But you have a new house and a new tractor," I said. "Why can't you afford a television set?"

Liu Si scoffed. "I didn't buy a television set because I can't afford the time to watch it, because I have to work until midnight every night." He turned to look at me. "If I watched television, who would watch my ducks?"

Liu Si epitomized the success of the first reforms that Deng Xiaoping set in motion. The changes featured the *zeren zhi* or new "responsibility system" under which Chinese peasants who worked harder earned more. The policy doubled farm output, nearly tripled peasant incomes, and wrought a social and economic transformation of the Chinese countryside. Like Liu Si, other peasants were building new houses and buying walking tractors, bicycles, television sets, and furniture.

Yet the real impact was political. In starting with agriculture, Deng won the loyalties of China's 800 million peasants simply by unfettering their industriousness and letting them keep some of the results. As meat and fresh vegetables filled the free markets, city dwellers realized the reforms would improve their living standards too. When Deng crushed the democracy movement in the cities in 1989, he did not have to worry about the peasants who make up four-fifths of China's population. His reforms assured their loyalty.

Here lay a critical distinction between the attempts to reconstruct the Soviet Union and China. The Russians I knew were fond of embracing ideas. My Chinese friends conformed their idealism to the realities at hand. So Gorbachev set about to win hearts and minds while Deng appealed to the stomach.

One of the sturdier political anecdotes I heard in Moscow involved an allegorical train bound for Communism, with Stalin, Khrushchev, and Brezhnev aboard. The train stalled, so Stalin ordered the entire crew taken out and shot. But the train didn't move. Khrushchev had the crew posthumously rehabilitated and awarded medals. Still nothing happened. At length, Stalin and Khrushchev turned to Brezhnev. "We'll pull the curtains shut and pretend that we are moving," Brezhnev said. Some years later, I was told the same joke with an updated punch line. In the postscripted version, Gorbachev had joined Stalin, Khrushchev, and Brezhnev. After the other three failed to get Communism's train moving, Gorbachev told all the passengers to get out and push. "I'll pay you later," he promised.

That is pretty much how Gorbachev launched his *perestroika*, with lots of promises but no hard cash, or the ready means of earning it, offered up front. Russians, who have learned to be one of the world's most patient people, were told that they would have to work harder, and only afterward would the benefits come. For all of Gorbachev's bold vision, in the first years of *perestroika* living standards in the Soviet Union declined, as attempts to impose quality control in factories choked the output of consumer goods and confusion over the new policies stifled food deliveries. "In fact, most families in the country haven't benefited so far," I heard Abel Aganbegyan, Gorchabev's top economic adviser, admit nearly three years after the Soviet leader took over. When the quick fix didn't come, when the situation in the markets and stores actually worsened, disenchantment set in.

The difference in the Soviet and Chinese approaches has gone to the heart of the debate over the future of Communism. It involves how far, if at all, individualism should be encouraged over the collective will, and to what extent personal decisions should be permitted to replace those made by the Party. The Chinese have professed to see no contradiction as long as it didn't lead to subversive notions about political freedom. "In a socialist society in which the exploiting classes have been eliminated, egalitarianism only lets laggards share the fruits of the diligent," the New China News Agency explained in one commentary.

Nowhere has this been more important than in agriculture. One of the attitudes shared by Russian and Chinese farmers was an aversion to their collectivization. When the Marxist revolutionaries promised land to the tiller, the farmers assumed it would go to them.[9] Instead, they were rounded up by the state to toil as indentured hands. Stalin's collectivization of the Ukraine and southern Russia amounted to genocide. Western scholars guessed that 5 to 10 million peasants were starved to death to break the will of the kulaks, comparatively wealthy farmers who balked at collectivization. Up to a quarter million Ukrainians, by one Soviet estimate, were declared "not suitable for the conduct of farming" and shipped like cattle off to Siberia or Central Asia. Khrushchev told the 20th Party Congress in 1956 that Stalin might have deported the entire Ukrainian population but for lack of enough boxcars.

The number of Chinese peasants who perished from hunger and related illness in Chairman Mao's Great Leap Forward from 1958 to 1961 has been similarly estimated to be from 14 to 30 million victims, extrapolated from gaps in the census figures and other indirect evidence. Such estimates are inadequate when loss of life is so immense. Communist governments that can rattle off the number of tons of rolled steel, coal, cement, crude oil, sulfuric acid, and chemical fertilizer they produce do not seem to keep similarly scrupulous records on people. In the case of the Soviet famine and China's disastrous Great Leap Forward, the governments long denied that such deaths even took place.

The Chinese peasants I talked to were unanimous in their experience that "eating from the big pot"—*da guofan*—didn't work because it stifled initiative. When Chairman Mao promulgated his slogan of "taking grain as the key link" to increase grain output, some farmers said they were forced to stop cultivating crops more suitable to the climate and soil and plant rice or wheat instead. "Our peasants used to laugh at 'taking grain as the key link,'" recalled the deputy director of a former commune outside Canton. "They joked about 'taking a stick as the key link' because the slogan meant nothing."

China's grain output lagged so badly that a government report in 1977, the year after the Cultural Revolution ended, disclosed that 100 million Chinese peasants did not have enough to eat. They went hungry because of arbitrary directives from Party cadres who knew little or nothing about farming. Peasants who had been planting and harvesting rice since childhood were told how to transplant the young plants, and if the specified intervals between stalks was not exact, the entire paddy had to be uprooted and replanted, according to Du Shubing, an agricultural specialist in Sichuan. "The big defect was that the cadres who knew nothing about agriculture also bore none of the consequences," he told me.

I had watched a film, *A Corner Overlooked by Love*, about the ordeal of a peasant family in Sichuan during the Cultural Revolution. The Red Guards ordered the father to cut down his orange orchard to make space for grain. When the old man tried to save his favorite tree, he was hauled out in his ragged clothes and publicly reviled as a class enemy. I asked Du, who had seen the film too, whether the political climate was really that bad. "The suffering in Sichuan was even worse," he replied.

After the misery engendered by Mao's irrational policies, China's peasants welcomed a chance to do what they knew best. But Soviet agriculture, since the Stalinist collectivization of the 1930s, limped along without personal tragedies or rewards. Everyone on a collective farm was housed, fed, and clothed, even if he didn't work very hard. Only in autumn did Soviet farms go into a frenzy, and the rest of the country was mobilized to help as if confronted by an unanticipated disaster.

I did encounter a few conspicuous exceptions to this stasis, like the Sergei M. Kirov Collective Farm and Fishery, which occupied a wedge of Baltic shoreline with a splendid view of the slender spires of Tallinn. It had no connection with Sergei Kirov, the Leningrad Party chief assassinated in 1934, probably on Stalin's orders. His name was picked as ideological camouflage for gambles running counter to the conventional mind set on Soviet agriculture. The Estonian *kolkhoz,* or collective farm, was among a few dozen selected by Khrushchev in the early 1960s to experiment with *khozraschet,* an accounting system that made an enterprise responsible for its own profits and losses, instead of having them absorbed by the state. After Khrushchev's overthrow in 1964, the plan was formally abandoned, but the Kirov *kolkhoz* kept tinkering with the kind of reforms that Gorbachev endorsed over two decades later.

In processing the catches brought ashore by its nineteen ocean-going trawlers, the *kolkhoz* found its canning factory awash with fish by-products. State-run fisheries dumped them back into the sea. The Kirov *kolkhoz* turned them into a natural shampoo, which it marketed successfully to the tune of two million rubles annually. The notion that Soviet citizens would pay to wash their hair with something extracted from fish guts would hardly have occurred to the central planners in Moscow, but the *kolkhoz* built itself a shampoo factory and recouped the investment in little more than a year.

"No state enterprise would have taken such a risk, and the person who had to give permission would not have given it because the risk would be too great," said Evald Pelli, the vice chairman. "If the people in government offices who make the decisions did nothing, they would not be punished. But if they made mistakes, they would be removed."

Pelli, an engineer with steel-rimmed spectacles and a busy manner, said his *kolkhoz* had been practicing profit-and-loss accounting on a practical basis since 1963. "And we feel now that from the beginning of this year"—it was now 1988— "it has become easier for us to work. The most important thing is the possibility of having direct links with other enterprises. I can contact the other enterprises directly and ask what they need and tell them what we need to order from them."

A month earlier, he had ordered some supplies that would have taken months to requisition through the pipeline of state distribution. "We agreed upon delivery in twenty days and we received it in twenty days. Now we hope that everything will be done like this."

In practice, there did not seem all that much difference between the *khozraschet* formally ushered in by Mikhail Gorbachev and the *zeren zhi*, China's responsibility system devised by Deng Xiaoping. Both relied less on ideology than on hard work and more than a little courage. "The success of *khozraschet* depended on the strength of the chairman's neck and how many blows he could survive," said Pelli. "And there were many of them."

Had the Kirov *kolkhoz* failed, it would have been told to get in step with the rest of the Soviet Union. Instead, Gorbachev urged the country to look to such enterprises that were proving what could be done with a little imagination.

"We do not pay someone just to show up at the workplace," Pelli continued. "Everybody must work, and as for management, we have reduced it very radically compared to the state enterprises. That is why some managers earn twice what a state manager would get. The wages are very dependent on quality." The fishing-boat skippers, for example, earned 600 to 700 rubles, or more than $1,000, a month, and an ordinary fisherman 350 rubles, or nearly $600, which was well above the average in Estonia.

In the sunlit workshop where women crafted the heavy fishing nets, the supervisor said that 40 percent of the wages were linked to quality. If a net was poorly made, the worker had to redo it without pay, but the best workers could earn 250 rubles, over $400, a month. "Many workers at state enterprises saw our success and said, 'I would like to come here and make more money,' " the supervisor said. "But they didn't realize they would have to work harder. They came here, didn't like it, and went back to their old jobs."

It seemed ironic that such maverick practices had metamorphosed the Kirov *kolkhoz* into a model enterprise where visitors now were taken to show off what could be achieved under Communism. A Soviet reporter asked one of its retired workers the secret of its prosperity. Her answer, as it was told to me, delighted the reformers. "When you meet the sun rising every morning and see it off every night, you will have it too," the old lady replied.

The small plots tilled by Soviet farmers in their own backyards made clear the insufficiency of their collective experience. When I lived in the Soviet Union, private plots covered only 3 percent of the country's sown acreage; yet they provided 64 percent of the potatoes, 53 percent of the vegetables, 41 percent of the eggs, and 22 percent of the meat and milk consumed by the country.[10] The dependency on private plots has, if anything, increased since. Yet in June 1987, Gorbachev expressed astonishment that over half of rural Soviet families did not own cows and a third did not keep any livestock; they bought food at the store like city folk.[11] Soviet farmers got permission to use the farm equipment to improve their private plots and to lease pastures for livestock. By 1989, the government was desperate enough to offer hard currency for the extra grain farmers produced over their quota.

An economist I met at a Moscow research institute admitted that it was "illogical" for Gorbachev not to have implemented reform first on the farm as Deng did in China. "Agricultural reform creates both the political and economic conditions for larger reforms," he told me. "The market becomes more balanced in terms of supply and demand."

For the sake of comparison, even before Gorbachev assumed power in March 1985, China had dismantled its 55,000 communes, reviving in their administrative place the *xiangs*, or townships, abolished by Mao. The government paid bonuses for what peasants delivered above their quotas. Or they could sell their surplus at the farmers' markets. The peasants went back to family sharecropping, with the state as landlord. In time, they could buy and sell the rights to their land. Chinese agriculture differed radically not just from its Soviet counterpart but also from what it had been less than a decade earlier.

The secret of China's agricultural successes lay in its willingness to lunge beyond the sort of half measures timidly devised by Soviet bureaucrats. The new direction was not taken without considerable skepticism from Chinese peasants, who had been kicked around so often over the years that they distrusted anything the Party or government offered.

"At first, the peasants engaged in farming were unwilling to adopt the responsibility system because they didn't know what the outcome would be," said Chai Yanlin, the deputy director of Dali commune. So he let them test the *zeren zhi* at team level; the rice output shot up 50 percent within three years. "They lost interest in eating from the big pot," Chai said.

The directors found that the peasants became more reliable once no one told them what to do. Liang En, who led one of the production teams at the commune, told me that "before the new system, many peasants didn't take care of the equipment and facilities, because they thought it was public and not their own. They didn't have the sense of responsibility and it caused a lot of waste and damage to the farm tools and the irrigation network. Now, I don't have to shout at them to get out to work."

At the old Leiliu commune, which raised silkworms and fish in Guangdong's Shunde county, Huang Baoying explained that everyone chafed under the old policies. "Each peasant was given a fixed number of work points per day," the deputy director said. "The working day was eight hours, but some people only worked four hours, because they knew they would get the same pay, no matter how hard they worked. There was no initiative. There wasn't any direct connection between work and pay."

Even so, the trauma of the Cultural Revolution inhibited the peasants. "Especially at the beginning, they didn't trust the new policy wholeheartedly, because they feared they would suffer through the whole experience again and be branded as capitalist roaders," Huang said.

I asked him whether peasants had to attend political study sessions as in the old days. "They used to be held three times a week or even once a day," he said. "But now every production team meets once a month for general discussions, on policy and so forth." My hunch that they did not waste much time studying Party policy was confirmed when I asked a peasant named Wu what the discussions were like. "Oh, we meet the team leader once a month to discuss the use of insecticide and fertilizer," he said.

I supposed that he would not want to go back to eating from the big pot. "It was unfair," Wu replied. "Some people worked hard and they got paid the same as the lazy ones. Some people just stood around and they got paid the same as the busy ones. Now everyone has the same chance to work."

But as with other reforms, success brought its own problems. Peasants used up scarce farmland as they enlarged their old house or built brand-new ones and opened sideline factories. China's arable land shrank by more than 1 million acres a year between 1981 and 1985, and by more than 1.6 million acres during 1968 and 1987. An agricultural official in Guangdong estimated that the province had lost over 300,000 acres of arable land to construction in little more than three years. During the initial years of reform, at least a third of peasant families built new homes.

Farmers no longer let their sons join the People's Liberation Army, once an enviable career for a country boy, because they were needed in the fields. The government's family-planning program eroded as peasants gave birth to more children to help them. Even young boys and girls were kept out of school to tend the livestock. The new prosperity led to greater demands for kerosene, bicycles, and television sets, which the state could not meet.

Once the farmers were allowed a choice, many of them switched to more lucrative cash crops like tobacco or rapeseed at the expense of the country's grain output. Du Runsheng, director of the Central Committee's Rural Policy Research Center, blamed low prices paid by the state for the fall in grain output in 1985 and 1986, which led to urban rationing of pork, the basic meat in the Chinese diet. Conservatives in the Party have used the politically volatile grain issue to argue for a return to more central planning, because harvest failures historically meant famine in China.

And yet when there was a bumper harvest, China's backward infrastructure often could not handle it. If the state marketing cooperatives had nowhere to store the surplus, they sometimes refused to buy it and the crops rotted. When agents cut back the purchase price for bumper crops, some farmers refused to hand over what they owed the state or went back to growing only enough to feed themselves, and shortages developed. After officials in Liujia, a village in Shandong province, changed the purchasing contracts for apples and apricots in 1987, some peasants revolted, thrashed the officials, and organized their own alternative Party committee. The rebellious peasants controlled Liujia for nearly six weeks until the police moved in.[12]

Moreover, the communes, for all their defects, had provided social services that now began to unravel. In Yunnan province and elsewhere, I heard peasants lamenting the disappearance of "barefoot doctors." These were peasants who, after rudimentary medical training, became indispensable as public-health workers in the countryside. They quit because they could make more money farming.

Under the responsibility system, some farmers were making a lot more money than government and Party functionaries or urban white-collar workers, who resented it. "I can't compete with the peasants," confided a cadre in Guangdong, where farm incomes doubled in five years. "Even the ministers in the State Commission can't compete with the peasants."

Some prospering peasants alienated others suffering from what Chinese call *hong yanbing* or "the red-eyed disease" of jealousy. I heard stories of farmers bound for market who were stopped by highwaymen and forced to hand over part of their produce. The Urumqi radio station in western China reported the suicide of an "honest, diligent and competent" apple farmer named Liu Guozhi. When he reaped a bumper harvest, jealous neighbors stole his apples, poisoned his chickens, threw stones at his home, and beat him up. Unwilling to live among his tormentors, Liu poisoned himself.

It was more common for the neighbors to sponge off those who did well. A farmer in Gansu, one of the poorest provinces of China, earned 18,000 yuan growing mushrooms and building beehive boxes. But he had to lend his earnings to forty other families and wound up in debt. Elsewhere, local officials insisted on being made "partners" in enterprises once they turned a profit. Even those who were not harassed felt social pressure to spread their wealth around. I read about a peasant named Feng Zuhui in Guangxi who saved enough to buy a twenty-inch color television set; Feng was praised for toting it about on the back of his bicycle so other families in his village could borrow it.

Some local authorities tried to penalize farmers who reaped too big a surplus by jacking up the quota they owed the state, a practice the government compared disapprovingly to "whipping a fast ox." The farmers responded by reporting less than they produced. Other functionaries demanded bribes to approve contracts or supply farm machinery.[13]

But as one official in Guangdong also observed, "cadres can always go back to being peasants," and many did, with impressive results. Some of the more successful farmers I met had been commune cadres who got the jump on the other peasants. They often made more money by specializing on a specific commodity or service, rather than just planting rice.[14]

In the village of Changbei in rural Sichuan province, I came across two specialized households locked in a fierce if amusing rivalry. Ma Tianying, a middle-aged peasant who wore a white tee-shirt and baggy blue trousers held up with an army belt, was sawing up trees in his small sawmill when we met. A former production brigade leader, he told me he was one of the first cadres to go into business for himself. He also operated a tractor-repair shop and a small factory making concrete building slabs. Ma wanted to expand into trucking, where he could make real money. "I work seventeen or eighteen hours a day," Ma said with a grin. "It's not too much because I am in good health."

But for all his ingenuity and stamina, Ma had not caught up with Zhang Daishen, who lived in a new house with a fishpond in her courtyard and a chicken coop out back. Zhang used to be a fieldhand and she had also pulled a cart delivering coal and charcoal. "I got rich with building materials and asbestos tiles," she declared to us foreign reporters who crowded into her living room, trying not to knock over the television set and cassette recorder. Zhang was the first in Changbei to make prefabicated slabs and she owned a truck to deliver them, but this was not what gave her the edge. Zhang paid 300 yuan, the equivalent of seven months' average income for a local farmer, to have the village's only telephone installed in her home. When a builder in the provincial capital of Chengdu one hundred miles away wanted concrete slabs, he could phone in his order and get prompt delivery. Poor Ma was stuck with the vastly slower Chinese mail, for Zhang did not share her telephone with the competition.

Our Chinese handlers delighted in introducing us reporters to the clever Mas and Zhangs, though some success stories turned out to be fairy tales. The Chinese press fussed over the first peasant wealthy enough to buy a private car; the automobile, it turned out, already belonged to her husband, a local cadre. Another peasant in Henan province earned enough to buy an ultralight aircraft, which he wanted to use for crop dusting to eliminate locusts. Henan authorities promised to build a small airfield and send three peasants to Beijing for flying lessons. They never got around to it, and the aircraft sat in a hangar at the provincial capital of Zhengzhou for two years before it was given away to a tourist resort.

There were bleaker rural areas of China, where peasants

still lived in mud-brick houses with floors of pounded earth and oilpaper stretched across the windows. They ate coarse millet and yams cooked over manure or dried grass for lack of firewood. They borrowed draft animals to plough the stony fields because they could not afford their own, and they pulled their own carts harnessed like beasts of burden, walking barefoot in faded and patched denims. They were not to blame for lagging so far behind the wealthy peasants praised by the official press. They lived in places too empty and remote to exploit the reforms that had swept the lusher coastal regions. Farmers in Guangdong could get 15 to 20 percent more for their produce merely because they were close to the Hong Kong market. Backward areas were victims of a widening prosperity gap, though since they were usually closed to foreigners it was difficult to gauge how much poverty persisted.[15]

After I persuaded officials that I wanted to write about their irrigation projects diverting water from the Yellow River, I got permission to enter some of these poor areas in Qinghai, Gansu, and Ningxia, where thousands of peasants had been mobilized to dig the ditches. I pointed out that Mao Zedong, who was still useful for the supporting quotation, had called poverty a virtue because it created conditions for change. From harsh conditions the authorities let me see in their best areas, I could infer how desperately poor the others must be.

In Gansu, a desert expanse of barren hills and ravines that looks like Nevada, agricultural officials showed the brown water sloshing through the newly dug canals. "This place was so poor that when you visited someone's house, you could ask for a piece of steamed bread but not a bowl of water," an official named Ai recalled. "Some people used donkeys to fetch water far away or got bitter-tasting water from underground. And after people cooked the noodles in it, they would throw the water on the ground, because if you drank it you would get diarrhea or stomach trouble. Now," Ai gestured, "every household has its own cistern, which it fills up from the irrigation canal."

Tian Weiwan, a sun-wrinkled peasant in his sixties, greeted me with a gap-toothed smile and waved me into his adobe home in Mawan village. Its mud-brick floor had been swept clean in preparation for my arrival. A brick *kang* or sleeping platform drew its heat from the cooking stove. An alarm clock sat on a shelf made of empty pork cans, and a few plastic flowers stuck out of an old bottle. Tian and his wife had done all they could afford to brighten up their small home. They offered me some tea.

"We had nothing to water the fields with. It was all dry land. If there was rain, we would have a harvest. Otherwise, we would have nothing to eat." Tian gestured toward the dust bowl outside with heavily callused hands. "Before the water came in, we didn't have enough food to eat. Now we have enough." He hoped to be able to feed his family. Another farmer named Chen Qingfan recalled that "in this place, we had no rain for nine out of ten harvests. We relied on the weather and we lived by the weather. If there was rain, we got a harvest. If there was no rain, we got nothing."

I traveled down to southern Ningxia, where poor peasants were being moved down to the river diversion, rather than the other way around as in Gansu. Everyone wore a white skull cap and seemed to be named Ma, a common Moslem surname derived from the Chinese pronunciation of Mohammed. The plan had been to bring 5,000 peasants in from the desiccated mountains, but 50,000 applied and 11,500 were relocated, a cadre explained, "because people insisted on coming." Ma Shangqing, a Party secretary in the new village of Tangfang, said that farmers in his old area struggled to earn 40 or 50 yuan a year—barely a dollar a month—growing millet. "No, I don't miss my old home at all," he said. "Nobody wants to go back. More people there want to come here, but this space is limited, because the water isn't enough."

Deng's reforms had doubtless improved life in rural China, but by 1987, 60 million peasants, more than the combined populations of Britain and Ireland, still earned less than 200 yuan a year, which was not much more than a dollar a week. There was little likelihood that life in the backcountry would improve as fast as it had near the cities, however hard the peasants tried. In a mountainous region of Sichuan province, sometimes called the breadbasket of China for its abundant harvests, a young peasant told me that arable land was so scarce that officials doled out seed and told the farmers to find some level ground to plant. Other peasants were held back by a combination of ignorance and Maoist egalitarianism. They had neither the skill nor the desire to take the kind of risks more aggressive peasants assumed.

The growing disparity in incomes created a dilemma for the Chinese leadership that was ideological as well as practical. When people went hungry under Chairman Mao, they all were hungry together, or at least they were told so. Once the "big pot" was broken, it was taken for granted that some would do better than others. Du Runsheng argued that if successful peasants were restrained everyone would remain mired in poverty. "So some peasants have become better off first, and the others will be helped to catch up, with the goal of achieving common prosperity," Du told us at a briefing in Beijing.

Though it had been officially repudiated, the need for the old collective did not disappear. In one village I visited in Qinghai, the farmers elected to keep working in three production teams, which had been disbanded almost everywhere else. "If each family worked alone, they would have had to send members to town to sell their vegetables, and it would be a great waste of labor," explained the village head, Zhang Shengshou. Family farming on too small a scale also proved inefficient, particularly in the grain-growing expanses of north China. The government encouraged farmers there to take over land from less-productive neighbors, but some peasants declined because the land offered was too far from their fields. Or, mindful of the Maoist years, they knew they would need hired help to work a larger spread, and feared being accused of exploitation if the liberal policies were withdrawn.

The best way for the countryside to move forward, Du consistently argued, was to shift up to 30 or 40 percent of China's peasants out of farming and into new rural industries, in which they could be more productive and make more money too. Before, they lacked such mobility because they were tied to the communes. One consequence was that up to 200,000

CHRISTOPHER S. WREN

poor farmers hit the road, according to an estimate in 1988, looking for work in more prosperous areas. The migrants over-crowded the trains and slept in the railway stations.[16]

The dirt-poor farmers I talked with in Gansu and Ningxia tried to be philosophical about the prosperity gap. "At the moment it is difficult to catch up, because we still have more dry than irrigated land," said Tian Weiwan. I assumed that their conditions would get better. But in reading about the National People's Congress in April 1988, I was struck by a remark from a delegate from Gansu, whose backcountry I had toured, that more than five million people at home did not have enough grain to feed themselves, even in a new era when getting rich was declared glorious.

8

FLOWERS IN THE SUNSHINE OF THE PARTY: MEASURING THE SUCCESS OF COMMUNISM'S SOCIAL SERVICES

> Study is essential if we are to smash the bourgeoisie and reach communism and this goal must be our lodestar that gives us unerring guidance.
>
> —VLADIMIR ILYICH LENIN, 1920[1]

> At present, there is too much studying going on, and this is exceedingly harmful.
>
> —MAO ZEDONG, 1964[2]

THE LEPERS LIVED AT XIUNING in a small colony set at the edge of the rain forest a dozen miles outside Haikou, the administrative capital of Hainan. The leprosarium itself was a rambling old colonial villa with a gray tile roof, wide veranda, and bare concrete floors that evoked the tropical setting of some Somerset Maugham story. The stucco walls had been newly whitewashed in anticipation of our visit. The Japanese reporters in our group refused to go, pleading various excuses until it became clear they were afraid of catching leprosy. Most of the other foreign correspondents accepted; I was curious to see how the Communists had contained one of the grimmer diseases of the tropics, and the chance of catching leprosy on an afternoon's sojourn seemed remote.

The late George Hatem, a Lebanese-born physician, better known here by his Chinese name of Ma Daihe, estimated that China had a half million lepers when the Communists took over in 1949. Hatem helped lead the campaign to eradicate the disease, reducing the number of lepers to 150,000 in 1981 and only 70,000 in 1987. Hainan, with its hot, moist climate, once had the highest incidence of leprosy in China. The leprosarium at Xiuning had been established sixteen years before the Communists took over. Its government staff included thirteen physicians trained in Western and traditional Chinese medicine and eight nurses. Of 658 lepers treated in recent years, 288 still lived at the leprosarium and in a small village nearby.

"In the last decade, more and more patients who recover are willing to stay on here," said Huang Huiming, a slender man with a somewhat bureaucratic manner, who ran the center. "We have organized their life in a better way. We have encouraged those who are fully recovered to get married, after they are fully sterilized of course."

Sterilization, he explained, was necessary to avoid exposing children to the disease, though he conceded that the risks were not great. "We do the sterilization, which is entirely voluntary, because we consider two factors. First, some recovered patients who settle down here worry that if they have a baby it will get infected. And second, we couldn't ensure that genetic problems wouldn't occur if a baby was born."

The village population included seventy-two couples who had mostly married at the leprosarium. They remained because lepers were still generally unwelcome elsewhere. "Society is still not clear about leprosy," Huang said. "There is some discrimination in some areas. So they prefer to stay here."

Slogans were daubed in big characters on the leprosarium walls. "Create a new situation in socialist construction and struggle for the basic elimination of leprosy by the end of the century," said one. Another quoted the late Prime Minister Zhou Enlai: "Daring to treat lepers is an act that characterizes a whole-hearted devotion to serving the people."

The lepers' village looked no worse than other rural hamlets in southernmost China. The wide dirt street was faced with basic two- or three-room houses, built mostly of poured concrete and roofed with corrugated iron. Behind them carefully tended gardens stretched up to the jungle undergrowth.

A few pigs grunted inside ramshackle sties fashioned from split bamboo. Scrawny chickens scratched in the dust. It was clear from the way its residents spilled out of their houses to greet us that they didn't get many visitors.

Tang Zhaishun, a sturdy thirty-three-year-old peasant, invited me into the tidy cottage he shared with Yun Zhaishun, his twenty-nine-year-old wife. They had met and married at Xiuning, and then trained together as barefoot doctors. Together they earned 70 yuan a month—now about $20—looking after other lepers, plus another 9 yuan each in a disability pension from the state. To make ends meet, they raised pigs; Tang had just sold three the previous week.

Tang contracted leprosy on his right hand when he was seven, but, he said, "I was too young to understand the seriousness of the disease. When I was twelve, I came here and got proper treatment." I asked why he and his wife stayed on once they had been declared cured, for the scars on his hand were not noticeable. Tang replied that he went home sometimes to visit his mother, but "my wages and the facilities are better here, and I also get along better with these people."

Across the street not quite in the shade of a banana tree sat Wu Menghua, an eighty-year-old wisp of a woman with a plaid scarf wrapped bandannalike around her head. To attract our attention, she hoisted up one leg of her baggy black pajamas and thumped on the exposed left leg. It was made of steel and clunked like a badly made gong. In an instant, she had four of us squatting around her with open notebooks.

"I caught leprosy when I was thirty-seven," she announced, tapping her floppy canvas shoes for emphasis on the sun-baked dirt. "And nobody cared, nobody wanted to come near me. I was cast away by the community. I had been married before my leprosy was discovered. My husband died and I was left with no children."

All this happened before the Communist Liberation, she said. "Nobody supported me. The villagers all wanted to drive me away. They said I had the 'evil disease.' "

In the rain forest beyond her village, she built a bamboo lean-to for shelter, but once she began cultivating the land, she said, "they discovered me and I had to move again." The villagers, afraid to approach too closely, threw rocks to drive her off. She created another homestead further in the forest and lived alone until health workers conducting a survey for the new Communist regime found her and brought her to the leprosarium. The old woman had been there twenty-seven years when I met her. "I have a relative, a very remote one, who sometimes comes to see me," she said wistfully, "but not very often."

With nowhere to go, she sat every day on her small bench in the sun. Time had not erased her bitterness, and her parting words were more eloquent than all the slogans painted on the leprosarium walls. "If only I had had treatment in time," she said, "I could have kept my leg."

If a society's worth is measured by the care bestowed on unfortunates like the leprous old woman of Xiuning, the Soviet Union and China have made an impressive start. The social contract under which citizens of a Communist state surrender their free will in return for a guarantee that their physical needs will be met has formed the cornerstone of tranquility under socialism. Yet the inadequacies that daily confront ordinary Russians and Chinese have spread into the recesses of their social-welfare systems. Even in medical care there is never enough to go around, and so the real beneficiaries have become the élite, because they have first claim on anything in short supply.

Moscow, like other major Soviet cities, has an emergency ambulance network called *Skoraya Pomoshch* (literally "swift aid"). Our son Chris was playing with a friend in their school-yard one Saturday when his friend tripped and knocked himself out on the asphalt. We called *Skoraya Pomoshch* and an ambulance arrived within minutes. The husky attendants were accompanied by a matronly doctor in a white cap and smock who revived the boy, inspected him thoroughly, and offered to take him to the hospital overnight for observation. The emergency treatment cost nothing, nor would the hospitalization had the parents accepted it.

This free care extended to more serious medical problems.

When the brother of our bureau driver Ivan underwent six hours of complicated coronary-bypass surgery, followed by a lengthy hospital stay, he paid nothing for what would have cost thousands of dollars in the United States. And in the Crimean resort of Yalta, I visited a waterfront sanatorium for workers who rested at the expense of their trade unions. "The socialist countries grant and ensure for every one of their citizens the right to health care, to medical aid and treatment in the event of sickness," announced a pamphlet given me at the trade-union headquarters in Moscow.

At its best, medicine in Communist countries compares favorably with that in the West, and at vastly less cost to the beneficiary. Soviet surgeons pioneered new techniques in laser eye surgery, which corrects severe nearsightedness by slicing the cornea. And Chinese surgery is sometimes so meticulous that teams of surgeons in Shanghai labor for hours reattaching fingers and toes severed in industrial accidents. An American surgeon told me such operations consumed too much time and labor to become common in the United States.

Even so, Soviet and Chinese statistics focus on quantity achieved at the expense of quality. The Soviet Union, for example, claims twice as many doctors and hospital beds as the United States. The Soviet health indicators in 1988 counted 1.3 million doctors in all specialties, eleven times the number in 1940. But the late Theodore Shabad, a colleague who read the Soviet press voraciously, pointed out that only 43,000 of these held doctorates in medicine as American physicians do. Almost all the rest went from high school into a five-year medical course that qualified them as a *vrach*, or physician, but without the ultimate degree.

And what gets counted as a hospital bed in the national statistics may be nothing but a cot in the corridor of an overcrowded ward that lacks running water and toilets.[3] In the Soviet Union and China, I heard stories of long queues in public clinics, shortages of medicine, perfunctory treatment, and even extortion by underpaid doctors and overworked nurses. Because Soviet hospitals are short of equipment needed for coronary-bypass operations, Soviet males are statistically twice as likely to die from heart disease as men in the West. Kidney dialysis machines are nearly as hard to find. Modern drugs as well as simple bandages and aspirins run out because not enough are manufactured under the state plan. And patients are more likely than those in the West to contract hepatitis because of a lack of disposable syringes.

The best medical professionals understandably gravitate to grander facilities reserved for the élite, where a doctor's patient load may run a half or even a third of that in regular hosptals. A Moscow physician was quoted by the weekly *Medical Gazette (Meditsinskaya Gazeta)* as saying that the shortage of doctors and nurses at her Polyclinic Number 75 had worsened "because a certain percentage of them leave for special polyclinics, where they receive a higher salary for less work [and] have privileges and advantages in obtaining housing and passes to health resorts."[4]

Another woman named Ivanova told the newspaper *Moscow Communist Youth (Moskovsky Komsomolets)* how her twenty-one-month-old son had been taken to Children's Hospital No. 9 in Moscow. Unable to find out about his condition, she donned a white medical smock and walked into the ward, where she found her son lying naked and neglected. The other women in white she met turned to be mothers caring for their own children. The hospital administrator admitted that the hospital let mothers don white coats and do the nursing and cleaning in return for being allowed to tend their children, because the hospital lacked nearly a third of its required nurses and nearly two-thirds of its hospital workers. Its doctors and nurses refused to work longer hours because they did not get paid for overtime.[5]

Medical problems have been compounded by poor sanitation and diet, especially in rural areas. Under *glasnost*, the Soviet press disclosed that the Soviet Union had one of the highest rates of infant mortality in the world, two and a half times that of the United States and Western Europe. The trade union newspaper *Trud* reported in 1988 that 25 infants died for every 1,000 live births, and this rose to 70 deaths per 1,000 in regions of Soviet Central Asia.[6] A prominent surgeon, Dr.

Svyatoslav Fedorov, said that Soviet men lived on average sixty-five years, or eight years less than American males.[7]

The Soviet Union's health care has come under sharp criticism by its own specialists. Dr. Fedorov, writing in *Pravda*, said the health budget allocated little more than $100 a year per Soviet citizen, a quarter of what was needed to raise the Soviet Union to current world standards. "The Soviet physician today is a soldier armed with bows and arrows," he wrote, "and it is not within his power to fight against complex diseases." The Health Minister Yevgeny Chazov told Radio Moscow that defects in health care cost the Soviet economy 90 billion rubles annually—nearly $150 billion—in lost productivity. The government promised to boost its spending on health, which fell during the 1970s, by 25 to 30 percent.

But medical care is also affected by the larger inadequacies of the Soviet and Chinese infrastructure. Nearly a quarter of the 39,000 Russians killed in traffic accidents in 1986, *Izvestia* said, died because of tardy or inadequate medical treatment, delayed in part by a shortage of telephones along the highways. The risk of dying from a traffic accident in China is doubtless worse because the lack of telephones combines with a chaotic prevalence of bicycles vulnerable to collisions.[8] Outside Chengdu, I came upon a cyclist hit by a truck; he died surrounded by a ring of curious strangers long before the police arrived.

Socialized medicine in the Soviet Union and China encourages waste as well. Dr. Chazov observed that Russians were less conscious of fitness than Americans because "free medical care leads people to stop thinking about their health." Though many Chinese engage in early-morning exercises like *taijiquan*, a slow-motion shadow boxing, they also tend toward hyprochondria. The *Beijing Daily* reported that a Chinese doctor was likely to prescribe too much medicine for patients because "he doesn't really care what money is spent and how." A carpet factory in Beijing that was spending 40 yuan a year on medicine for each employee (Chinese workplaces often have their own dispensaries) decided to give the workers 18 yuan each to buy their own medicine. Not only did visits to the factory dispensary decline, but half of the employees didn't spend all the money.

In China, I encountered a more curious aspect of this disregard for medical resources, which were not squandered but never used at all. On Hainan island, I visited a hospital that had received a sophisticated X-ray machine from West Germany. It sat in a room of its own, sealed in the original crates, covered with dust. I could not get an explanation from the hospital director. Perhaps he was afraid it would break down with use, or maybe the hospital didn't have a trained X-ray technician. Just outside the wing containing this technological marvel, relatives squatted in the shade waiting to carry food to patients in the wards while a flock of turkeys pecked at the sparse grass in the yard. I had seen the same contrasts in Yunnan province a year earlier, but there the imported medical equipment was already rusting.

One of the consequences of the willingness to rethink socialism in the Soviet Union and China has been a limited return to private medicine. For years it had happened *na levo* in the Soviet Union, where off-duty physicians make house calls on private patients willing to purchase individual care. A trip to the doctor at a Soviet state clinic costs less than a dollar, but Muscovites willing to pay 10 rubles, or almost $15, at a cooperative clinic, have their choice of doctors, who in turn earn two to three times what they would be paid by the state.

This desocialization of medicine has become more conspicuous in China, which had over 135,000 licensed private health practitioners by the end of 1987. According to Public Health Minister Chen Minzhang, doctors and nurses in cooperative and private practice accounted for a fifth of China's 4.6 million health workers.

I spent a day visiting several such doctors in the industrial city of Lanzhou, the capital of Gansu province. Lanzhou, a city of two million people, had sixteen hundred doctors already practicing privately. "The original medical system was based on egalitarianism and it was no good," said Zhang Ting, the public health official who made the rounds with me. "In getting rid of rigid ideas and as part of the reform system, we think the reforms will not only benefit the health of the patients, but also increase the income of doctors."

Zhang and I found Kong Xianghe sitting at a small desk inside a pharmacy selling traditional herbal medicine on Lanzhou's busy Zhangye Road. He had chosen the location. "When the patients come to get medicine, they can see you at the same time," Dr. Kong explained. As many as fifty patients a day stopped at his desk to be examined. They paid about eight cents for an initial consultation and six cents for a return visit. Dr. Kong, who also collected a small pension from his old dispensary, had to give the government 20 percent of his earnings.

Yang Zhengying, another doctor, whose crew cut, spectacles, and gray wool suit gave him the demeanor of an affable monk, worked out of his home, administering acupuncture to patients on his double bed for eight to twelve cents a session. He had practiced in a hospital attached to the city's construction-engineering bureau, but quit so one of his children sent off to the countryside could return to Lanzhou and take his job. (China lets retiring workers pass state jobs on to their children.) When he went into private practice, Dr. Yang said, "at first I was at a pharmacy, but when it moved I came back and worked in my home." Every day, he saw twenty to thirty patients, who preferred him to the state-run clinics, Dr. Yang said, because "if they go to the hospital, they have to travel a long distance and then wait in line."

Such private doctors help plug some of the gaps in China's health care. Doctors paid by the state wouldn't make house calls, Dr. Yang said, while private physicians were prepared to hop on their bicycles and pedal across the city to visit a sick patient. "Even at midnight, I have to go, because my purpose is to be convenient for people," Dr. Yang told me. He insisted that he didn't mind. "If a patient calls you, that means he trusts you. In China, we still practice revolutionary humanitarianism."

Private medicine became so popular an alternative, not just with patients but also with the local government, that some villages in Gansu handed their clinics over to such doctors. Liujiatan, one village I visited, saved money by giving inhabitants an individual health subsidy of about forty cents a year and telling them to pay their own medical bills. Jin Faquan, a doctor at the local clinic, said he was earning two-thirds more than his old state salary. His clinic had seen thirteen thousand patients the previous year, which he said was still fewer than in the old days. "Under the old system, everything was paid by the state and they would come even if it was unnecessary," Jin explained. "Now they have to pay for a visit."

Education in China and the Soviet Union has undergone problems akin to those afflicting health care, with a conspicuous exception. The reformers' penchant for discarding outworn ideological precepts without offering anything significant to fill the void has introduced uncertainty into education as well. In 1988, I visited Moscow's School No. 31, where some high school pupils told me their textbook on the Soviet Communist Party was now worthless because it had been published under Stalin in 1937. With final examinations looming, a dark-eyed fifteen-year-old girl named Veronika said, "Our teacher told us that if we use only our textbook, we would get nothing more than a grade 3"—equivalent to a C—"so I am using all newspapers." Sixteen-year-old Vladimir said he was studying by listening to news reports on the BBC's shortwave radio broadcasts and attending open lectures at Moscow State University.

A few weeks after my visit that year, the government canceled the nationwide history examination and substituted classroom discussion, because it couldn't figure out what questions to ask its high school students.

In the first years after their respective revolutions, the Soviet Union and China made impressive strides toward eliminating illiteracy and providing free schooling. Lenin, believing that the survival of Communism depended on the education—and indoctrination—of the young, had spoken of the creation of a new school system as one of his most urgent tasks.

While Soviet statistics imply that education barely existed before the 1917 Revolution, Czarist records showed that two years before the Bolsheviks seized power, over half of all Russian children between eight and eleven years old were attending school and that more than two-thirds of the draftees in the Czarist Russian Army could read and write. In 1915, 10.6 million Russians were enrolled in schools and colleges. By the 1979–80 Soviet academic year, this number had climbed to over 99 million, including adult-education programs, outpacing the growth of the population.

In China, the precepts of Confucius treated wisdom and learning as cardinal virtues. The Qing Dynasty, before its collapse in 1911, regarded education as essential to help China catch up with the West. Foreign missionaries introduced Western-type education in the nineteenth century. The Communist government initially denounced the mission schools and colleges as alien to China, but subsequently conceded their usefulness. "Although the missionary schools had produced some lackeys and compradors of foreign aggressors, they educated a greater number of people who lately rendered good services to China," said the *Guangming Daily* newspaper.

But unlike their commitment to health care, the attitudes of the early revolutionaries in the Soviet Union and China toward education were ambivalent, for all the lip service they have paid it. They understood its value in disseminating ideas and indoctrinating rising generations in the faith. Yet it carries somehow a stigma of intellectual élitism and unearned leisure synonymous with learning in prerevolutionary Russia and China.

Marxist theoreticians predicted that schools, like other capitalist institutions, were destined to disappear in the Soviet Union. Until then, they said, youngsters should balance their classes with manual labor to absorb its dignity. The Soviet pedagogue A. P. Pinkevich declared in 1927 that "the center of all of the work of the school should be human labor."[9] As the country's industrialization faltered from a shortage of skilled workers and engineers, the Central Committee in 1931 attacked what it called "the anti-Leninist theory of the 'with-

ering away of the school,'" and made seven years of formal
education compulsory. In time, the Soviet Union embraced
traditional education, down to the old Czarist customs of
school uniforms and autocratic classroom discipline.

During the Cultural Revolution, which lasted from 1966
to 1976, China came close to destroying its educational system. Teachers were persecuted and their classrooms emptied
as adolescents were sent off to work in the countryside. University entrance examinations were abolished. A blank exam
paper handed in by one rebellious student was elevated to a
model of politically correct thinking, and outside agitators
were given free run on campuses. Maoist sophistries polluted
what classes were left. English-language textbooks, for example, were reduced to stilted translations of Chairman Mao's
speeches. The smug ignorance encouraged by the Cultural Revolution stunted a generation and more. A national census in
1982 found that nearly four-fifths of the country's industrial
work force had a junior high school education or less and that
23.5 percent of the population still could not read or write
thirty-three years after the Revolution.[10]

It would be hard to underestimate the damage that the
Cultural Revolution inflicted on Chinese education. Yang Li-
jian, headmistress at Shiyan primary school in Shanghai, re-
minisced with me one afternoon about the hard times that she
and the other teachers underwent. "In the time of the Gang
of Four, children didn't like to study, because that would be
considered as putting intellectual education first," she recalled. "Also, discipline wasn't good. Those children who
disrupted class were praised as heroes. It was considered revolutionary spirit. We kept on teaching but it was very hard on
the teachers. The Gang of Four encouraged children to cut
classes and pushed them toward outdoor schooling at factories
and communes. It took us about a year to restore order and
discipline afterward."

By comparison, the Soviet educational system has drawn
accolades for its emphasis on mathematics and related skills—
two years of calculus for high school students is mandatory—
and its workload of up to twenty-two subjects for a student is

far heavier than at American schools. What has suffered is creativity. The Soviet learning process, like that in China, relies more on passive memorization than intellectual inquiry. Wang Yibing, a researcher for the State Education Commission, wrote in the *Beijing Review* that "because of the traditional spoon-fed method of teaching in China, students lack the ability to think and study independently."

This began to change in the Soviet Union once Gorbachev encouraged more public discussion. I was struck by the spontaneity in the second-floor classroom I visited at School No. 31 in Moscow, where the mood seemed altogether more candid than the polite tension in other Soviet schools I had visited in the previous two decades. The students boasted almost joyously that they were introducing Gorbachev's reforms into their own school. "The plan of the school council is prepared by the children, not the teachers," said Veronika. "It gives new opportunities to our life. We are tired of subjects we don't need." A plump brunette named Rita added, "Now we feel *perestroika* in our society, but we want to feel it in our school, to make our subjects more interesting, to make it easier to listen and to learn."

But I suspect that their school of well-dressed, well-fed teenagers specializing in English was more dynamic than most others in Moscow. The former Moscow Party chief Boris Yeltsin, in a blunt speech in September 1986, disclosed that alcoholism and drug use had become serious problems among the one million secondary and vocational school students in the Soviet capital.

Yeltsin was particularly scathing about the neglect of vocational education, the institution dearest to the heart of the early revolutionaries. "The state of many vocational schools is so miserable that young people refuse to go there," said Yeltsin, who estimated that one in four vocational schools in Moscow had become useless.

In China, where the late President Liu Shaoqi once advocated a two-track school system that combined teaching with factory and farm experience, fewer than a tenth of China's secondary school students in 1985 were going on to vocational

230 CHRISTOPHER S. WREN

school. As a result, over one million Chinese a year have graduated from high school, and six million have left junior high school, without marketable skills.

Because a college degree ranks next to a Party card in providing upward mobility into the new caste, it is not surprising that higher education too has suffered from favoritism and corruption. Gaidar Aliyev, the former Party chief of Azerbaijan, was quoted in 1977 as saying that "the opinion was widespread in the republic that without patronage, without a bribe, you could not get into university." Ten years later, the Soviet Ministry of Higher and Secondary Education and the Party's Control Committee decided to close down Azerbaijan's Economics Institute because of rampant nepotism in admissions and cheating on examinations.

As with other sectors of Communist society, the discrepancy between the best and worst in education can be startling. Moscow State University, despite its Stalinist architecture, looks as impressive as a Big Ten university in the American Midwest. But outside the big cities, the facilities I saw were often archaic. I was taken through a technical institute in the Moldavian capital of Kishinev as ramshackle as anything I had seen in rural Mississippi.

The bureaucracy's preoccupation with statistical results in education, as in other fields, steers funds away from those areas where progress is less visible. In Moscow, I was moved by the attention lavished on handicapped children at the Institute of Defectology. I watched Raisa Mareyeva, a middle-aged miracle worker, coax a little boy without sight or hearing into making his first sounds. "Never give a child prepared knowledge," she told me afterward. "Make him discover it for himself."

Yet the rest of the Soviet Union had few such remarkable facilities. In a typical province of southern Russia, *Izvestia* subsequently reported, "There is not a single school for children with arrested psychological development. Nor are there any special schools for children with aftereffects of poliomyelitis or cerebral palsy." Only one teacher in ten, it said, was trained to deal with handicapped children.[11]

Special education was even more backward in China, according to my sister Virginia Wren Moore, a speech pathologist who toured Chinese schools in 1983. Ginny, who directs special education at Lake Forest High School in Illinois, had read glowing descriptions of Chinese education, and she was surprised to find no special facilities in the half-dozen major cities her delegation visited. "When I described learning disabilities, neurological deficits, autism, other emotional disorders, cleft palate or cerebral palsy, I would receive answers that these children were not in school," she reported. Two Chinese teachers told Ginny privately that retarded or physically handicapped children in rural areas were sent out to beg.[12]

Central economic planners in the Soviet Union and China have lavished resources so intensively on development of industry and agriculture that education, like other fields of social welfare, are bound to have been neglected. Similar complaints have been expressed about American education, of course, but Moscow and Beijing pretended for years that everything in their classrooms was superior to things in the West and suppressed evidence to the contrary. "In the last thirty years, there has been a gradual reduction of investment in education," Gorbachev's economic adviser Abel Aganbegyan admitted at a seminar I attended in 1988. "Now that gradual decline is recognized as having been an error." Aganbegyan said Moscow hoped to increased its educational spending 1.7 times, with a 30 percent pay raise for teachers.

When the state of Soviet education was reviewed by the Central Committee in February 1988, Gorbachev argued that hopes for restructuring the country rested on the teachers, not schools or curricula. "The teacher is a major protagonist of *perestroika*," Gorbachev said. "If he supports us with conviction, sense, and passion, *perestroika* will gain many new sincere supporters and champions, successors to the revolutionary socialist cause. But what if the support is formal, and the teacher remains indifferent, neutral? Who will be able to predict what social stagnation and backward movement this indifference may produce?"

Westerners visiting China before the Cultural Revolution

considered its educational system a major achievement. "The Communists have poured into it vast effort, imagination and money," wrote Mark Gayn, a Canadian, in 1965. "The visitor is constantly delighted by such experiences as finding twenty-five microscopes in a provincial secondary school." Twenty years later, the *Economic Daily* told an altogether different story, reporting that 40 percent of children in some rural areas were dropping out before they completed the first five years of school (nine years is compulsory). The newspaper blamed the problem mainly on "limited funds, poor teaching equipment, and unqualified teachers." The newspaper disclosed that 53 percent of primary school teachers and 18 percent of those in high school were unsuited for their jobs. "Because of such deficiencies," it said, "some parents are unwilling to put their children through school. Other parents ask their children to drop out in order to make money."[13]

Another survey done in 1987 found that China needed thousands of new classrooms and that fewer than 10 percent of existing primary and secondary schools had the scientific equipment, like microscopes, required by their curriculum. The State Statistical Bureau reported that Chinese teachers, ill-paid in the best of times, ranked tenth among twelve wage levels in the economy. To make ends meet, China has pared back the old guarantees of a free higher education—the state spends about 3,000 yuan a year educating each university student—and employment after graduation. It wants to make 70 percent of students start paying for tuition by 1993 and let them find their own jobs.

China tried to export part of its educational crisis to the West, dispatching armies of graduate students to study there, often on the charity of foreign scholarships. In 1988, 40,000 Chinese students were estimated to be studying abroad, 27,000 of them in the United States, compared with about 1,500 Soviet students overseas. The consequence was a "brain drain" of educated young Chinese who now want to stay in the West, especially after Deng's crackdown on their student peers in 1989.[14]

The gap between official word and deed has engendered

enough youthful cynicism to discredit Marxism in the Soviet Union and China. The traditional fabric of both countries was shredded after their revolutions to make children conform more quickly to socialism. "Children belong to the society into which they are born, not to their parents," wrote Nikolai Bukharin and Yevgeny Preobrazhensky in their 1920s handbook *The ABC's of Communism*.[15] As late as 1984, new Soviet legislation on educational reform stated: "The unshakable foundation of Communist education for schoolchildren is the formation in their minds of a Marxist-Leninist world outlook."

In 1949, China's new Communist government called for a "scientific, historical viewpoint" in education—meaning a Marxist one. The *Youth Newspaper (Qingnian Bao)*, defending state boarding schools in 1959, said that "it is for society to raise and educate the young into a new generation and give the kind of love that no maternal love can ever hope to compete with."

Logically, then, children raised by the Party would grow up into model Communists. I decided to test the thesis by visiting the Yuhong orphanage in Shijiazhuang. The orphanage was created, supervised, and funded by the Chinese Communist Party for the children who survived the devastating Tangshan earthquake in July 1976. The orphans, some as young as three months, were pulled out of the rubble of Tangshan and sent to Shijiazhuang, the provincial capital 225 miles to the southwest.

"I am a flower in the sunshine of the Party," exults a nursery song taught to Chinese toddlers, in a kind of Communist variation of the "Jesus Loves Me" sung in American Sunday schools. If so, the orphans in the Party's hothouse at Yuhong should have been unfolding their petals as perfect little Communists. As I rode the slow train from Beijing to Shijiazhuang, I wondered how the orphans differed from other Chinese children, who were buffered against relentless indoctrination by the nourishment of their own family and home.

Chinese Communism's ideal child had been capsuled during the Cultural Revolution in a comic book relating the fictional exploits of "heroic little Dai Bilun," a cheerful moppet

234 CHRISTOPHER S. WREN

in the mold of Little Orphan Annie. While gathering water-cress, she spied a runaway freight train bearing down on three other children, whom she pushed to safety at the cost of serious injury. When Bilun regained consciousness after an emergency operation, she serenaded her surgeons by singing "The East Is Red." Lying in her hospital bed, she memorized radio broadcasts of Chairman Mao's directives. "Daddy, Sister, don't feel sorry for me," Bilun reassured her family. "I still have one arm to write the thoughts of Chairman Mao. I can still serve the people." Such ideological fairy tales ring hollow today but they were believed at the time and emulated sometimes by credulous Chinese youngsters.

When I arrived at the orphanage, some of the boys were playing a raucous game of soccer. Tang Huizheng, the motherly gray-haired woman who ran the orphanage, dispelled my preconceptions almost immediately when she pointed out a rubber factory beyond the gray wall from the orphanage. In the evening, the factory showed movies to its workers, she said, "and sometimes the children break discipline and sneak out to watch the film." They were also inclined, she said, to watch a lot of television on weekends.

Miss Tang led me through the whitewashed barracks. The floors were of poured concrete and the furnishings spartan, but in one dormitory for teenage girls, colored calendar pictures of favorite movie actresses were tacked up on the walls behind the tidy rows of beds with folded quilts, foot lockers, and enamel washbasins. There were no pin-ups here of Karl Marx, Mao Zedong, or Deng Xiaoping.

Outside the dormitory, a quiz on patriotism was written on a blackboard, but other blackboards along the dirt path gave pointers on chemistry and physics. "At the moment, the teachers are studying Deng Xiaoping's works, especially on education, to improve our ideology and to train the children in ethics," the director said. "We are reading Deng Xiaoping's works to the children to teach them the four Cardinal Principles." These, as set out by Deng in 1979, pledged everyone to (1) keep to the socialist road, (2) uphold the dictatorship of the proletariat, (3) uphold the leadership of the Communist

Party, and (4) uphold Marxism-Leninism and Mao Zedong Thought. When I later asked a slender seventeen-year-old how her study of the Four Cardinal Principles was going, she looked confused. "We plan to study Deng Xiaoping's works, but not yet, because at present we are very busy with our school exams," she explained.

Though the Tangshan earthquake came at the tag end of the Cultural Revolution, Miss Tang said, "the children were so young that they were not directly influenced by the Cultural Revolution. But they were influenced by the lack of discipline at the time. Some children followed the rules and some didn't, so we had to educate them. They didn't have their mother and father to educate them, so we had to do it, and the discipline improved."

"Of course, the children appreciate the deep feelings of the Party," Miss Tang said when I asked where the Party fitted in. "They realize that without the concern of the Party and the teachers, they couldn't grow up." But their real affection seemed reserved for the latter. In the early years, the teachers slept in the dormitories to reassure the orphans that the thunderclaps or wind outside did not mean that the earthquake was returning. "We had to take on the responsibilities of both parents and teachers," Miss Tang said as she passed among her charges, pausing to caress one or bundle up another. "So our teachers have deep feelings for the children."

Before the Chinese New Year, the local Party secretary and his counterpart in the Communist Youth League joined the children in making *baozi* or meat dumplings, a holiday tradition akin to dying Easter eggs in the United States. Some local textile workers who had been orphans themselves were invited to recall an orphan's bleak life before the 1949 Revolution. The children liked such avuncular visits, which had no overt ideological agenda, but they loved the orphanage staff members who lived among them. I asked Du Mingyan, a doll-like child, whom she regarded as her parents. "My teachers," she whispered.

When I visited the orphanage, only 176 children were left. Most of the graduates had left to work in factories, though some also enlisted in the army or went to college. "A few of them haven't behaved very well," Miss Tang confided. "According to the letters we receive, some pay too much attention to their appearance and style of living, and some don't work very hard." I assured her that they sounded like most adolescents.

A musical performance had been arranged for me. I sat on a folding chair and a chorus of orphans wearing the red scarves of Young Pioneers, the Communist equivalent of the Boy and Girl Scouts, filed in. I suppose I expected to hear "The East Is Red" or "The Communist Internationale." Instead, I was regaled with "Jingle Bells" and "Row, Row, Row Your Boat," sung out lustily in Chinese to the beat of a metal triangle tapped by a chipmunk-cheeked girl in a white sweater. In return, I had to stand and sing "Do Re Mi" from *The Sound of Music*, which Chinese dote on for reasons I never understood. I was not Julie Andrews but they clapped politely when I finished, though I had to fake some of the words.

The children seemed charming and well adjusted, but I figured it was because of the old-fashioned love lavished by their teachers, not because socialism offered any superior formula for child raising. Contrary to my fears, there wasn't an ideologue among them.

"We wouldn't say that our political consciousness is higher than that of other children," said Zhang Lihua, a bespectacled teenage girl who wanted to study English. "The sense of the collective is higher for children like us simply because we live and study together."

9

THE FRAUDULENT FLYING PIGEONS: THE CHRONIC SHORTAGE OF ALMOST EVERYTHING

▬▬▬▬▬▬▬▬▬▬▬▬▬▬

When there is enough goods in a store, the purchasers can come whenever they want to. When there is little goods, the purchasers are compelled to stand in line. When the lines are very long, it is necessary to appoint a policeman to keep order. Such is the starting point of the power of the Soviet bureaucracy.

—LEON TROTSKY, 1937[1]

Why do we spend our working hours, strength, raw materials, and energy producing a worthless product?

—MIKHAIL S. GORBACHEV, 1987[2]

THE KITCHEN, cozy and slightly unkempt, was where Andrei Sakharov and his wife, Yelena Bonner, liked to entertain visitors in their small Moscow apartment. "I hope you don't mind getting photographed," said Mrs. Sakharov, gesturing a little wearily toward the kitchen window. The KGB, she said, kept a camera trained on her kitchen table. I had visited the Sakharovs often enough so that I figured the security police already had my photo on file.

I dropped by the Sakharovs' that night in March 1977 because of a news reports made all the more fascinating by its seeming banality. Sakharov, who died of heart failure in

1989, is best remembered as the inventor of the Soviet hydrogen bomb, winner of the Nobel Peace Prize, and patriarch of the struggling Soviet human rights movement. But on this occasion, he was embroiled in a struggle more familiar to ordinary Russians. He was trying to move into a better apartment.

His efforts might have escaped notice had not Tass assailed Sakharov for trying to wangle a "considerable increase" in his living space. "On somebody's assignment, Sakharov must have needed to attract again scandalous attention to his person from a section of the foreign press and at the same time to cast aspersions once again on Soviet laws," Tass said, sniffing yet another plot.

As Mrs. Sakharov poured everyone strong black tea, the Nobel laureate explained that there was less to the tale than the official news agency had implied. Before they emigrated to Massachusetts, Mrs. Sakharov's daughter and son-in-law, Tanya and Efrem Yankelevich, lived with her mother, Ruth Bonner, in another apartment. The Sakharovs wanted to move with them into a larger four-room apartment communally occupied by three other families. In return, the Sakharovs and the Yankeleviches offered to exchange their two smaller apartments. One apartment would go to a family in the communal apartment. Their fellow tenants would move to two other apartments, whose current occupants would move together into the Sakharovs' apartment.

Yelena Bonner Sakharov had to sketch me a diagram on the kitchen table before I understood the intricacies of this multiple swap, which involved seventeen people and five apartments and had taken a year to choreograph. As she explained it, their arrangement satisfied everyone involved. Two of the women sharing the kitchen and the bathroom of the communal apartment were quarreling. A widower in another room wanted to move into a separate flat with his three-year-old child, who now lived with his mother-in-law. And the others who signed up thought that the move would improve their lives.

The local housing exchange approved the plan and so did

the housing commission of Moscow's Cheryemushky district. But the district's executive commission overruled both on grounds that one of the women in the communal flat already had 172 square feet of living space. Moscow's housing regulations allowed only 10 square meters, or 107 square feet, per person. By moving, the woman would get another 8 square feet. "That she lives in a communal apartment and quarrels with the other woman doesn't interest them," Mrs. Sakharov said, sighing. "She doesn't have permission of the executive committee to change her life."

Perhaps the Soviet authorities did not want to make life easier for the nation's most celebrated dissident, who in 1980 was exiled to Gorky for six years. Or perhaps the KGB balked at having to bug another flat so thoroughly. But the episode's real significance here was that seventeen people had to go through such contortions to make their lives a little better and that their hopes could be dashed by bureaucratic arbitrariness over a bit of space no larger than the Sakharovs' kitchen table.

Because its system of central planning was not designed to give people priority over the state, Communism has become synonymous with chronic economic shortage. The insistence of the Soviet and Chinese governments upon doing for people what they could do more easily for themselves has been exacerbated by what the Chinese call "metal-eating," meaning the preference for heavy over light industry.

The Russians and Chinese I knew wanted a greater abundance of food, better consumer goods—which usually meant Western imports—their own apartments, and the chance to travel abroad. Most had little or no interest in moving to the West (this is not necessarily so in Eastern Europe as emigrants from East Germany have shown). Accustomed to the idiosyncrasies of a Communist society, they were not enthusiastic about finding their own jobs or being confronted with other choices demanded in a pluralistic society. They conceived a life in the West as more ruthless because it lacked a safety net. "I'd love to be able to visit the United States," a university student in Moscow told me, but afterward, he said, "I want to be able to return home."

The exception was Soviet Jews who dreamed of going to Israel, where they could observe their own traditions and religion freely. A survey directed by James R. Millar, a University of Illinois economist, of 2,793 Soviet immigrants in the United States found that 64 percent had been satisfied with their former jobs in the Soviet Union and 60 percent with their overall standard of living. They generally left for family or religious reasons—most were Jewish—not political ones.[3]

In guaranteeing jobs and cheap food and apartments, but not of sufficient quantity or quality, Communism has created a life comforting in its reliability if not reliable in its comforts. The relative contentment, whether out of docility or resignation, is a mixed blessing for reformers in Moscow and Beijing, because it makes it harder to change the way things get done. "Chinese cities have been turned into day-care centers and the inertia has set in," observed an American banker with whom I lunched one day in Beijing. "If you're assured of sustenance without working, why hurt yourself?"

The late Soviet dissident Andrei Amalrik contended that this indolence engendered among his fellow Russians extended to Western-style freedoms. "Even in the idea of pragmatic freedom a Russian tends to see not so much the possibility of securing a good life for himself as the danger that some clever fellow will make good at his expense," Amalrik wrote in his 1969 essay "Will the Soviet Union Survive Until 1984?"[4] When I got to know Amalrik in 1975, he insisted that his observation remained valid.

It seemed to me that material shortage and not lack of democracy in the Soviet Union and China created the flash point for instability. The biggest wave of strikes to hit the Soviet Union in more than six decades happened in the summer of 1989 when coal miners from Siberia to the Ukraine walked out in protest over the lack of basic necessities like the soap needed to wash away the daily grime accumulated down in the shafts. Of course, economic sufficiency can lead to rising political expectations, though the vast majority of Chinese did not support the students in Beijing and other cities who mounted the ill-fated democracy movement of 1989.

Abel Aganbegyan, the Soviet economist, once described housing as his nation's most serious social problem; China's housing shortage is hardly better.[5] "Trying to find an apartment to rent is harder than finding a spouse," the People's Daily lamented a few years ago. Yet public complacency has also frustrated a solution. In the Soviet Union and China, token rents are taken for granted as a socialist birthright, and the leadership has been reluctant to raise them for fear of triggering new resentments. Today, a two-room apartment in Moscow rents for about 15 rubles, or $20, a month, as it did back in 1928. Rent accounts for only 3 percent of the average Soviet family's expenditures. An apartment in China rents for even less. Housing officials in Canton told me that a two-room flat with kitchen and bath went for about $2 a month—if one was available.

In the wake of the Bolshevik Revolution, the Soviet Union's temporary solution was communal living in the apartment houses and mansions confiscated from the middle and upper classes until inexpensive housing could be built. Because Stalin spent money on factories, power dams, and battle tanks instead, by 1955, two years after his death, average per capita living space amounted to less than 54 square feet, or not much larger than a king-size bed. In 1961, Khrushchev promised every Soviet family its own home by 1980. It didn't happen. Despite Brezhnev's call for builders to erect "good, high-grade, and handsome houses," the construction rate for new apartments dropped more than 40 percent between 1960 and 1985. In 1986, when the Party pushed the 1980 deadline back another twenty years, one-fifth of all urban families were still packed into communal apartments. In Moscow alone, nearly 1.9 million residents were waiting for new apartments.

It is hardly surprising that an apartment of one's own has become a status symbol. Moscow's taxi drivers sarcastically referred to an upscale neighborhood inhabited by senior Party and government functionaries as Tsarkoe Selo ("the Czar's village"), after the residence of Russia's last Czar.

Apartments are allocated to ordinary Russians through work units or places of employment. "Money doesn't work as

242   CHRISTOPHER S. WREN

it should here," said a Russian scientist friend who had been waiting years for a better apartment. "You get your apartment not on how well you work but on how good you look in the eyes of your boss. Of course, it is better to work well than badly, but it is even better to look good."

When I lived in Moscow, high rises kept sprouting up around the city's perimeter, but when I visited friends, their apartments seemed tacky and hastily assembled. The worst were the six-story walkups thrown together during the Khrushchev years; such a flat was nicknamed *khrushchyoba*, a word that rhymed with the Russian word for slum. Flats from the Brezhnev years were a little more substantial, but the plaster still flaked, the doors and windows rattled, the toilets leaked, and the walls were paper thin. When I visited the Moldavian city of Kishinev, my taxi driver pointed out a large housing complex on the road in from the airport. Cracks had opened in the concrete façades like earthquake fault lines and the small balconies drooped. I assumed they were at least twenty years old, but the driver corrected me. "Three years," he boasted.

The drab state of Soviet housing was satirized in a Soviet film comedy, *With Some Light Steam.* The film's amiable young hero spent the afternoon drinking with his buddies in a Moscow steam bath and wound up on a flight to Leningrad booked by his friend. Upon arrival, he assumed he was in Moscow and hailed a taxi to his apartment on Avenue of the Builders. His key opened the door of an apartment with the same address, but inside was a lovely blonde who mistook him for a burglar. He wooed and wed her in the end, but not before the audience enjoyed some credible gags about the anonymity of Soviet housing.

I saw the best and worst of it. Lithuania, which always seemed of independent mind, mixed up the limited prefabricated designs to create an appealing neighborhood at Lazdynai, a postwar suburb of Vilnius that won a Lenin Prize for architectural imagination. The towers of blue, pumpkin, and violet looked like a high-rise neighborhood of Helsinki, set among pine trees and enlivened with pedestrian malls, flower beds, and abstract sculptures. Only when I walked up to the buildings did I recognize the components common across the Soviet Union. I could not help but compare Lazdynai to the Siberian city of Bratsk, where the forest was razed to make way for barracklike housing laid out like dominoes. The state invested its money and ingenuity in the adjacent hydroelectric project.

After the Communists took over China, many urban dwellers also lived in hovels or dormitories. I got an insight into the continuing problem when we invited some British friends studying in Beijing to dinner in our foreigners-only apartment building. I thought they would enjoy a home-cooked meal, but what they really came for was a hot bath. In time, we learned to keep a pile of clean towels waiting for dinner guests, including our Chinese acquaintances.

Though the Communists meant to solve the housing crisis, the resources were diverted for showcase projects that highlighted China's industrial progress. Not until the Cultural Revolution ground to a halt in 1976 was housing taken seriously. When I first visited Shanghai in 1981, its per capita living space averaged about forty-three square feet. Such cramped conditions explain why Chinese, who are naturally gracious hosts, usually avoid inviting foreigners home. When one couple I met overcame this reluctance, the husband, a pediatrician, cooked us dinner on a communal hotplate shared with a family living on the other side of a curtain dividing the small flat. We ate sitting on a double bed that almost filled the room allotted to him and his family.

Chinese mass housing, which has traditionally been distributed through work units, was modeled after the Soviet Union's and inherited many of its characteristics of dreariness, poor workmanship, and corruption. In Beijing, the state built a row of new high rises, some sixteen stories high, so relentless in their monotony that locals nicknamed them the New Great Wall. In early 1988, the *Beijing Daily* reported that many of the buildings still lacked electricity, running water, natural gas, telephones, and automatic elevators. Nearly half had no gas pipelines, which forced residents to carry heavy propane cylinders up to their apartments. Only two of the thirty buildings surveyed had telephones, and these were public ones.

The pre-revolutionary buildings in Moscow and Beijing were not much better. Even the grandest mansions deteriorated through lack of maintenance. As I rode my bicycle down some narrow *hutong*, or back alley, in old Beijing, I imagined at first that it would be fun to live in one of the gray brick houses behind the high walls, looking out into some nineteenth-century courtyard with its delicate garden. The Chinese I knew scoffed at my naïveté, for who would want to live squeezed in with four other families, lacking central heating, running water, and indoor toilets?

Moscow's most romantic neighborhood is the Arbat, which has been around since the fourteenth century. I visited an acquaintance living on the second floor of one of the pastel-colored houses and was disenchanted by the cracking plaster, sagging staircases, and leaky plumbing. In 1985, the city renovated the Arbat with a lovely brick pedestrian mall and wrought-iron streetlamps. When I walked through the restored neighborhood past folksingers and sidewalk artists, I assumed that the houses had been included in the renovations. But a couple of reporters sent by the magazine *Ogonyok* to look behind the Arbat's painted façade found the apartments rotting from lack of repair and crammed with communal tenants still waiting for better quarters. One resident fetched her own water; another complained about rats. In cleaning up the Arbat's exterior, the Moscow city authorities had created another Potemkin village. The disparity was not unusual. As late as 1987, nearly one in three Soviet apartments owned by the state lacked hot water, nearly one in six lacked indoor toilets, one in eleven had no central heating, and one in twelve no running water.

Most Russians I knew didn't bother fixing up their apartments because home-improvement items were so scarce. A teacher wrote *Pravda* that his city of Kursk received only two shipments of wallpaper a year, "something dull, insipid, and sparsely floral—and not in very large amounts." Still, the demand ran five times the supply. In Dnepropetrovsk, another Ukrainian city, a cooperative began renovating apartments only to find that it had to go to other cities and neighboring republics to scrounge such basic fixtures as radiators and bathtubs.

For a long time, the Soviet Union blamed its chronic housing shortage on the devastation of World War Two; China used the Japanese occupation and the ensuing civil war as a similar excuse. Neither explained why the Germans and Japanese, whose countries were also devastated, live so much better today. In November 1987, the economist Abel Aganbegyan attributed his country's backwardness not to the war but to outmoded and wrong economic and social policies.

The unalleviated apartment shortage has contributed to the Soviet Union's falling birth rate and rising divorce rate, as young couples postpone marriage or bunk for years with in-laws. To qualify for a flat in the better cities, Russians marry spouses they don't love, take jobs they don't like, or bear children they don't want. The lack of housing has even retarded economic development because it restricts labor mobility. The Soviet government has talked of shifting superfluous workers to other labor-hungry regions, but cannot find them places to live.

The dire straits of Soviet housing was suggested in one *Pravda* article I read about a new employee hired by a movie theater in Gelendzhik, a resort on the Black Sea. Because the town was full up, the manager let him sleep temporarily in the box office. Moviegoers were soon complaining about odors of soup and fried potatoes wafting from the small stove that the man had set up behind the cinema screen. The employee refused to dismantle his housekeeping because, he said, he had nowhere else to live. "Who is to blame?" *Pravda* concluded, implying that the real culprits were the economic planners who scrimped on housing.

The need for a residence permit, called a *propiska*, has prevented Russians from looking for better accommodation in other cities. Without permission to move, it becomes nigh impossible to get an apartment, a job, even ration coupons to buy basic foodstuffs. Similar controls exist in China. I knew a young woman who was deprived of her residence permit in Beijing after she took a job in southern China. She missed Beijing and came home illegally, cadging food coupons and living nights with her parents and other relatives and friends. She said she knew other young Chinese who did the same, including former Red Guards who marched off to the countryside during the Cultural Revolution and were refused permission to come home.

In China, the social strains were compounded by the bureaucratic habit of assigning husbands and wives to jobs in different cities. A language translator I knew working in Beijing tried to rent a hotel room for a reunion with his wife, who was due for vacation from her job in Shanghai. But his Beijing residence permit showed him to have accommodations in a bachelors' dormitory, which made him ineligible to stay at a hotel. His sympathetic employer eventually produced a *banfa* by sending him to Shanghai on an ostensible business trip.

The residence restrictions created a pattern of formidable commuting that is quite the reverse of the American custom. In the Soviet Union and China, it is the poorer and less privileged who commute into the cities, where social and cultural life is livelier and consumer goods are more plentiful. To research a story on Soviet commuting, I went to the Yaroslavl and Belorussky stations in Moscow and watched the commuters surging on and off the trains. Some carried flapping leather briefcases; others lugged sacks of produce. They were either taking it to sell in the local farmers' markets or buying goods downtown that were scarce in their own communities. I later asked a middle-aged woman why she didn't shop in her own neighborhood, but she said the shelves of the local stores were nearly bare. "I can buy milk, cheese, and bread, but I buy the other consumer goods downtown," she explained. "I spent an hour and a half waiting in line here for meat once, but it was half bone."

Some Soviet social scientists like Viktor Perevedentsev, a respected demographer, have called for an end to residence controls, which Stalin imposed more than a half century ago, arguing that they perpetuate inequality and corruption because Russians will do almost anything to acquire or keep the right to live in cities like Moscow and Leningrad. Perevedentsev proposed controlling the expected influx through available jobs. Some outside workers, called *limitchiki*, are already allowed into Moscow and other major cities to fill crucial jobs on a probationary basis; they must stay in dormitories and are not allowed to look for other work or an apartment before they get a residence permit, which can take at least five years.

One solution has been to ask those who want their own homes to start paying for them. Soviet economists suggested charging more for space in excess of the legal minimum. China has offered some state apartments for private sale. In Canton, I visited some private apartments being built by the Guangzhou Urban Construction Company. "The housing problem has put too big a burden on the goverment," said the general manager, Zhang Haochun. "In this country, because wages are low, rents are also very cheap, so it takes a very long time for the state to recoup its investment." His company was selling apartments with kitchen, bath, balcony, and up to three bedrooms, starting at 11,000 to 15,000 yuan, depending on location and floor. "We didn't put up any advertisements. We only let the newspapers release the news and people came over," said Chai Binshu, a company planner. "More than one thousand people showed up the first day. Our office was so crowded that they couldn't fit in." Because the flats were too costly for anyone with a low-paying state job, some buyers borrowed the money from relatives in Hong Kong or overseas.

The Soviet Union has also tolerated more private or cooperatively owned homes. But Russians, more than the Chinese, have retained a skittishness about private ownership, particularly since they can use the state's property for a pittance. After more than seven decades spent living under Communism, they found it hard to disregard the dictum of Marx and Engels that "the theory of the Communists may be summed up in the single phrase: abolition of private property."

· · ·

The plight of the long-suffering consumer was illustrated in 1989 by a news item in *Pravda* about a farmer in the Soviet Far East who realized on a trip to Vladivostok that he had left his shaving brush at home. The farmer, Nikolai Vasilenko, looked in vain for another in Vladivostok and two other cities. He also could not find the other items on his shopping list, which included a sewing machine, a milk separator, a colander, a jacket for his son, and some tights for his daughter. That same year, the Soviet government acknowledged that shortages existed in 1,000 of 1,200 basic consumer items produced by the state.

The size of personal savings in the Soviet Union is the result not of Russian frugality but of the shortage of consumer goods. In 1988, Sergei Grigoryants, the editor of the Soviet dissident journal *Glasnost,* said private savings in the Soviet Union amounted to 300 billion rubles in bank accounts and another 100 billion rubles squirreled away in mattresses and holes in the ground, while the products available for sale countrywide totaled about 82 billion rubles. In other words, Mr. Grigoryants said, 75 percent of the rubles saved were worthless because there was nothing to spend them on. In 1989, the Soviet Union quietly instituted emergency imports of such Western consumer goods as razor blades, toothpaste, soap powder, pantyhose, knitwear, and leather shoes, to compensate for substantial shortfalls in its own production.

Tourists arriving in Moscow for the first time comment upon its drabness. I grew accustomed to this gloom, which could be offset by the Soviet capital's interior cultural glitter of ballet, opera, drama, and symphony concerts, but something else was missing. For a long time it eluded me until I realized that it was the restaurants. Virtually every other world capital I had visited had a wealth of international restaurants. Moscow had none when I lived there, nor did any other Soviet city I saw. In Moscow, restaurants of dubious quality offered ethnic cuisines from the Soviet republics of Uzbekistan, Georgia, and Armenia, but there were no French, Italian, or Japanese restaurants. The dining rooms at the Berlin, Belgrade, and Peking hotels and the Prague restaurant served Russian borscht, sturgeon, and chicken Kiev, but not specialties from the capitals after which they were named. The unfettering of private enterprise gave rise to some cooperative restaurants, but except for an Indian and a Chinese restaurant I heard about, their cuisines still come from the Soviet republics.

Beijing also lacked restaurants specializing in foreign cuisine when we arrived. The dining room at the Xinqiao Hotel did an adequate borscht, chicken Kiev, and Pakistani chapatis. A few French restaurants later opened in hotels patronized by foreigners. Strictly for the challenge, Pierre Cardin helped create a replica of Maxim's in Paris ("if I can open a Maxim's in Beijing," he boasted to me, "I can open a Maxim's on the moon"), but ordinary Chinese could not afford to go there. Shanghai, a more cosmopolitan port city, had the Hong Fangzi, or Red House, a cheerfully tacky French restaurant that had survived the 1949 Revolution; it was frequented by youths who took their dates to show off their dexterity with knives and forks. The Chinese didn't seem as threatened by Western cuisine because they considered their own superior. It may be a mistake to read too much into restaurants, but their absence seemed evidence that foreign food, like foreigners themselves, was deemed superfluous. For whatever reason, a discriminating palate became one of the first casualties of the Revolution, as was evidenced by the poor quality of domestic cuisine. The best Russian and Chinese restaurants I patronized during my tour in Moscow and Beijing were located respectively in Helsinki and Hong Kong.

The perennial search for food in the state stores is well known outside the Soviet Union, though most Westerners cannot fathom the daily frustration. "There are no chickens anywhere, and when there are, there is a long queue. And pork, I have forgotten how it looks," complained the wife of a Russian computer specialist when I dropped in one evening. "You can't eat the sausage because it is made with artificial ingredients, and after several hours, it tastes like medicine. You can't fry it. If you put it in a pan with some butter, it shrinks and you can't eat it at all."

Even spending several hours a day shopping for food, she was better off than other Soviet housewives because she lived in Moscow. Another friend received a letter from an aunt in the Urals who wrote that the only produce available that winter was potatoes and onions; meat did not exist. This happened before the shortages worsened in the initial years of *perestroika*.[6] The disparity between city and countryside gave rise to a joke in which the chairman of a collective farm promised everyone a helicopter once true Communism arrived. "Why would I need a helicopter?" one farmer asked. "When there is no sausage in our stores, you can fly to Moscow and buy some there," the chairman said.

Raiding other cities for scarce items has become an accepted Communist custom, to the irritation of locals, who feel the state sends them too little. A Moscow woman who went shopping in Riga a few years ago found the clerks in one department store would only sell children's shoes to customers who produced a Riga residence permit along with their child's birth certificate.[7]

For some months in Moscow, we lived with a calendar of "fish days" when meat was not available. In 1988 when I returned to Moscow, the food situation had improved in one respect. In the meat section of the giant GUM department store on Red Square, dozens of Russians had lined up to buy some well-made sausage for what a hand-lettered sign said were "cooperative prices," or nearly double the state price. By injecting privately produced goods into the state system, the government let Russians have more of what they wanted, but at higher prices.

Even in an economy characterized by want, some products are so poor as to overstay their shelf life. Food shops, for example, halved their prices on fish that had been canned five years earlier, but consumers still turned up their noses.[8] Other stores have made customers buy something undesirable, like outdated fish, to get what they do want. When good produce is available, it seldom lasts long because customers buy all they can for friends and relatives. On Lenin Street in Kiev, I watched a farm woman open a large crate of lettuce she had carried in from the countryside. The passersby pulled out string shopping bags and queued up. Halfway around the block, I realized that we hadn't seen lettuce in Moscow so I turned back to buy some, but the lettuce was gone and so was the vendor.

The habit of snatching up whatever appears on sale, which has led to hoarding of products as mundane as soap, is not confined to the Soviet Union. In China, the potential spending power also exceeds the goods available. When rumors of price rises triggered a spate of panic buying in 1988, an elderly Beijing resident stepped into a long line outside an electrical appliance store and told the salesclerk that he wanted what everybody else had queued up for. He spent 2,500 yuan on two stereo sets, the *China Daily* reported.

Such oddities are the government's own creation. The prices set by the Soviet state for most food staples have not risen since 1955; meat and dairy prices have remained frozen since 1962. Subsidized meat sells for half of what it costs to produce, and bread remains so cheap that Gorbachev reminded an audience in Murmansk, "You can see children using a loaf of bread as a football." But in 1987, *Izvestia* drew a flood of irate letters after it reported that the average Soviet family spent only 28.3 percent of its income on food (Chinese budget twice as much).[9] One reader said he spent nearly all his wages on food, because he had to turn to higher-priced cooperatives and farmers' markets for produce absent from the state stores. Criticism of tardy and inadequate distribution of vegetables and fruit is leveled even by the Kremlin. The Soviet Union loses one billion rubles, or more than $1.4 billion, a year in vegetables that become too rotten to sell.[10]

Such incompetence would suggest that the state should get out of the grocery business, but Russians view the government as their first line of defense against inflation. Their frustration is vented instead on private and cooperative entrepreneurs, who become scapegoats on the assumption that costs would skyrocket without existing price ceilings.[11]

To circumvent its own price controls, the Soviet government has replaced existing goods with ostensibly newer ones at higher prices. Prices were hiked in 1986 for a supposedly better loaf of bread, though I was told the improvement was not noticeable. The government has also cut back on the size or ingredients of a price-controlled item, or introduced a costlier substitute. For example, a fancier woman's blouse went on sale for 15 rubles, while the 5-ruble blouse sewn from the same cotton disappeared. Since enterprises were told to make themselves self-sufficient, bait-and-switch tactics have become more common. An audit in 1987 of some Moscow enterprises found that half of the industrial enterprises, a sixth of the retail stores, and a seventh of the food-catering firms examined had illicitly hiked some prices set by the state.

The Soviet government promised that any price rise would be offset by wage increases, but the assurance was not enough to forestall panic buying in 1987.[12] A year later, Chinese consumers responded to rumors of price rises by hoarding grain, soap, matches, and clothing. Shoppers in Beijing stocked up on so much toilet paper that the authorities had to limit customers to one roll a month.[13]

When the Chinese government began lifting some price controls, the outcome was mounting inflation, once dismissed as a phenomenon unique to the discredited old Kuomintang regime. Indeed, the Communists made themselves popular by shooting speculators in the early days. In 1987, food prices rose 9.1 percent in the cities, or five times more than urban incomes. In some cities, the cost of vegetables jumped 30 percent, and pork,[14] which rose 60 percent in Shanghai, had to be rationed. "Some people who are very happy with the reforms are very unhappy with the prospect of higher prices," a Chinese editor told me. "The government has been making up the difference with subsidies, and the economy cannot develop if this continues." By 1987, China's subsidies reached 50 billion yuan a year, which was twenty-four times the total subsidies in 1965.

The extent of Soviet consumer goods that are *defitsitny*, or in shortage, encourages petty theft. Whenever we parked our car in Moscow, we adopted the Russian habit of locking up the windshield wipers, because they would otherwise be stolen and we couldn't replace them. During a lunch with two Soviet editors, I remembered that I had parked my Volga with the wipers intact. They nodded sympathetically when I explained why I had to dash out of the restaurant.

With the exception of its cheap prices, a Communist economy is seldom user friendly. In Moscow, we were always short of paper products because much of what was produced under the state plan went to print political tracts. One winter, we imported our stationery, napkins, and toilet paper from Helsinki—and paid Soviet import duties—after the available paper went into propaganda material for a Party congress. In 1989, a shortage of newsprint forced the more popular Soviet magazines and newspapers to limit their subscriptions to the 1988 level, despite the increased readership. *Izvestia* confirmed that paper and printing facilities were being wasted on turgid ideological stuff that nobody wanted to read.

The reliable reputation of Soviet armaments does not extend to the country's consumer goods. "You rarely find so much junk, lack of taste, and technical ineptitude as you do in the toy sector," *Pravda* complained in 1987. The article went on to cite dolls with uneven legs and hair that fell out, razor-sharp sandbox pails and lethal chemistry sets, all of which taught children early that shoddy craftsmanship was the norm in Soviet society.[15] My own children's toys in Moscow fell apart after a few days, or hours, of play. The bindings on my Russian cross-country skis snapped a mile out in the woods. When Russian teenagers begged to buy my Levi jacket and jeans for the equivalent of $200, they were not just preoccupied with the American label. Unless a product bore a *znak kachestva*—star-shaped quality seal certifying it as fit for export, it was usually not worth acquiring.

The chronic problem of quality control, running a gamut from housing to consumer goods, goes to the heart of the socialist production process. Quantity determines the fulfillment of a five-year plan; the result has been a plethora of what Russians call *brak* or junk. The deficiencies range through the production process. When Gorbachev visited the northern port of Murmansk in 1987, the dockworkers complained that their loading machines would not function because they were so badly made.

But when Gorbachev introduced tougher quality-control standards at fifteen hundred selected factories, a Soviet editor told me, nearly a third could not get their products past the new inspectors. After the Party published a draft plan in 1985 calling for a radical improvement in the variety and quality of consumer goods, the production of some products like dishes declined because much of what came off the assembly line was rejected. Even so, 2.3 billion dollars' worth of the goods appearing in 1987 were shoddy or unattractive enough so that no one would buy them.

In Moscow, we owned a perky red Zhiguli sedan, marketed abroad as the Lada, which was built on a tested if old design bought from the auto maker Fiat. When Soviet designers made their own hatchback model, the new rear window got caked with slush spun up by the tires. The windshield wipers to clean the rear window only came with the export version.[16] It is not hard to understand why Russians with money and connections opt for the West German Mercedes or the Swedish Volvo.

The hazard poor quality poses to the consumer has been dramatized by the unpredictability of Soviet color-television sets.[17] Aside from the need for frequent repairs, the sets demonstrated an unfortunate tendency to explode and were blamed for 18,000 fires between 1980 and 1986 that killed 927 people and seriously injured 512 others, according to the magazine *Ogonyok*. Not until 1987 did the manufacturer trace the hazard to a badly made transformer component. The owners, who could not demand a refund or buy from a competitor, learned to unplug their television sets if they weren't watching. When I stayed at Moscow's Intourist Hotel in 1988, I wondered why the maid kept disconnecting the television set in my room. It turned out to be a routine safety precaution following a fatal fire caused by a television set at the Rossiya Hotel across town.

We had a similar problem in the Soviet Union and China with light bulbs, which tended to pop when they burned out, raining shards of glass. Occasionally, new ones also shattered when they were inserted into a socket. I traveled around China with a spare light bulb because the lighting in most hotel rooms was too dim for me to work. I stopped after the bulb blew up in my face in Xian and the splinters ricocheted off my glasses.

Given such deficiencies, cooperatives and private artisans have been presented with a virgin market for quality goods. At a Soviet department store, I bought a box of ten metal soldiers with crudely stamped helmets and rifles for the ruble equivalent of about a dollar. Two days later, I visited the artists' market in Moscow's Ismailovo Park, where one artist was selling toy soldiers hand-molded and painted in the green coats of Imperial Russian cavalry and infantry in the Napoleonic wars. He charged 2 rubles—nearly $3—for a horseman and 1 ruble for a foot soldier, and by the time I reached the front of the queue, he was auctioning off the last pieces.

Consumer products in China seemed better made, with deft touches like hand-painted flowers on thermos bottles and soft floral patterns on thick woolen blankets. Chinese manufacturers watched quality not out of concern for the consumer but because they wanted to break into the world market, like South Korea and Taiwan. Even so, Zhang Jinfu, the head of China's State Economic Commission, estimated in 1988 that a quarter of domestic products were of "unstable" quality. Near Tianjin, I wrote a story on a small vineyard producing Dynasty wine, a muscatel with a fruity bouquet, in a joint venture with France's Remy-Martin. The local grapes were good enough but the bottles had to be imported with precious hard currency, first from France and then from Australia, because, the production manager said, "our local bottles can't take the pressure."

Chinese consumer goods also have suffered from rising expectations created by the new prosperity. In 1981, when I arrived in China, new brides were content with the traditional "three rounds"—a bicycle, watch, and sewing machine. By the time I left at the end of 1984, young women expected their dowry to include a television set and small refrigerator. Over half of Chinese households now have television sets, thousands of which have been smuggled in by fishing boat from Hong Kong and Taiwan along with the majority of videocassette recorders in China. On Hainan island, some ethnic Li dancers entertained a group of us visiting journalists with a performance titled "A Dance of Joy at Receiving the First Television Set in the Village," with the slender sloe-eyed girls prancing and genuflecting before a one-eyed cardboard box with protruding wire antennae.

As the Chinese became more affluent, they frequently wanted imported goods. Even foreign labels afforded status. I flew to visit Huangshan, a mountain celebrated for its sharp peaks sprinkled with pines, on the same plane as a honeymooning couple from Shanghai. The bride proudly wore new sunglasses with a "Made in Hong Kong" label pasted on the left lens, a popular affectation. A Chinese newspaper ridiculed this trendiness with a cartoon of a pair of lovers gazing at the moon. "It's so beautiful; is it foreign?" the girl asked. But the real appeal of foreign-made goods lay in their reliability.

The demand encouraged a widespread counterfeiting of quality consumer goods, not least in the production of bicycles. At the top of China's line were the Phoenix (Fenghuang) and Forever (Yongjiu) from Shanghai and the Flying Pigeon (Feige) from Tianjin. Owning a Phoenix, as I did, involves more than snobbery. Over 45 percent of the other bicycles produced in China flunk government standards. So some peasant entrepreneurs in Hebei province began scavenging damaged or rejected parts from local bicycle factories and assembling them with prestigious counterfeit labels. Their rural customers were so impressed by the trademarks that they overlooked the defects, which sometimes included wooden spokes and patched inner tubes.[18]

The scam spread. A convicted swindler in Tianjin named Jiang Fugui shipped over a thousand fake Flying Pigeons to neighboring provinces. The counterfeiters at first used genuine decals, which sold on the black market for up to $10 apiece, until thousands of Forever decals were stolen from the Shanghai factory. In time, rural enterprises in Zhejiang and Guangdong provinces began printing bootleg labels.

With not enough good bicycles to go around, some respectable retail outlets collaborated. Five stores in Shanxi province were accused of selling more than two thousand fraudulent Flying Pigeons. Legitimate manufacturers were slow to object because they couldn't produce enough bicycles to meet the demand anyway and were getting more for reject parts than the pittance paid by scrap-metal dealers. The real victims were socialism's perennial losers—the state and the consumer. When last I heard, counterfeit bicycles had turned up in fourteen provinces and municipalities and unsuspecting riders were still pedaling damaged goods.

In fairness, the Chinese seemed to respond faster to quality problems than their Soviet counterparts. A refrigerator factory in Shanxi province drew so many complaints that the government shut it down. In 1987, the Ministry of Light Industry even organized an exhibition of inferior products in Beijing, but canceled it after some factories promised to do better.

China also has done more than the Soviet Union to resurrect the concept of fashion, particularly in Shanghai, a textile center whose reputation for style dates back to pre-revolutionary years when it was known as the "city of three scissors," for the skill of its tailors, barbers, and noodle-making chefs. The watchword for style under the Maoists, who considered fashion bourgeois, was "three years new, three years old, and three years patched and mended," meaning that a baggy blue or olive jacket and trousers should last for at least nine years.[19] Once it was no longer a crime to look well dressed, brighter clothing and smarter tailoring became the norm.

Whether for scruples of ideology or fashion, most Chinese I knew were wary of looking too dapper. And new styles were not available quickly enough or in sufficient shapes and sizes. Because of a shortage of tailors, customers in Beijing waited up to five months to have a suit or dress made. I heard of peasants who headed for Beijing's outdoor markets and bought up to a hundred pair of trousers to outfit their village. One fabric that did not catch on, except among some city youth, was denim, because it was too reminiscent of the proletarian old days.

The Russians seemed hungrier for fashion, and less fortunate. In 1976, I returned to Moscow from a month's home leave in New York to find young women parading on Gorky Street in ankle-length skirts. The new *maksi* look, as it was called, had been borrowed from trend-setting Poland and whipped up overnight on sewing machines by young women who knew that the fad would be over before it made the next five-year plan. It took at least a year and a half to get a new design into the stores. Ludmilla Turchanovskaya, the head of Moscow's House of Fashion, which had been caught off guard by the *maksi* look, sniffed that "it's a good thing that girls have started to do more with their hands now—that is to sew for themselves, to knit and to embroider."

The House of Fashion has its own stable of designers like Slava Zaitsev, who has created smart dresses for Gorbachev's wife, Raisa, but their fashions don't make it into state stores where ordinary Russians must shop. In 1987, a seeker of summer clothing in Novosibirsk wrote *Pravda* to complain that "there are only winter clothes in black and gray for all ages. . . . Where are the white colors, bright cottons, and light materials?"

The chronic shortage of almost everything in the Soviet Union has strained the credibility of Gorbachev's reforms. In June 1988, Veniamin Yarin, a steelworker from the Urals, reminded the Party work conference that "now we have sugar rationed. There wasn't any meat before and there still isn't. Consumer goods have entirely disappeared."[20]

The lack of material improvement in an era of major political change spawned a fresh wave of Soviet jokes, like the one about an American dog who asked a Russian dog what his life was like under Gorbachev's *perestroika*. Replied the Russian dog, "Now they feed you once a day instead of twice, but the chain is three feet longer and you can bark all you want."

10

IN THE EYES
OF THE STATE:
SEX, LOVE, AND
MARRIAGE WITH
YOUR GOVERNMENT
AS VOYEUR

▬ ▬ ▬ ▬ ▬ ▬ ▬ ▬ ▬ ▬ ▬ ▬ ▬

The relation between men and
women in the Communist
society of tomorrow . . . will
assure to humanity all the joys of
so-called free-love ennobled by a
true social equality of the mates,
joys which were unknown to the
commercial society of the
capitalist regime.

—ALEKSANDRA MIKHAILOVNA
KOLLONTAI, 1920[1]

Dissoluteness in sexual life is
bourgeois, is a phenomenon of
decay. . . . Self-control, self-
discipline is not slavery, not even
in love.

—VLADIMIR ILYICH LENIN, 1922[2]

DURING THE CULTURAL REVOLUTION, a diligent
study of Chairman Mao Zedong's thoughts was considered a
panacea for almost anyone suffering from emotional problems,
though the strain of those chaotic years was manifested in
suicides and breakdowns. After China returned to relative nor-
mality, there was a revival of concern about mental health. In
1984, I visited Dr. Zhao Gengyuan's new walk-in clinic in a
suburban Canton hospital. Dr. Zhao was a neurologist, but on
Monday and Wednesday mornings he assumed the role of psy-

chiatrist and examined the compulsions, phobias, and psycho-somatic ailments of those bold or desperate enough to bare their souls to a stranger.

"We let them talk about their problems, let them unburden the secrets in their minds," said Dr. Zhao, a stocky man in a white smock.

It was the first time that most patients had confided in someone other than family or close friend. Dr. Zhao estimated that of three hundred cases he had handled over the past year, 40 percent involved phobias, compulsions, and sexual inhibitions. Another 10 percent entailed sexual dysfunction, and 20 percent were more serious mental disturbances, for which the patients were sent to a regular psychiatric hospital. The remaining 30 percent had sundry physical or psychosomatic complaints. Dr. Zhao did not see many cases of depression. "Depressed people do not like to come here because they do not like to go out and be active," he told me. Most patients came once a week for two or three months. During their treatment, Dr. Zhao asked them, he said, "to write down in a diary everything they experience, whether they feel more comfortable, whether any results have been gained."

Dr. Zhao dealt not in Freudian or Jungian analysis, but in common sense buttressed by liberal doses of Valium. He directed a college student suffering from claustrophobia to stand in a crowd breathing deeply for a half hour and later to read a newspaper aloud to passersby. "He did so and he recovered," the doctor said. A young woman was contemplating suicide after a failed love affair. "I told her to think in a broader perspective," the good doctor said. "She was cured in two months."

The case most revealing of Chinese cultural inhibitions involved a fourteen-year-old girl who was crazy about boys, an adolescent condition hardly abnormal among Western teenagers. She became so embarrassed that she wouldn't go to school or ride a city bus for fear of acting forward toward a young man. Her anxious father brought the girl to Dr. Zhao, who advised her to wear a rubber band around her wrist. Whenever a boy distracted her, she was to transfer her sexual feelings to the rubber band by pulling it. At first, the doctor said, the girl was yanking her rubber band as many as two hundred times, but eventually ten pulls were enough to curb the untoward emotion. "We have worked with her for a half year," Dr. Zhao said proudly, "and she recovered and is back in school."

I asked what other sexual problems he had encountered. "We haven't had success in treating sexual inadequacy because we have a tradition in our country of shying away from discussing sex," the doctor replied. "These problems should be solved together by the couple, but many of them won't come to see us together. It is just one spouse or the other. We say, 'You both must come together or we can't solve it.' We say, 'If you come together, we will make you happy.' "

Some employers and judicial officials had dropped by to ask him about homosexuality, Dr. Zhao said, but he had no gay patients. Like the Soviet Union, China had made homosexuality a crime, a definition from which he did not dissent.[3]

Communism's innate conservatism becomes most obvious in its priggish attitude toward love and sex, which has reinforced China's cultural puritanism and provided a fig leaf for the Soviet Union's promiscuity. (Russian and Chinese sexual mores differ sufficiently so that I must deal with them in turn, while noting where they converge.) What the two countries do share is the Party's unwillingness to respect even this last bastion of privacy.

Sex has the distinction of being one of the last pleasures not organized by the state, though it has tried. Its universal popularity aside, sex also allows for the assertion of individuality in a collective society, creating a breathtaking double standard. Marxism's first sexual hypocrite was Karl Marx, who got the family maid pregnant in London, even as he accused capitalists of seducing each other's wives. Friedrich Engels, his friend and collaborator on The Communist Manifesto, agreed to acknowledge paternity.

Lenin expressed a distaste for sex in its looser manifestations. When a militant German Communist tried to enlist prostitutes in her struggle, Lenin told Clara Zetkin, a visitor from Germany, that while whores should be viewed as victims of bourgeois society, "still, that is not at all the same thing as considering prostitutes—how shall I put it?—to be a special revolutionary militant section. . . . Aren't there really any other working women in Germany to organize?"

Aleksandra M. Kollontai, a well-born feminist who became the first Soviet Commissar of Social Welfare in the wake of the 1917 Revolution, argued that traditional marriage and the family were superfluous, even harmful bourgeois institutions and would disappear, leaving free love, open marriages, and offspring to be reared by the state.[4] To Lenin's despair, many young Bolsheviks embraced the new morality espoused by Kollontai, whose lithe beauty made her unorthodox opinions more glamorous. Lenin complained to Clara Zetkin: "You must be aware of the famous theory that in Communist society the satisfaction of sexual desires, of love, will be as simple and unimportant as drinking a glass of water. This glass of water theory has made our young people mad, quite mad."

"Of course, thirst must be satisfied," Lenin said. "But will the normal man in normal circumstances lie down in the gutter and drink out of a puddle, or out of a glass with a rim greasy from many lips?" The lusty appetites of youth, Lenin insisted, should be channeled into "healthy sport, swimming, racing, walking, bodily exercises of every kind, and many-sided intellectual interests."

Kollontai, who had left her husband and child for a succession of revolutionary lovers, was persuaded to clean up her act and went off to Oslo as Soviet envoy. Two of her paramours died in Stalin's purges a decade later. The lid clamped down on sexual expression, whether because it sapped the energy needed to build socialism or because it was reminiscent of prerevolutionary excesses, typified by the monk Rasputin. When I lived in the Soviet Union and China, there was no suggestive advertising or nudity on the movie screens. Commercial exploitation of sex was disparaged as a manifestation of moral rot in the West. What took place below the surface was a different matter.

Russians never really shared their government's public

puritanism, and some of the funniest jokes I heard played upon the rich scatology of the Russian language. A scientist tested my knowledge of Russian by posing a riddle: What three-letter word describes what women love, men take pride in, and small boys write on lavatory walls? My immediate answer was *khui*, a vulgarism of Tartar derivation for the erect penis. *"Mir!,"* the scientist announced instead, substituting the overworked cliché word for peace, and erupted into laughter.

Marriage and the family were still around when I moved to Moscow in 1973. So were divorce and extramarital sex. I spent an evening talking about sexual habits with an upstanding member of the Komsomol. "In our school, everybody slept around by the time we finished the eighth grade," he said. "By the tenth grade, one girl was already pregnant. But when I look at the kids today, I think we were quite moral." Sex was not hard to find, he explained. "I could walk out on the street and in less than an hour find a woman to bring to bed." He offered to prove it by fixing me up but I demurred.

The lack of privacy appeared to make little difference. Two students told me about a solution popular at their university. Soviet sleeping cars are not segregated by sex, so they would ride the night train to Leningrad and back with their girlfriends, booking four berths in the same sleeping compartment for two nights of passion interspersed with a day of fatigued sightseeing.

An American diplomat returned from Sochi, a popular Black Sea resort, and told me of an encounter that had dumbfounded him. He was walking one evening on the oceanfront promenade behind a pair of young women, who were approached by two apparent strangers. *"Devushki, davaitye nam ebyat"* ("Girls, let's go fuck"), one of the young men quipped. It was not the smoothest pickup line, and my friend assumed the tasteless proposition would be ignored. But the girls looked at each other, shrugged, and walked off with the boys into the darkness. Their compliance was not unique. A Soviet physician said she had seen a survey in which 70 percent of women interviewed approved of sex outside marriage and most of the others didn't care.

I was struck by the slapdash Russian approach to contraception, which was prompted in part by the failure of Soviet light industry to meet consumer needs in even this area. In 1988, 220 million condoms, not even one for every Soviet citizen, were manufactured by the Ministry of Petroleum Refining and Petrochemical Industry, not that it mattered. Though the state plan projected an output of 700 million condoms annually by 1993, the young Russians I met were contemptuous of the Soviet-made condoms, nicknaming them "night galoshes" *(nochnoi kalosh)*, for their thick, rubbery texture. A pack of five costs about a ruble, but the black-market price was much higher, because, as a young father said, "you don't always find them available." Imported condoms cost more, and a young man I knew boasted that those made in Japan wouldn't fit him anyway.

Vasectomies, I was told, were favored mostly by prominent officials who wanted affairs without the risk of blackmail. Birth-control pills, which can cause weight gain, were unpopular among Russian women already inclined to plumpness. And Soviet-made diaphragms and cervical caps were dismissed as ineffective.

Abortion became the most common method of birth control by default, because it was legal, cheap, and widely available at government clinics. Seven abortions were not uncommon in a woman's reproductive years. In 1989, the medical newspaper *Meditsinskaya Gazeta* disclosed that there were 106 abortions for every 100 births in the Soviet Union. My wife was once taken aside by an amiable grandmother in Moscow. Her daughter, who already had one child, was pregnant and didn't want another. Could Jaqueline get some American medicine to make her abort and avoid the nuisance of being scraped out at the neighborhood clinic? Jaqueline replied that she hadn't heard of such medicine. The old woman thought this unlikely, given the American reputation for miracle technology. "I've heard in America they have something you only have to drink"—here the grandmother waved her fat arms— "and WHOOSH!"

The relatively high rate of illegitimate births testifies to the extent of casual sex in the Soviet Union. In a story about Soviet sexual mores in 1977, I quoted the estimate that one in ten children, or about 400,000 a year, were born out of wedlock. In 1985, Viktor Perevedentsev, a social demographer, cited a survey that showed that one out of every seven babies in Perm, a Russian city east of the Urals, was born to a single mother. More than one in four babies were conceived outside marriage and as many pregnancies were terminated by abortion.[5]

The insouciance I found extended to venereal disease. "Of course, there is always the danger of contracting disease," said the free-spirited heroine of a novel written by Aleksandra Kollontai. "But no man will lie to you about that—no comrade, that is—if you look straight into his eyes and ask for the truth." It was not so easy. A Soviet specialist I interviewed on the subject estimated that 60 to 70 percent of Russians in the countryside had some form of hereditary VD, predominantly syphilis, before the Bolshevik Revolution. During World War Two, he said, venereal disease declined, which I suggested was contrary to usual wartime experience. "During the blockade of Leningrad, couples didn't have the strength to make love," he replied. And under Stalin, people were careful because they knew they could be punished for the slightest infraction. By the early 1950s, venereal disease was sufficiently under control, he said, so that medical students were advised to specialize in other fields. His own introduction to syphilis was a picture in a medical textbook.

But now, the physician said, "it is everywhere. In the time I have spent talking to you, I would have seen seven patients." He blamed the rise in venereal disease on contaminated foreigners, an increase in money that financed a freer life-style, and lessening fear of the Communist regime. His conclusions seemed biased—he singled out African and Arab students as carriers of VD—but he seemed to know his specialty, and the Soviet press has since expressed increasing concern about venereal disease spreading among teenagers.

China, too, has had to cope with the reappearance of venereal disease, which was all but eradicated after the Communist takeover. The Public Health Ministry was quoted by the *China Daily* as attributing its resurgence to "tourists who have brought the virus into China" and "the occurrence of promiscuous behavior in the country."[6]

This vulnerability to sexually transmitted disease may explain the panic in the Soviet Union over the spread of the Acquired Immunity Deficiency Syndrome, or AIDS. In 1986, the Soviet media alleged that AIDS was born in American biological-warfare laboratories, prompting a protest from the U.S. Embassy in Moscow. A cartoon in *Pravda* depicted an American scientist, surrounded by corpses, handing a giant test tube marked "AIDS virus" to a sinister general in exchange for dollars. Soviet scientists subsequently debunked this propaganda. Although Russians were quick to blame the appearance of AIDS on African students, who are perennial targets of prejudice, *Komsomolskaya Pravda* told of a Soviet diplomat who caught the virus in Tanzania and passed it on to twenty-four homosexual lovers after he came home. New legislation, possibly the world's harshest, made anyone who infected a partner with AIDS subject to eight years in prison. Foreigners staying more than three months in the Soviet Union are required to take an AIDS test. Similar testing was imposed on foreigners living in China, where AIDS was introduced by contaminated blood, not sex.

Alien influences were also blamed for prostitution, which the 1975 edition of the *Great Soviet Encyclopedia* insisted had been "liquidated as a widespread social phenomenon." This was about the time that I watched the whores hang around Moscow's Komsomolskaya Square, the terminus of three busy railway lines, charging 3 rubles, less than $5, for a tumble in the shadows of the trains. During the 1980 Olympics in Moscow, prostitutes were rounded up and banished from the capital; their temporary exile became the subject of a hit play in Moscow, *Stars in the Morning Sky*. In 1987, *Soviet Russia* interviewed a police major who produced an alphabetical list of more than 3,500 known prostitutes in Moscow, though a lot more existed in the rest of the Soviet Union, notably in the Baltic republics and the Far East.

Some of these "women of light behavior," as they are called, were alcoholics willing to rent their bodies for a bottle of vodka. Classier call girls worked the hotels where foreigners stayed, using part of their earnings, which could exceed 100 rubles a trick, to buy off the hotel porters. The Soviet press dug out stories of amateur hookers as young as thirteen years old who invaded restaurants, truck stops, dormitories, even army barracks.

But the Soviet authorities were confounded by their own rhetoric; prostitution had been declared nonexistent under Communism, so no specific Soviet laws had been enacted to prevent it. The authorities tried confiscating the residence permits of prostitutes, but this didn't work because some didn't have permission to be in the cities anyway. Efforts to prosecute them under the catchall charge of parasitism wasn't applicable because many had other jobs. Those who accepted foreign currency from tourists or sailors might be convicted, but under laws against speculating in foreign currency. The Russian Federation finally imposed administrative fines of up to 200 rubles for prostitution,[7] but it didn't seem to crimp business. Returning to my Moscow hotel about midnight in 1988, I was hailed from a parked Volga taxi by a rouged blonde who beckoned me to join her inside.

Prostitution resurfaced as well in China, where one of the first reforms undertaken by the new Communist authorities was to close down the brothels of Shanghai and pack the women, some of whom were sold into prostitution, off for reeducation. In September 1987, nearly three decades after the cleanup, China's domestic news service reported the execution of two pimps who were running thirty-five prostitutes in Canton and nearby Foshan.[8]

Traditionally, the Chinese approached sex as they did painting and poetry, with a refinement that did nothing to undercut the enjoyment. The euphemism for sexual intercourse, *yunyu*, literally means "clouds and rain." The Chinese language is rich with such delicate idioms. Concubines occupied an acceptable social niche in Imperial China, and bound feet, formed by breaking and binding the toes and arches of young girls, were considered erotic because the deformation made a woman appear more suppliant toward her master. Even today, Chinese medicine is full of herbal remedies for flagging virility. Proof that sex exists in China is reflected in the government's efforts to hold the population down to 1.2 billion Chinese by the year 2000. When my family and I walked home from supper at our favorite dumpling restaurant in Ritan Park, the bushes alongside our path rustled with the grappling of young lovers.

The Communists living in the caves of Yanan after the Long March could be libertine during the long winter nights. Jiang Qing, a sassy Shanghai actress with quite a few lovers behind her, migrated to Red Army headquarters in Yanan in 1937 and moved in with Mao Zedong, later becoming his fourth wife and amassing power as fearsome as that of the Qing Dynasty's Dowager Empress, who also rose through the boudoir. But after the 1949 Communist takeover, sexual urges were sublimated into ideological fervor, especially during the Cultural Revolution, when drab unisex clothing, short cropped hair, and lack of makeup made Chinese women almost indistinguishable from men. Beauty sprang from correct ideological thought, the Maoists said.

No one believes that anymore, but what remains is a modesty engendered by straitlaced cultural tradition. In Beijing, Liu Shaoqing, a wide-eyed, button-cute starlet, professed her distaste for the nudity that she had seen in American movies privately shown to China's élite. "I accept the idea that Western actresses can appear like that, but I cannot," she said, with a toss of her lustrous black hair. "I think the best actress should attract audiences with her own character rather than by disrobing. I don't think that disrobing shows off an actress's character."

Her qualms were not unique, as I found when I interviewed two nubile fashion models in Shanghai. Xu Ping recalled for me the start of her career. She was working in a button factory when a man walked up and offered to make her a model. She was startled and not particularly pleased, she said, because she assumed he was talking about those mannequins propped in a department-store window, and Xu Ping didn't think she could stand still that long.

Her employer persuaded her to try modeling, over the objections of her family, not to mention the neighbors, who felt that nice girls did not exhibit themselves in public. So Xu Ping, who was twenty-three years old when I met her, was plucked from the ranks of Shanghai's textile workers to become one of the first fashion models in Communist China.

The young women were called "fashion show performing actresses," which sounded less sluttish to Chinese ears. They had to be between five feet five inches and five feet seven inches tall, with bust measurements at least eight inches larger than their waists. Xu and her friend Shi Fengmei were unlike any Western fashion model I had met. They wore no lipstick, eye shadow, or other makeup when we talked at the Fashion Design Institute. They lived with their parents and commuted to their jobs by bicycle or public bus. "When there are no shows, we go back to the factories," said Shi.

They were also unwilling to model Western clothing that revealed too much skin. "Some fashions are very, very new but they are not acceptable in China," Shi said. I asked what she had in mind, but she blushed and fell silent. It took Jing Taijun, the Institute's vice president, to voice what Shi dared not speak. "Some fashions have their backs exposed, and so are not acceptable in China," Jing said firmly.

At one fashion show I attended in Beijing, the audience was packed with curious workers who looked as embarrassed as Western men caught sneaking into a pornographic movie during lunch hour. They sniggered when some models walked out in the old qipao, a tight-fitting dress, usually of silk brocade, with a high mandarin collar and a skirt slit up to the thigh. "People are laughing because this is what a Chinese landlord's wife used to wear," my Chinese companion whispered. One man drew a round of laughter when he catcalled in the dark: "Maybe some day but not now." When I left China, most orders for the *qipao* seemed to be placed by Western visitors who wanted something Chinese-looking to wear home.

Beauty pageants became acceptable at last in the Soviet Union; Mariya Kalinina was the first Miss Moscow in June 1988. That same month, a contest in Beijing selected a dozen so-called "girls of youth and elegance," but it happened privately at a tea party, and not publicly on television as originally announced. The Chinese authorities still thought it unseemly to admire the human body.

Self-consciousness, to be sure, depends on the occasion. At communal toilets I used across China, men squatted and grunted in chorus over the open holes as they relieved themselves, paying no attention to me or anyone else. A woman reporter friend assured me the ambiance was as nonchalant on her side of the partition. But Chinese women eschewed sundresses or skimpy bathing costumes. The beach at Beidaihe, a popular Chinese seaside resort, had surprisingly few women, none of whom wore a bikini. When a lissome Frenchwoman at our hotel came out to sun herself in a provocative bit of cloth and string, men and boys gathered to gape in such numbers that the hotel staff had to shoo them away.

By contrast, Russians never seemed embarrassed to shed their clothes. On Sunday outings in summer, flabby grandmothers stripped down to bras and panties like everyone else along the crowded banks of the Moscow River, and bikinis, often home-sewn, flourish on the beaches of the Black Sea, however rotund the sunbather's figure. I saw Russian girls embrace the miniskirt with a vengeance, even on bitter winter nights. In Siberia, I heard of a miniskirted teenager who underwent surgery to peel off the patterned stockings frozen to her legs.

Chinese archeologists have found nudes sculpted on pottery and knife handles, among other relics, and painted on tombs of ancient China. But under the Communists, nudes became decadent and artists who painted them were punished. When one artist included two bare-breasted women of the Dai ethnic minority in a mural at Beijing's airport, such a fuss ensued that they were quickly covered up.

This circumspection extends to the private lives of celebrities. In 1987, the *People's Daily* chastised a magazine for publishing "wanton exaggerations" about the first love of a famous writer, but so circumspectly that it identified neither the writer nor the magazine. And public displays of affection remained taboo. When the American director George White staged Eugene O'Neill's *Anna Christie* in Beijing with a Chinese cast, he was unable to get Anna and her sailor lover to kiss on stage. "Suddenly it was like an eighth-grade play. They started giggling," White told me. He had to change their kiss to a hug.

This is not to say that the Chinese don't think about sex. *Jinpingmei*, or *The Golden Lotus*, an erotic masterpiece written nearly four hundred years ago was highly regarded for its elegant language. The new prosperity engendered a proliferation of cruder pornography smuggled in from Hong Kong and Taiwan or churned out at home. Some of the worst offenders turned out to be legitimate publishing houses trying to avoid going bankrupt under the new system that made them responsible for profits and losses. The Workers' Publishing House in Beijing and the Yanbian People's Publishing House in Jilin province were fined 600,000 and 400,000 yuan respectively in 1988 for publishing up to 400,000 copies of translations of two undistinguished imports considered to be dirty.[9] The Beijing authorities, in moving to eliminate vulgar advertisements at bookstalls, found that more than seven hundred vendors were selling salacious books, often wrapped in innocuous jackets. In 1988, China's domestic news service estimated that seven million copies of pornographic publications were on sale around the country.[10]

Videocassettes of blue movies (nicknamed *huangse*, or yellow, in Chinese) arrived by fishing boat from Hong Kong. In one village in Fujian province, a few enterprising peasants invested in a videocassette recorder and turned a tidy profit showing pornographic films to their neighbors. The police raided the makeshift theater once they realized where all the men were disappearing to at night.

Soviet readers get their smut from the West, notably Scandinavia. An American security man assigned to protect visiting officials told me how his pals in the U.S. Secret Service bought cooperation from their counterparts in the KGB on one presidential visit by handing out copies of *Playboy*.

Notwithstanding the lip service that Chinese Marxism accords social equality, Chinese women, far more than Russian women, have remained trapped in a double standard of sexuality. In 1986, a sampling of one hundred divorce cases in Tianjin found that twenty-three of them were initiated by husbands who suspected their wives of having affairs but could offer no proof.[11] A few years earlier, I toured a reform school in Shanghai for juvenile delinquents, who sewed diapers, assembled bicycles, and patched cardboard boxes while they underwent "reeducation." The boys told me they had ended up there for fighting or stealing. But when I asked a plump girl toiling at a sewing machine what her offense was, she stuttered and began to cry. Most of the female inmates, it developed, had been caught engaging in sex.

Sex outside marriage, although less common than in the Soviet Union or the West, does occur in China, especially where traditional society has been dislocated. A high incidence of pregnancy was reported among the 250,000 unmarried women who came from Guangdong province to work in the Special Economic Zone of Shenzhen. In 1987, nearly one in twelve women working in the factories and assembly plants of Shenzhen's Shekou district got pregnant, according to the *China Youth News*, which explained that "they strongly desired satisfaction from the opposite sex." Shenzhen's work force is overwhelmingly female, and the local divorce statistics suggested that some women got sexually involved with married male superiors. The high pregnancy rate resulted from the shortage of other recreation at night as well as the influence of moral standards from neighboring Hong Kong. Shenzhen authorities took the exceptional step for China of distributing contraceptives to women workers, and I assume that those who got pregnant were badgered into having abortions.

A plea for tolerance of extramarital sex surfaced in a film from Xian called *Country Girl Xiaoxiao* (later released in the West as *A Girl From Hunan*), about a pretty sixteen-year-old in prerevolutionary China. Her peasant parents betrothed Xiaoxiao to a two-year-old boy, whom she had to carry strapped to her back while laboring in the fields. Bored with baby-sitting her fiancé, she strayed into a love affair with a young man her age and was punished for it. The film, by Xie Fei, ostensibly criticized arranged marriages but implied too that there were legitimate grounds for adultery.

In 1988, the *China Daily* related the ordeal of a Gansu woman whose rejected suitor took revenge by claiming that she had a string of lovers. She tried to sue him for slander, only to find her co-workers and even her boss rallying to his defense. "The traditional morality of this nation has always protected and even encouraged indifference toward discrimination and even physical abuse of women," the newspaper said. "And the victims are not allowed to resist in case they lose the tenderness and virtue that are supposed to be the characteristics of women."[12]

As a result of this, rape often goes unreported. An acquaintance at Beijing's radio station tipped me off when a grandson of Zhu De, the great Red Army commander, was tried and shot after committing dozens of rapes. He and several other spoiled sons of the Party élite held what they privately called "naked dancing parties," to which unsuspecting girls were invited. Those who resisted their advances were sexually assaulted. The evidence given at the closed trial was so sordid that Zhu De's widow declined to ask the authorities to spare her grandson's life.

China has accepted the need for sex education, which was once considered akin to pornography. By 1988, about 6,000 high schools were experimenting with sex-education classes. They were sorely needed. A survey that year of 242 Beijing students between twelve and nineteen years old found that only 6 percent had some accurate knowledge about sex, while 80 percent knew almost nothing.[13] This ignorance was not confined to youth. A pair of Shanghai schoolteachers visited a family-planning clinic to find out why they had not produced a child in two years of marriage. The counselor discovered that the couple, both college graduates, had never had sexual intercourse, assuming that "molecules" shared under the blankets would make the wife conceive.

A similar official prudishness in the Soviet Union left even the sexually active misinformed. During my tour in Moscow, the only regular source of information on sex was the magazine *Health (Zdorovye)*.[14] It declared that intercourse lasted about two minutes, that premarital sex caused neuroses, and that frigidity among women was natural, which did not foster much tenderness in bed. A reader wrote in to recall her wedding night: "He swooped down like a kite and fell fast asleep afterwards. In the morning when he woke up, he was surprised to see my eyes swollen with tears."

One issue of *Zdorovye* grappled with misconceptions about penis length. "The myth that the sexual function of a man depends on his anatomical build has existed for a long time and unfortunately hangs on tenaciously, although neither scientific data nor real life confirms anything of the kind," it explained. The few marriage manuals available incline toward similar vagueness, as in this one titled *Medical Aspects of Marriage:* "While the man arouses quickly and strives for sexual intimacy, the woman needs time in order to adapt to a new situation. A husband should not rush his intended [mate] into intimacy right away. Fear and shame may result, and the first sexual act done at the husband's insistence may cause in a young woman a disgust for sexual life."

Fortunately, the era of *glasnost* has wafted in more clarity. The magazine *Ogonyok* quoted Igor Kon, a sociologist, as saying that "sexual illiteracy" was driving up the Soviet Union's divorce rate, which reached 347 divorces per 1,000 marriages by 1986. In another study of 1,000 divorced Russians, 244 cited infidelity and 60 sexual dissatisfaction as reasons for their divorces.[15]

During the Brezhnev years, medical statistics were doctored to make Communist lovers look no less virile than those in capitalist countries. The first Soviet sex manual, issued back in 1974 and limited to 30,000 copies, asserted that a full 100 percent of Soviet men surveyed regularly achieved orgasm. A Moscow gynecologist subsequently told me the censors twice blocked publication of a landmark study on female sexuality until the statistics on frigidity were lowered. Even in the bedroom, the Kremlin could not keep itself from meddling.

Unlike in the Soviet Union, courtship is not undertaken lightly in China, hedged as it is with old customs and new realities, including the interference of the state. A Beijing woman told me of an engineering student she knew who was twenty-six but looked younger. For five years, he had dated a farmer's daughter from his village, which meant nothing more intimate than roller skating or seeing a movie together. But he decided that he wanted to live in Beijing after graduation, while she as a peasant had a residence permit that confined her to her village. Realizing that the bureaucracy would not let her join him legally in Beijing, he broke off their relationship. Her outraged family sued him for 200 yuan, claiming damage to her reputation. But the student received only 25 yuan a month from his college stipend. "Now he is paying it off with the help of his family," I was told. "And he has fallen in love with another girl from the countryside."

So I was unprepared for the urgent phone call I got one afternoon from a translator and sometime poet I knew in Beijing. He had to meet me, he said, because he had devised a scheme that required my help. The following afternoon, we sat on a bench among the willow trees in Ritan Park. The poet was desperate to get to the United States, where he had singled out a college that he was confident would hire him as a professor once he arrived on campus. Since the college had not invited him and he had no American relatives, the Chinese government would not let him out or the American government let him in.

"I want you to find me a wife," he told me, and interpreted

my stunned silence as license to continue. "If you find me an American wife, she can invite me to the United States and your government can give me my visa."

I replied that I was not a marriage broker, that I could not think offhand of any eligible acquaintances, and that I doubted that anyone I did know was looking for a mail-order spouse. He was at least sixty and age had helped neither his looks nor his temperament. He brushed my demurrals aside. "But I am an intellectual," he said. "I know American women would find an intellectual desirable." Having been kicked around so long under the Maoists because of his education, he assumed that the Americans would have to love him.

I promised to see what I could do and thereafter let our acquaintance wither. The poet was not alone in his search, though the others I ran across were content to look in China. Under Chairman Mao, Chinese were exhorted to marry late and then to seek a correct ideological attitude in a spouse. In fact, placing love second was never realistic—a spouse in modern Chinese is called *airen*, or literally "love person." When people reordered their lives after the Cultural Revolution, many started worrying about getting married.

China remains a straitlaced country where it is hard to socialize with the opposite sex. There are no bars or other singles hangouts. Most young people live in cramped apartments with their parents or in workers' dormitories, neither of which are conducive to courtship.

The problem is hardly confined to China. While living in Moscow, I read a letter in the *Moscow Communist (Moskovsky Kommunist)* in which a woman who called herself Nina K. described her difficulty. "In our factory, there are ten women for one man," she wrote. "And as a rule, he is married or approaching retirement age. So you can see for yourself, you won't meet your promised one at work. In the park perhaps? But even sociologists know that fellows do not go to the park looking for a bride. Perhaps you'll find a bridegroom on the dance floor. So you go and see. If a girl is attractive, she is grabbed by some half-drunken slob from the company of regulars. If you try to refuse, then only your long legs will save you."

Before I left China, some organizations took to sponsoring get-togethers. I crashed one mixer at the Workers' Palace of Culture that attracted several thousand Chinese on a muggy June night. Some partygoers, holding each other stiffly at arm's length, plodded through a foxtrot to the music of a small orchestra, while more sat on the sidelines and watched. Retired workers recruited to play Cupid bustled about, trying to dissolve the tension between the sexes with films, games, and even a calligraphy contest.

In Beijing's Chaoyang district, I later visited a marriage introduction bureau run by the Communist Youth League and the Women's Federation. The bureau, one of many proliferating across China, had attracted more than 11,000 clients, which was not surprising since estimates suggested that Beijing alone had 100,000 single people between thirty and forty years old. Xu Jiashe, the director, told me that the majority of applicants were in their thirties, though some were in their forties, and one was seventy-two years old.

"During the Cultural Revolution, many young people were asked to go to the countryside," Xu explained. "After they returned, their first priority was to find jobs or prepare for school examinations. Once they settled down, it was almost too late to get married." He said prospects were most bleak for educated women and men with menial jobs, like street cleaners or nightsoil collectors.

Xu let me look over some applications, which listed age, occupation, education, class background, and family. A smaller card bearing the applicant's photograph but not name—"we have to keep secrets," Xu said—listed the qualities he or she sought in a spouse. I picked up one with the snapshot of a young woman in an army uniform. "Morally decent, above average in looks, 1.72 meters [five feet seven inches] tall, with genuine education, plain life-style and manner," read the painstakingly handwritten characters. "Looking for someone to be a good friend and teacher to me." An institute researcher shown in sweater and pigtails said she was thirty-two years old and seeking a husband "dedicated to his profession, willing to learn and make progress, in good health, morally decent." No one here described himself or herself as sexy or fun, but neither did they have to profess a good ideological attitude.

Each client paid the bureau 2 yuan, then about 87 cents, to meet three prospective spouses; if these were not satisfactory, the client had to pay another 2 yuan and register all over again. "A few people have remained on our list without getting a proper partner because they have high standards and they don't like to lower them, particularly ladies who come from an educated background," Xu said. "Frankly, some people come to find partners because they feel it is hard to find someone in usual society, but they set their sights too high. If it is difficult out in society because of their high standards, it will be difficult here."

I asked what the standards were. "Generally speaking, women tend to want partners who are competent and dedicated to a profession, especially if the women are college graduates themselves. This is usually the first request," Xu said. "Men want women who are younger and of good appearance. In selecting a partner, it is customary in China to prefer competence in a man and beauty in a woman."

Xu began shaking his head. "We want to make it a success, but we can only provide the chance and conditions for these people to meet and get together," he said. "If both sides stick to their standards, that will make marriage less successful." Still, when I visited his introduction bureau, over nine hundred clients had reported so far that they were getting wed. There were probably more, Xu said, but "some people don't like others to know how they got married, so they don't tell us."

Some accounts I read in the Chinese press confirmed that many suitors were choosy. In Beijing, women usually requested a husband at least five feet eight inches in height, which is taller than the average Chinese. Men insisted upon wives who were not only younger but also less educated, applying the old adage that "no talent is a virtue in a woman." A computer operator turned down two prospects because he

considered both of them, at twenty-eight, too old; he himself
was thirty.[16]

The most eligible mate had relatives overseas who could
deliver scarce consumer durables like imported refrigerators
and videocassette recorders. When Arthur Miller directed his
Death of a Salesman in Beijing, he asked the actor playing the
character of Happy, the son who picked up girls by pretending
that he had gone to West Point, to suggest a pitch more com-
prehensible to a Chinese audience. "I would tell them I had
an uncle in Hong Kong," the actor said.

Some searchers, too shy to present themselves for public
scrutiny, hid behind intermediaries. The *China Youth* newspaper *(Zhongguo Qingnian Bao)* ran an advertisement by a
schoolteacher in Inner Mongolia on behalf of her twenty-five-
year-old cousin, a factory worker who was seeking a man who
was "well-built, good-mannered, independent-minded, hard-
working," no older than thirty and preferably a non-smoker.
The teacher offered to pass along letters and photographs.

The marriage introduction bureau that most impressed me
was in Harbin and tried to match up the handicapped. "The
job of matchmakers is something new to us and we have no
experience at all," said Li Yincheng, a motherly woman who
ran the small operation. When I visited her, one couple had
married and three pairs were seriously courting. "Physically
they are disabled but mentally they are normal and may be
even more considerate and careful than physically healthy people. They have the same desire for marriage and happiness,"
Li said. But her success rate was low. In one case, she introduced a promising young man disabled in both arms to a
woman whose legs were paralyzed; both were twenty-five
years old and were studying on their own to become language
translators. What's more, they liked each other. But the woman
decided that if she had a baby he could not carry it for her. "So
they didn't make it," Li said sadly.

Widows who want to remarry in China have also encountered resistance, not least from their children. "My younger
sister and I are ashamed of my mother's remarriage," a man
whose father had died ten years earlier wrote to a legal advice

column. ". . . Now that her sudden remarriage made all of us lose face, should we force her back and support her for the rest of her life?" The columnist replied that "it is heartless for you, as her children, to require her to comply with feudal standards."[17] Some marital experts suggested that second or late marriages would reduce the incidence of offenses like molesting women. In 1986, such sexual crimes accounted for a third of the convictions of elderly men in Shanghai.

The government has been less sympathetic to those who want to marry before the legal age of twenty-two years for men and twenty years for women, a minimum that was set to postpone childbearing. As the dismantling of the communes in the early 1980s reduced the state's daily supervision of the individual, underage marriages have increased, so that registered weddings in some rural areas are now thought to account for as few as one-tenth of the actual marriages taking place, many of them arranged by families. In 1988, the *People's Daily* reported that in three townships and one village in Anhui province, more than four-fifths of the couples who married in 1986 and part of 1987 failed to register as required by law.[18] Bigamy cases have been reported in which people remarried without bothering to divorce their spouses, usually to avoid the bureaucratic hassle. Some Moslems in Xinjiang still take more than one wife, and a Chinese doctor working in the backcountry of Tibet told me that he encountered polyandry, in which a Tibetan woman who takes a husband is considered married to all his brothers too.

The authorities in China are presented with a conundrum when unregistered couples decide they want to separate. Since they are not lawful spouses, there are no legal grounds for them not to do so. Yet turning a blind eye puts the government in the position of condoning adultery or bigamy. The typically Chinese *banfa* is that couples must register their unofficial state of matrimony in order to apply for a divorce.[19]

One disincentive is the shortage of romance at a Communist wedding, which pretty much consists of patriotic platitudes from a civil official and the signing of some pieces of paper. At a mass ceremony of several hundred couples in Beijing, three grooms I interviewed never bothered to take off their floppy winter pile caps. Weddings are conducted with a little more flair in the Soviet Union, though they still work on an assembly line. At the Central Wedding Palace in Kiev, twenty-seven weddings were scheduled on the Saturday I visited. One couple was ascending the staircase while another in the second-floor chamber exchanged vows to "share happiness and toil" and a third couple, clutching their complimentary champagne glasses, descended the back stairs to a hired Volga taxi. The ceremony lasted about ten minutes, if one included the optional performance by a choir of the patriotic hymn "My Country, My Motherland."

Russians and Chinese alike compensate for the dearth of ritual by blowing money at lavish wedding receptions, despite official disapproval. In 1987, the average cost of a wedding in urban China, including the dowry, was put at 6,000 yuan (over $1,600), which was equivalent to several years' wages for an average worker. A catering firm in Nanjing tried offering low-budget wedding receptions and attracted only five couples, including one of its own employees. In a satirical article in *Komsomolskaya Pravda*, which I quoted for a story about Soviet weddings, the reporter boasted that he crashed wedding parties regularly because the food and drink were so abundant. "The larger the debt, the greater the honor," the freeloader wrote. "The rare parent who manages to stage a dinner without going into debt begins feeling guilty and sits shamefully in the vestibule."

If change in the Soviet Union and China has injected a little more freedom into the private lives of its citizens, their governments have yet to figure how to mandate an end to the loneliness that they long contended could not exist in a collectivist society. In China's Anhui province, over a quarter of the men surveyed in 1984 confessed to having trouble finding a wife. In Wuxi county of Jiangsu province, men accounted for 97 percent of unmarried people over twenty-eight. The disparities result partly because many women raised in poor areas prefer to find a husband in town where life is easier; it also reflects some female infanticide practiced by families who did not want a daughter. As a result, women get bought and sold as chattels behind the back of the Chinese government, which has declared that the "feudal practice of slavery" ended with the Communist takeover in 1949.

I once researched a story based on a radio broadcast from Sichuan province about the smashing of a local abduction ring. As I combed through the press, I found cases in seven Chinese provinces where poor peasant girls were lured from their homes by the promise of a better life in the city. Instead, they were sold as wives and mistresses, often after being raped or sexually abused to discourage them from returning home, for virginity is still expected in a rural bride. The buyers of these broken women were often lonely farmers who could not find desirable wives or who felt they could not afford the costlier dowry that local custom dictated. The police who smashed the Sichuan syndicate arrested eighty-three traffickers and were hunting others when I wrote the story. The government reacted with such anger—the ringleaders were executed—that I assumed so horrendous a crime could not repeat itself. Five years later in 1988, I came across a story from the *Peasants' Daily* newspaper *(Nongmin Ribao)* about another abduction ring in Henan province that had sold more than two hundred women. The only difference was that the price for a healthy young female had risen to 2,000 yuan, or about $540.[20]

11

▀▀▀▀▀▀▀▀▀▀▀▀▀▀

> Millions of sins, filthy deeds,
> acts of violence, and physical
> contagion are far less dangerous
> than the subtle, spiritual idea of
> a god decked out in the smartest
> "ideological" costumes.
>
> —VLADIMIR ILYICH LENIN, 1916[1]

> Some positive moral standards
> advocated by religious groups can
> guide believers to paths benefi-
> cial to socialist society.
>
> —CHINESE ATHEISTS'
> ASSOCIATION, 1986[2]

THE COMMUNIST VIEW of religion is on exhibit at the Cathedral of Our Lady of Kazan on Leningrad's downtown Nevsky Prospect. The magnificent Russian Orthodox cathedral, 650 feet high to the tip of its gilded cross, was erected under Czar Alexander I to the glory of God, but in 1932, Stalin converted it to his purposes as the State Museum of the History of Religion and Atheism.

The neo-classical cathedral, never deconsecrated, was turned into a repository of the most damaging evidence the authorities could gather against organized religion's fanaticism, intolerance, and perfidy, the very flaws that have since afflicted Marxism. A fragment of a nineteenth-century fresco removed from a village church near Moscow shows Russia's beloved poet Mikhail Lermontov suffering in the flames of hell for some infraction. There are ornate crosses, chalices, and rosaries on display as "cultist objects," a pistol concealed in a hollowed-out Bible, and photos and documents identifying priests who collaborated with the Nazis. The museum has no sectarian bias; Christianity, Judaism, and the Eastern religions are dismissed as equally worthless historical phenomena.

"There isn't such a museum elsewhere in the world," bragged Vasily Y. Leshchenko, who was the museum's scientific secretary in the 1970s. I had surprised him by walking into his office, jumping the queue of visitors outside the cathedral's bronze doors.

"We have a long line because of school vacations," apologized Leshchenko. "We find a great interest among young people." The youngsters I saw, fresh-faced and wearing dark school uniforms enlivened by the red scarves of the Young Pioneers, seemed particularly fascinated by the Spanish Inquisition, which was summed up in a life-size wax tableau showing a heretic under interrogation by clerics in sinister robes. To one side of the dungeon, the grisly instruments of the heretic's imminent torture sat on a brazier of glowing coals. I listened to a couple of schoolboys shrilly debate how long he could hold out before the agony killed him.

Leshchenko, who worked for the atheistic Znaniye (Knowledge) Society, didn't agree with me that the museum disparaged religion. "We objectively try to give the whole picture," he said. He rambled on about Lenin's directive in 1918 separating church and state and the freedom of religion guaranteed under Article 124 of the Soviet Constitution.

"Separation of church and state is a great plus for the church," he said, "because someone who belongs to the church now is a genuine believer." I asked whether such freedom of conscience extended to Communist Party members. "That is entirely different," Leshchenko said.

There is a desperation to orthodox Communism's intolerance of organized religion. The two are competing for souls, and by not winning, the Communists, however much they have stacked the odds, have lost.

THE END OF THE LINE

At its roots, Marxism is a Christian heresy, a protest against man's failure to create the Kingdom of God on earth. Marxists would argue that the political and economic materialism of their belief precludes it from being a religion. Yet similarities abound, from the prophecies of Marx to the propagation of the faith and the warnings of a judgment day when capitalism in collapse will give rise to an incorruptible new world. Marxism, no less than Christianity or Islam, believes in devotion and martyrdom, salvation and damnation.

Marx viewed belief in God as symptomatic of a sick society. "Religion is the sigh of the oppressed creature, the sentiment of a heartless world, and the soul of soulless conditions. It is the opium of the people," he wrote. Lenin called it "a kind of spiritual vodka in which the slaves of capitalism drown their human shape and their claims to any decent life." The Communists assumed that religion would disappear as socialist society developed. "The liquidation of the religious wreckage and of the most important of this, faith in God, constitutes one of the objectives of the Communist education of the Soviet people," the *Great Soviet Encyclopedia* said in its 1961 edition.

Stalin closed churches and murdered or jailed tens of thousands of priests; Khrushchev unleashed a fresh wave of persecutions, but it didn't wipe out religion. A guide at the Museum of the History of Religion and Atheism told me that visitors kept asking him about the state of the Russian Orthodox Church.

The Chinese Communists were, if anything, more suspicious of religion. Mao Zedong lumped it with political, clan, and masculine authority as the four "thick ropes" binding Chinese to their feudalistic past. In 1940, nine years before he came to power, Mao Zedong proposed a competition between religion and Marxism. "If Communism is beaten, we Communists will admit defeat in good grace," Mao said.[3]

The Communists proved to be sore losers. The fragile guarantees of religious freedom in China's 1954 Constitution were whittled down in the Anti-Rightist Campaign in 1958 and, more brutally, in the 1966–76 Cultural Revolution, when the Red Guards trashed houses of worship and persecuted believers.

In China as in the Soviet Union, the Communists knew the older religious believers would die off. They did not expect younger ones to take their place. The *People's Daily* acknowledged after the trauma of the Cultural Revolution that "many young people find their old political and moral beliefs shattered and new concepts have yet to replace them. As a result, they feel spiritually empty." I came across Communist Youth League members in Beijing who were threatened with expulsion if they went to church. During required political study sessions at Beijing and Qinghua universities, students were told to say whether they went to church and to turn in religious material and the names of classmates who were churchgoers.

The failure of religion to wither away has forced the Soviet Union and China into a spiritual stalemate. It is their religious believers and not atheists who demonstrate the virtues, lauded by the Party, of industry, honesty, and selflessness needed to make the economic and political reforms work. Mikhail Gorbachev promised new protections for religious freedom, which Article 52 of the Soviet Constitution already guarantees. In 1989, the Soviet leader dropped by the Vatican for an audience with the Pope. The Anglican Archbishop of Canterbury, the Greek Orthodox Patriarch, the Reverend Billy Graham, and Mother Teresa have all been guests of the Soviet Union, though none of their itineraries, as far as I know, included a visit to the State Museum of the History of Religion and Atheism in Leningrad's profaned cathedral.

Even before Gorbachev, Deng Xiaoping moved away from confrontation and toward coexistence. Some religious believers, among them aging graduates of Western missionary schools in pre-revolutionary years, had the skills needed to modernize China. The government also realized that it could not afford to offend potential friends in countries where faith in Islam or Buddhism ran deep. In 1982, the old ideological journal *Red Flag* observed that contacts with religious believers abroad could "play an important role in raising our country's political influence." This change of strategy led to milder treatment of China's Buddhists and, more conspicuously, of its Moslem ethnic minorities, who live on the strategic frontiers with the Soviet Union, Afghanistan, and Pakistan.

China has come a long way from the days when the Red Guards paraded Moslem clergymen through the streets with bloody pig's heads tied around their necks in a sacrilege against Islam. Now, where Moslems predominate, Han Chinese have been asked to fence in their pigs rather than let their foraging offend Moslems. The result is that Islam appears to be flourishing, albeit under the watchful eye of the Bureau of Religious Affairs, which was modeled after the Soviet Union's Council on Religious Affairs. Some Chinese Moslems have even been allowed to make the pilgrimage to Mecca.

I found the new vitality of Islam most evident in Xinjiang, China's westernmost region, where Islam arrived by caravan on the Silk Road in the ninth century. In Kashgar, I watched Uighurs, Kazakhs, Kirghiz, and Tadjiks remove their shoes and kneel on small rugs, or even a piece of cardboard, when the loudspeaker atop the whitewashed Id Kah mosque summoned the faithful to evening prayer.

Uighurs farmed the former commune of Pahatekli outside Kashgar, where the first green sprouts of the spring rice planting had appeared. Among the fields were a number of stucco buildings with small minarets each crowned by a sliver of moon. Yes, Pahatekli's administrators confirmed, they had 43 mosques, one for each production brigade. "We are 100 percent practicing Moslems here," boasted the Party secretary, Abdullah Ahmed. And how many belonged to the Communist Party? There were 240 Party members, he said, and they attended the mosques like everyone else because they were Uighurs. Ahmed saw no contradiction.

"It is according to their custom and does not mean that they believe in religion," insisted Mehut Amin, an official in the Religious Affairs Bureau in Urumqi. The local press was complaining at the time that Party officials in southern Xinjiang went to the mosque and let parents teach their children about Islam. It was a complaint not uncommon on the other side of the frontier in Soviet Central Asia, where officials have taken a tougher line on the resurgence of Islam, fearing a spill-over from both Iran and Afghanistan.

More than Christianity, Islam threatens Marxism because both have translated faith into a consuming way of life. While the Soviet Union kept its Moslems on a tight leash during the war in Afghanistan to forestall Islamic fundamentalism, China was allowing Moslems greater freedom. I found Chinese Moslems less likely than the Buddhists to mince words about co-existing with a Communist state. "The Prophet only gives one heart to every individual. He only gives one belief," said Imam Karaji, Kashgar's venerable Islamic patriarch. "Either you believe in Islam or you believe in Communism."

But there seemed a deeper and more lingering fascination with religion in the Soviet Union than in China, especially among young people bored with the implausible cautionary tales of the Soviet authorities. *Science and Religion (Nauka i Religiya),* an atheistic journal published by the Znaniye Society, warned parents that religious upbringing of children "provokes a grave split in their mentality and personality" and makes them prone to lie at school and contract mental disorders. This heavy-handed approach only provoked more curiosity. "Often people have come to religion through the journal *Science and Religion,*" a Russian priest explained to me. "They were told there was no God, but through the reading of anti-religious publications, they would acquire God. Many of the students in our theological schools found their faith through these anti-religious journals."

The Young Communist League, or Komsomol, has lamented more than once that religious customs linger, like the sign of the cross that Russian mothers make over their children. Baptism is so ingrained that Mikhail Gorbachev, by one account, was christened as a baby at his grandmother's insistence. Konstantin M. Kharchev, the chairman of the Kremlin's Council on Religious Affairs, estimated in 1988 that seventy million Soviet citizens, or a fourth of the Soviet population, adhere to some religious faith. What makes this significant is that most of these believers were born after the

Revolution and had been indoctrinated with atheism from childhood.

On my first Easter in Moscow, in 1974, I walked over to Red Army Park with Hedrick Smith, my predecessor as bureau chief, and we passed a company of army recruits marching in ragged formation. Shorn of their hair and dressed in baggy brown uniforms, they still looked for the most part like country boys. Out of mischief, I suppose, we called out the Easter greeting, *"Khristos voskres"* (He is risen). From the Soviet Army ranks rose the antiphonal response, *"Vo istinu voskres!"* (He is risen indeed).

Sometimes the Russian fascination with religion amounts to little more than rebellion, like the casual fad I saw among girls of wearing crosses as jewelry. More often, it reflects disillusionment with atheism. A survey of more than a thousand Ukrainian workers published in the Soviet press back in 1975 found that a third of them stayed away from such indoctrination sessions because they were boring, and over half didn't think that religion was so bad. Among more educated Russians, militant atheism has become socially gauche. "No intelligent person could possibly adopt a position like that," explained a Russian woman. "It is considered a sign of ignorance, not ideological steadfastness."

Where the Communist authorities have succeeded is in eroding memories of the Russian religious heritage. Even those with no time for atheism may have but fading acquaintance with religion's contribution to their history and literature. The poet Yevgeny Yevtushenko lamented that ignorance of the Bible prevented most young people from appreciating the symbolism of Tolstoy and Dostoyevsky. Aleksei, a gifted musician who taught me classical guitar in Moscow, lingered after one lesson to admire a wood carving of the Crucifixion that I had just brought back from Poland. Aleksei studied the painted carving, which showed a Jesus crowned with bloody thorns stumbling under the weight of His cross, and turned to ask amiably, "Some historical event, I suppose?"

The monotony of life under Communism, and the nagging

sense that there must be some force beyond the Party, has sufficed to enhance religion's mystique. One young Russian told me that until he got interested in religion, "something was missing in life."

Marxism-Leninism has been conspicuous in its inability to console ordinary people afflicted by tragedy or failure. And the ideology has proven unsatisfactory in denying the possibility of an afterlife, particularly for the Russians, who like to keep their spiritual options open. I never attended an event more depressing than an official Soviet funeral, not just because of its mournful dirges and black armbands, but because once the deceased comrade got sealed up in the Kremlin wall he was expected to stay there forever, unless history awarded his niche to a rival. This may be why as many as 40 percent of Russians who die receive church funerals.

Russian folk traditions also appeal to a people who make natural mystics. In the Soviet collective farmers' markets, peasant women sell hand-painted wooden eggs with the Cyrillic initials X B, representing the traditional Easter greeting, "*Khristos voskres.*" Easter, the holiest day in the Orthodox calendar, never failed to bring out an innate Russian sentimentality. Even those who never go to church might carry a traditional Easter cake, called a *kulich*, and dyed Easter eggs to be blessed by the local priest. "People have nothing to believe in, nothing to rely upon," explained one woman I knew, though she was not religious. "Easter offers something very spiritual and very beautiful. It is interesting, and life is not filled with interesting things."

On Easter eve of 1977, I joined the crowds converging on the Church of St. Nicholas of the Weavers on Komsomolsky Prospect in downtown Moscow. Policemen manning the metal street barricades sorted out the faithful from the curious, letting in only the elderly. The Soviet authorities were most afraid that religion would infect young Russians, and every Easter eve they scheduled rock-music concerts and Western films on television to keep them from straying off to church. Not until 1988 did Soviet television begin broadcasting part of the Easter service.

I was allowed through the barricades outside St. Nicholas's after I showed my foreign correspondent's credentials. Behind me, ordinary Russians jostled each other as they argued with the sullen policemen. Within the fenced church grounds, deputized volunteers from the Young Communist League were rounding up some teenagers who had sneaked in. The church door opened and the Easter procession filed out, carrying crosses, icons, and candles that illuminated the midnight darkness in the symbolic reenactment of the search for the resurrected Jesus. The crowds outside the church pushed forward for a better look. The bells pealed and the shout rang out, "*Khristos voskres*," followed by the antiphonal response, "*Vo istinu voskres!*""

In Old Russia, so many bells would have rung as to awaken all of Moscow, but the working churches have been winnowed down under the Communists to a few dozen. Because the others were razed or turned into factories and warehouses, not enough churches are left to hold everyone who wants to attend an Easter service.

As I stood outside St. Nicholas of the Weavers, policemen in gray overcoats flanked the Easter procession, in part to discourage heckling from some drunken youths. A cluster of old women charged a side door, hoping to get in, but the *druzheniki*, vigilantes, deputized by the police, drove them back. A husky blond plainclothesman in a trenchcoat blocked the main door; he kept announcing that there was no room inside. A disabled man pushed through the crowd and held up some credentials. "Please let me through," he beseeched. "I am an invalid and I come here to worship every day."

"Splendid, simply splendid," the blond man replied. "Go and tell your problems to the Party respresentative over there."

"Who are you?" the supplicant asked. "Are you a believer?"

"Listen, comrade, I'm a policeman," said the blond man and went inside, slamming the door behind him. The invalid limped off. A few minutes later, the policeman opened the door again to let in four colleagues. "These guys work here," he explained in answer to my question.

Eventually, I despaired of getting inside, and left. Behind me, an old man and his wife, each cupping a dripping candle against the night wind, maintained their own Easter vigil outside the locked door.

When it is tolerated, religious worship has been circumscribed with secular restrictions. "One should bear in mind that the Russian Orthodox Church is not a missionary society," said Archbishop Peterim as he defended his church's docility. Policing the faithful is the task of the Council on Religious Affairs, the watchdog body created by Stalin. The Council ensures that congregations register with the government as religious cults, that they do not proselytize for members or publish religious literature without state approval, and that they refrain from giving religious instruction to anyone younger than eighteen. In June 1988, in honor of Christianity's millennium in the Ukraine, the Kremlin made a substantial concession and let priests, hitherto limited to holding religious services, administer their own parishes, though the state retained ownership of the buildings.

But believers have remained fettered to a system intolerant of true religious freedom. Suspicions that police informers infiltrated the churches were confirmed in 1987 when Aleksandr Shushpanov, a translator for the Russian Orthodox Church, came forward to reveal how the KGB had recruited him.[4] Priests who stepped out of line have been disciplined as often as not by the church itself, which feared they would jeopardize the modest gains achieved. Some men of conscience, like Father Dmitri Dudko, were all but crushed for loyally dissenting with the church. Others, like the Reverend Rostislav Galetsky, turned their backs on state-controlled religion and became outlaws.

Father Dudko, a Russian Orthodox priest I knew in Moscow, was first called to task in 1974 after he preached some question-and-answer sermons that examined the role of Christians in a Communist society.

On one spring evening, he began his sermon by talking about an eleven-year-old girl who came with her younger brother to confess that she was a sinner. Father Dudko, startled, wondered what kind of sin it could be. The overflow crowd hushed as he related his story:

" 'It's like this,' she says. 'I believe [in God], but they make me wear a Pioneer's tie. Isn't that a sin?' she asks me very fearfully." Father Dudko referred to the red scarf of the Young Pioneers, a Communist version of the Boy and Girl Scouts.

"If it had been a grownup in front of me, I'd have thought it was some kind of provocation," he continued, "but since she was just a child, it couldn't be. At any rate, I kept silent. The girl continues: 'Of course, we're powerless. They make us do it. So this is what we did. First we blessed it with holy water, and then put it on. . . .'

" 'Oh Lord!' I thought. 'How the Lord makes children wise! O.K., so they make you wear it. We'll wear it, but first we'll bless it.' "

And with that, Father Dudko launched into a criticism of the Young Pioneers. "It would seem there's nothing bad here," he said. "It's a children's organization that trains in decency. But there's one catch. After all, it's an atheistic organization. What happens with the children of believers, with children who believe? Do you teach him a dual existence from childhood, one thing in school and another at home? Once he's grownup he can choose his own path, but while he's a child, while he's made to do things, he has to be tossed between his parents and the Pioneer organization."[5]

So many young people flocked Sunday evenings to the suburban Church of St. Nicholas to hear Father Dudko that the district Komsomol office complained. He was summoned to the Patriarch's office and told to confine himself to conventional sermons. He was reassigned, first to a church in Kabanovo and then to another at Grebnevo, closer to Moscow. It was out of bounds to foreign correspondents, but some of his followers commuted out to hear him.

The stocky, balding priest seemed amiable when I visited his apartment on the outskirts of Moscow. As a theological student, Father Dudko recalled, he had served eight and a half years in prison on trumped-up charges of anti-Soviet activity. He served out much of his sentence loading trucks at a labor camp in the Arctic. His maverick reputation had followed him to Grebnevo. "I had a lot of painful experiences there," he said. "They would suddenly say I was not allowed to participate in the divine liturgy." Pressure was applied to his son Misha and daughter Natasha to disown their father. Misha was warned at school that his religious belief would be noted on his *kharakteristika*, the character reference needed for a job or higher education. Misha was subsequently grilled by psychiatrists because he showed up at his medical examination for military induction wearing a small cross around his neck.

After I left the Soviet Union, Father Dudko got into worse trouble. The KGB searched his apartment, and one morning in January 1980, when he emerged from his church at Grebnevo, they arrested him. The priest was interrogated in prison for two months and then transferred to a hospital for "medical" treatment. In all, he spent more than six months incommunicado, with no one to talk to but his KGB handlers.

I was working in Cairo when a couple of Dutch reporters looked me up to report that Father Dudko, five months after his arrest, had denounced me and Arkady Nebolsin, an Oxford-educated art historian, on prime-time Soviet television. Some Russians who watched the priest's abject performance said it reminded them of the Stalinist show trials of the 1930s. Father Dudko confessed that his behavior "took on a more anti-Soviet activity because it was stimulated at first and later directed from abroad." He named those who had led them astray as "*The New York Times* correspondent C. Wren, the American professor A. R. Nebolsin, and the [Russian Orthodox] Archbishop Vasily of Brussels."[6]

The confession, which *Izvestia* published, lacked his characteristic eloquence and included some theological inconsistencies apparent to anyone attentive to the language of the church.[7] My initial outrage at having been smeared quickly turned to sympathy for what Father Dudko must have undergone before the KGB released him from Lefortovo prison, forty pounds thinner and numbed by depression. Evidence that his recantation was involuntary emerged when Father Dudko smuggled a cryptic letter out to Brussels hinting that he had broken under interrogation. "My heart is torn asunder seeing your confusion and hearing the garbled interpretations," he wrote Archbishop Vasily. "...I overestimated my own strength and fell lower than anyone else has ever done."[8]

Such tragedies notwithstanding, I heard Russian religious dissidents claim that they were more blessed than Westerners whose religious convictions had never been tried. At one of Father Dudko's crowded vespers, someone asked when the church had its finest hour. "Right now," he responded. "The church is powerful when she is on the cross, when she is persecuted. When she has a 'guardian,' she becomes weak."

By contrast, Rostislav Galetsky was the most engaging criminal of my acquaintance in a society that had no shortage of lawbreakers. Galetsky had earned a place on the *gossysk*, or most wanted list of the police, for bootlegging the Word of God. He traveled around the Soviet Union preaching to his fellow Seventh-Day Adventists, collecting their complaints of persecution, and distributing religious literature that he had printed on an illegal press.

In late 1977, I met him at the apartment of a Moscow dissident. Galetsky's broad Slavic face radiated serenity. His sober tie was offset by a pink shirt brighter than anything I had seen in a state store. Galetsky cheerfully admitted being a fugitive. "The only thing that I am guilty of," he said, "is that I want to serve God faithfully and will not accept this dictatorial system of coercion."

In the two weeks or so that we stayed in touch, Galetsky turned out to be a tough character underneath his Sunday-school demeanor. Like a New Testament apostle, he always seemed in joyful motion, distributing his tracts out of a worn leather briefcase and seldom spending two nights in the same place.

"We are people who don't need a warm chair," he said. "We can be on the move all the time. Sometimes we sleep only four hours. We are very busy because there is so much to do. We have to travel around and counsel the flocks."

In his restless fervor, Galetsky reminded me of Anatoly Shcharansky, a friend who would telephone at all hours to coax me into meeting some Soviet Jew suffering persecution for trying to emigrate to Israel. The KGB had picked up Shcharansky earlier that year; his real crime was speaking English well enough to bring the plight of Jewish refuseniks alive to Western correspondents. Anatoly survived prison and now lives in Israel as Natan Sharansky.

When I met Rostislav Galetsky, he had not seen his wife and three children for more than six months. The KGB kept them under surveillance in Voronezh in the hope that he might risk a visit. A few months earlier, the police surrounded a building where he and several other pastors were preaching. "I was besieged for thirteen hours. Thirty *gebeshniki* surrounded the building," he recalled. He used the contemptuous nickname taken from the last two initials of the KGB. "We were on the third floor and we didn't open up. At midnight when we finally unbolted the door, the first ranks of old men and old women rushed out as a diversion. The believers surrounded the *gebeshniki* and we ministers got away."

Galetsky and his fellow worshipers belonged to a militant minority that considered their faith none of the state's business. The prisons and labor camps held hundreds of such unrepentant Baptists, Pentecostals, and Seventh-Day Adventists. A former inmate of a Siberian labor camp told me that Jehovah's Witnesses had converted scores of his fellow convicts, using Russian-language copies of the *Watchtower* publication smuggled through the barbed wire.

"In our country, there are approved Seventh-Day Adventists," Galetsky explained one crisp autumn morning as we cruised around Moscow in my Volga sedan. "The sect split in 1924 and again in 1928. The larger part is official now, but the smaller group decided not to make any concessions. Our sect exists illegally. Arrests and jail have followed. Almost all the ministers in our church find themselves in illegal situations. The older people have been in prison for up to ten years at a stretch."

He mentioned Vladimir Shelko, the white-bearded patriarch of the All-Union Church of True and Free Seventh-Day Adventists. Shelko had served twenty-five years in prison, some of the time under sentence of death, and was on the run again. The old man was caught and died in a labor camp at the age of eighty-four. "To be a minister, one has to live a high level of morality. We use the example not only of Christ but also of men like Shelko," Galetsky said.

Galetsky's own troubles with the authorities started at thirteen, when he decided that there must be more to life than what the Young Communist League promised. He began cutting Saturday classes at school to go to a Seventh-Day Adventist worship service. The officials in his Ukrainian village threatened to send him to a reformatory. "They said there were murderers, thieves, and wastrels there.' They said, 'They'll soon straighten you out.' I said I would be very happy to go there so I could speak to them about God and reform them," Galetsky recalled. The officials dropped their threat.

His father was told to discipline the errant teenager, but when he was beaten, Galetsky said, "I didn't cry out at all." The outcome was that "now my father is a very strong believer." But the harassment was relentless, he said, and "at fifteen, I had to leave home and begin earning money for my own food and clothing."

As he wandered, Galetsky linked up with other dissident Adventists. He was ordained a deacon and then a minister, but his talents lay in underground publishing. Galetsky showed me his line of prayer books and devotional manuals, skillfully bound and stamped with gilt titles. He would not say how many presses he operated because it might help the KGB find them. "We can assure full availability of material to our congregation," Galetsky said like a good salesman. "All the books our church distributes are free." He pressed his samples on me. "Take what you want," he urged. "We can print more."

His customers were farmers and workers, the oppressed and exploited proletarians in whose name Lenin had launched his Revolution and for whom the Party now had little time. Galetsky was there to convert them, though he would not say how many they were. "As soon as the number of members or ministers becomes known, the repression will begin," he said.

"The members are located throughout the Soviet Union, and we have central control. We meet for services illegally. We have our own tactics in the search for souls. The KGB says of us, 'They're like mice. You can hear them but you can't find them.' "

But the KGB kept trying. "There are many attempts to infiltrate us. If they send an informer, we will find out if he is a wolf and divest him of his sheep's clothing. There have been cases where KGB agents have gotten to know the faithful and have ended up joining us. Others say, 'We are not believers, but we cannot work against you.' "

The Adventists, he said, were vulnerable through their children. "Our children don't go to school on Saturday so that opens the family up to repression. They have taken the children away from some believers and put them in special boarding schools. It is a dreadful situation, with old clothing and lice."

Among Galetsky's underground publications was a book with a dignified green cover that spelled out a "holy silence" for Adventists who were found out, much like a code of conduct for soldiers taken prisoner. Galetsky paraphrased it:

We are aware that we are innocent.

We are ready to suffer and even die for our faith. We don't have a cult of suffering, but everyone must be prepared.

In contacts with the KGB, we say we don't know anyone but ourselves, not even our wives.

We believe that turning against the sect is a great sin contrary to the Sixth Commandment, "Thou shalt not kill."

We won't answer religious questions because it is state interference in our religious affairs. We won't even answer whether we are believers.

We deny charges of treason or anti-state activity as lies and deception. We say, "Give us the facts."

We don't simply refuse to give evidence but we cite as our reason the guarantees of religious freedom of conscience [in the Soviet Constitution]. We say, "You are performing a criminal act by invading the Constitution, and if we were to answer, we would be accessories."

We defend our civil rights. We have printed up the International Convention on Human Rights and other international legal documents on the rights of man. You see, we have to be lawyers too.

Galetsky went on to describe how the faithful were taught how to act during searches and interrogations. "Our people are courageous. The KGB broke into one home and found a typewriter and said they would take it. The old woman refused to give it up. She said it was not hers. It took eight *gebeshniki* to wrest it away from her."

The prospect of capture by the KGB did not seem to disturb Galetsky. In fact, he expected it. "My only crime is that I believe in God and want to serve Him," the fugitive said. "The service of God is the highest form of life, and striving for justice is a form of serving God. If it is hard to do, it means God approves.

"From the age of thirteen, there have been occasions right up until today when God delivered me from their jaws. It gladdens and strengthens us. We understand that if God permits it, it will be for our personal good."

In July 1980, five KGB agents grabbed Galetsky at Moscow's Kazan station. He served five years in a labor camp on charges of slandering the Soviet state and "infringing the rights of citizens under the guise of performing religious ceremonies." The harshness of his sentence suggested that Galetsky had withstood nearly nine months of interrogation in pre-trial detention. Then in 1987, two years after he was released, the magazine *Oktyabr* published a bitter attack on the True and Free Adventists, accusing them of disseminating "slanderous fabrications" about religious persecution. The article singled out Rostislav Galetsky. God's outlaw in the pink shirt was back in business.[9]

I was reminded of his parting words when I dropped him off on Moscow's Ring Road after our last furtive rendezvous.

"Khrushchev said, 'I will go on television and show you the last believer,' " Galetsky remarked. "But he didn't manage to do it."

. . .

The carved wooden monkeys crouching between yak horns on the eaves of Ta'er monastery were there, I was told, to ward off evil lurking beyond its high walls. This was in 1984, when I drove from Xining, the capital of China's Qinghai province, for an audience with the resident living Buddha. Ta'er monastery venerates the founder of yellow-sect Buddhism, who was born here in 1357 on the northeastern flank of the Tibetan plateau. Over the centuries, the monastery became renowned for its yak-butter sculptures of Buddhist life. Present-day Tibet lies to the south, but Qinghai is hardly less isolated, especially when the heavy winter snows arrive, and Ta'er monastery looked authentically Tibetan with its curving tiled roofs and interior *tankas*—colorful religious art embroidered on heavy cloth.

The pilgrims had pitched their dirty white tents outside the monastery gate. They were mostly Tibetan herdsmen, who wore sheepskin coats hanging off one shoulder for ventilation, high leather boots, and daggers in their belts. The hair of the women was plaited with strings of turquoise and coral. The pilgrims poured yak butter from their glass jars or teapots into the votive lamps burning before the looming Buddhas. They piled other gifts of small coins, boiled candy, unshelled peanuts, and grain-ration coupons on the altars. One family prayed with their heads pressed to the stone floor. The mother guided her toddler through the ritual that her three older children knew by heart. In the courtyard outside, the pilgrims spun giant prayer wheels or gaped at cautionary murals, in which the wicked suffered vivisection and hanging while small devils ate their black hearts (the virtuous had red hearts and were spared eternal torture).

The living Buddha was named Dianbaijianzang, as best I could transliterate it from the Chinese. Gentle and rotund, he wore a maroon cloak over his brown robe and yellow undergarments. We pulled our chairs up to the glowing metal stove in the chilly reception room and sipped yak-butter tea.

"With the care of the Party, the monastery is well preserved," he said in careful Chinese. It was the first of his paeans to Communist rule.

"All Buddhist believers are very happy in the care of the Party," the living Buddha said.

He belonged to the fourteenth generation of his line of living Buddhas, chosen in childhood for reincarnating the qualities of a revered predecessor. "I came here when I was five years old, and now I am seventy," he told me. "My home was in Haiyan country in Qinghai, but I am Mongolian. My parents were herdsmen. I can't remember coming here"—his small hands fluttered toward the courtyard outside—"because I was so small. I had an uncle who was a lama here and he looked after me."

I asked about his life now. "Before Liberation, the rules were strict. People were cursed and beaten and the lamas had no freedom," he replied. "Now, the monks and people are free to believe in Buddhism or quit. So more people are coming to Buddha as believers."

After the Cultural Revolution was launched in 1966, Red Guards rampaged through China's temples, churches, and mosques. Ta'er was only slightly damaged but it did not readmit worshipers until 1978. Now four hundred lamas and monks were in attendance. "Before, the lamas and monks went out to collect contributions from the Tibetans," he said. "Now, we have to work to eat, so we feed ourselves. We are self-reliant. We don't rely on exploitation as before."

I couldn't decide whether he was phrasing his words for the benefit of a foreign reporter or whether his fulsome gratitude was the accumulation of more than three decades spent looking to the Communists for spiritual and physical survival. He seemed not unlike the Panchen Lama, now dead, who stayed to collaborate when the Dalai Lama, the paramount authority of Tibetan Buddhism, fled into exile. I asked the living Buddha whether life in an atheistic state suited him.

"The only thing that disappointed me was the Cultural Revolution. I didn't have much freedom," he replied. He had been held inside the monastery for a dozen years and forced to do manual labor. "Otherwise, I feel happy with my life since Communist Liberation. I receive a high salary and am given special treatment, thanks to the Party," he said. "Before Liberation, though my life was well off it was not honorable because we lived by exploiting others. Now there is no more exploitation, so my life is not only better off but also more honorable."

When I asked what future he saw for Buddhism in China, he said he was optimistic. "Since I myself am Buddhist, I hope it will continue and develop. Whatever we do now is seeking truth from facts." He managed to insert into our conversation Deng Xiaoping's favorite slogan.

The living Buddha was not the only holy man I met who had made his peace with Marxism. The Soviet government co-opted the Russian Orthodox Church for its own ends. During World War Two, Stalin halted his persecution of the churches to win the support of religious believers for the war effort against Nazi Germany—the Russian Orthodox Church even bought the Red Army a column of tanks. Tame clerics have since been trotted out at forums like the World Council of Churches to deny the existence of religious repression at home. The Russian church has sponsored peace and disarmament conferences at which it praised Soviet foreign policy effusively. Though the Orthodox Church claimed to lack money to print more Bibles or open more churches, it was contributing about 35 million rubles, or over $50 million, a year to the Soviet Peace Fund, which supports the government line. "All these sums come from the offerings of the faithful," confirmed Fyodor Bulyevsky, a spokesman I met from the Russian Orthodox Church.

Gorbachev conceded that his predecessors persecuted religion. "Mistakes made with regard to the church and believers in the 1930s and the years that followed are being rectified," he said. Complaints by church congregations of official mistreatment have been raised in the official press but not by the church hierarchy, whose fealty to the Kremlin predates the 1917 Revolution. At the celebration of Christianity's Ukrainian millennium in 1988, Patriarch Pimen was awarded the

Red Banner of Labor, a medal more appropriate for overachieving coal miners or tractor drivers.

In a society suffocating under official statistics, church leaders tolerated by the Kremlin have resisted saying how many members they have. "It is not the practice here, as it is abroad, to count parishioners or connect them to this or that parish," said Bulyevsky, when I asked how many members belonged. "Every day, thousands of churches open their doors and thousands of people go in." In late 1988, the church did acknowledge having 6,893 parishes.

Archbishop Yuvenaly rationalized the paucity of working churches, which dropped from over 51,000 to fewer than 500 in the first few decades of Soviet power. "It is more convenient for us to have one church and increase the number of priests and services to keep down the extra cost," he said. And I heard another ecclesiastical official, Metropolitan Peterim, shrug off the scandalous shortage of Bibles. "In my house, I have several Bibles from my father and grandfather, not a collection but an inheritance," he said. "Bibles have been in religious families for many years."

The Chinese government has kept its eight million or so Christians on an equally short leash.[10] Christianity was viewed by the Communists as a subversive religion imposed by foreigners. (It is not lost on some Chinese Christians that Marx and Lenin were imports too.) The unequal treaties forced by Western countries on the Qing emperors in the nineteenth century included provisions safeguarding the propagation of Christianity by Western missionaries.

After the Communists came to power, they insisted that Christians sever their ties with the West. Protestants complied by founding the Three-Self Patriotic Movement, a church that was effectively self-administering, self-sustaining, and self-propagating, as well as loyal to Beijing. In 1957, Catholics were compelled to join a new Catholic Patriotic Association, which proclaimed its independence from the Vatican. (The Chinese treat Protestantism and Catholicism as different religions because they were propagated by competing Western missionaries.)

Some Christians told me they felt more at home in an indigenous church. "Our aim is to free ourselves from foreign domination," explained the Reverend Chen Zemin, the vice principal of China's sole surviving Protestant seminary, in Nanjing. "It used to be that for the church to gain one Christian, China would have to lose one Chinese. We realized we must make Christianity really Chinese, so we could bear witness and bring the gospel to the Chinese people. Now that we have identified with the Chinese people, Christianity has gained new respect in China."

The Nanjing Union Theological Seminary resembles a Bible college in the American South, with a tidy library upstairs and modest chapel downstairs adorned with a simple cross. It opened in 1952, only to be sacked and closed down in 1966 at the onset of the Cultural Revolution. "The Red Guards came and wanted to burn all our books," Chen recalled. "We said some of them were important for our studies. They were kind enough to give us forty-eight hours to select some books. Then they changed their minds and said we had only twenty-four hours. We only saved ten percent of the books." The rest were burned or carted off for pulping. Chen, a former Baptist minister, spent the next five years at farm labor.

The seminary, which became an agricultural bureau, reopened in 1981. Despite the fifteen-year hiatus, more than one thousand young Chinese applied for barely fifty places. "Their knowledge of the Bible and Christianity was rather meager, so we had to start at the beginning," Chen said.

It struck me as remarkable that so many young Chinese who grew up under Communism should come forward after their elders had been so persecuted. Luo Chenfang, a professor of New Testament at the seminary, said he was not surprised. "Out of more than one billion Chinese, it would be quite natural that a few hundred young people felt called to serve the church," he said.

Most Chinese Christians I met, though they graciously found room for me in their crowded services on Christmas and Easter, were skittish of foreigners, whose well-intentioned solicitude they feared might jeopardize their spiritual survival. "We ask for them to pray for us, but not to drown us in Christian love," Luo said. Chen was upset that some Western evangelists had tried to smuggle Chinese-language Bibles into Guangdong province.

Despite the guarantees of religious freedom in the Chinese Constitution, I kept hearing about Chinese who were in trouble for disobeying the laws circumscribing religion. At one church in Beijing, two Chinese were arrested on suspicion of receiving unapproved religious literature from foreigners. More often, church leaders were intimidated into keeping their churches above reproach. One pastor at a Protestant church in Beijing played it safe and discouraged young people from getting baptized. I later heard of a church warden in suburban Moscow who demanded the identity documents of anyone being baptized, so their names could be given to the Soviet authorities.

When the Anglican Archbishop of Canterbury, Robert Runcie, visited Beijing in December 1983, a neatly dressed young man tried to enter the church where the Archbishop was preaching in the Chongwenmen district. The deacons intercepted him and asked him to leave, one told me, because the youth admitted to membership in the Communist Youth League and the elders didn't want to incur its displeasure.

As in the Soviet Union, the legal churches in China survived by deferring to the state, but the Chinese churchmen I met insisted that how they practiced their religion was their own affair. "Christianity came to China by the grace of God, not by the grace of foreigners," said Father Shen Baozhi as we talked in the vestry of the Xujiahui Catholic Cathedral in Shanghai. I had reported some months earlier on four elderly Jesuit priests in Shanghai who finished long prison terms, only to be rearrested on new charges of maintaining clandestine ties to the Vatican. When I mentioned their plight to Father Shen, he was unsympathetic. "The reason is not that they are priests but that they use their positions as priests to sabotage society," he said. "Even religious people can violate the law."

During the Cultural Revolution, some Christians met secretly in private homes to whisper their hymns and prayers together, lest the neighbors turn them in. I had heard that these so-called "house Christians" still existed in some areas and I chanced upon one in Suzhou. I had gotten lost and a passerby, sensing my uncertainty, offered to guide me back to my hotel.

"Ten years ago, I couldn't talk to you. Someone would spy on me and follow me home," he said as he wheeled his bicycle alongside me through the darkening streets. He proudly identified himself as a Catholic. I asked if he had visited the cathedral in Shanghai. No, he replied, he wouldn't go to a state-controlled church "because it is against the Pope." He and his friends celebrated mass in their homes.

"There are churches in Beijing and Shanghai, but they are for foreigners," he said. Until 1979, local Chinese were not permitted inside. But now, I said, he could worship openly. "It is better now, but not entirely," he replied. "I hope that someday our church will be as free as it is in America." And he disappeared into the dusk without daring to invite me to a house mass.

In the Soviet Union and China, religious believers are valued in the blue-collar trades because they are hard workers, good family folk, and seldom touch alcohol—in short, the model of socialist man. But they cannot rise to real responsibility. In the Soviet resort of Yalta, I fell into conversation with a couple of burly Ukrainians on holiday. When they learned I was American, they identified themselves as Baptists and peppered me with questions about American Baptists. In turn, I asked about their lives and their smiles faded. Gesturing with his callused hands, one worker related how he and his friend were given the dirtiest factory jobs. The Baptists were never promoted to foremen, he said, despite their reliability, and lazier workers resented them. And of course, the Party, the surest route to success, was closed to Christians. By the time we parted, they looked so dejected that I was sorry I had asked.

And yet by merely enduring, these *veryayushchi*, or "believing ones" as the Russians call them, testify to Marxism's inadequacies. Shortly before I left China, I traveled to the Buddhist monasteries on Wutaishan, a remote cluster of peaks rising up to ten thousand feet in Shanxi province in northern China. More than 360 monks and 20 nuns lived there and young novices arrived almost daily. One lama from Inner Mongolia, Dang Gatasai, was only thirteen. "I thought that he was too young," apologized Da Erji, his religious master at Xiantong monastery. "But without getting my permission, his parents sent him here because they believe in Buddhism."

I was more intrigued by Yuan, a nineteen-year-old monk wearing granny glasses who also came from Inner Mongolia, because his father had joined the Communist Revolution back in 1930 and was honorably retired as a Party veteran. "I'm the only one in my family who believes in Buddhism," Yuan said as he made room in his small cell for some visiting correspondents. "The others believe in Marxism. But my father has not interfered in my personal affairs."

Yuan downplayed his conversion as undramatic. "My mother died when I was a year old and I was raised by my grandmother and sister," he said. His grandmother took him regularly to the local Buddhist temple. "I worked repairing cars for only nine months before I became a monk," he said. Yuan, who had belonged to the Communist Youth League, had to pay his way twice to Beijing to persuade Buddhist authorities to accept him.

His life was ascetic even by the standards of rural China. Yuan rose at 2:30 A.M. before morning prayers, washed in cold water, wore a rough gray robe, and subsisted on a spartan vegetarian diet. He explained that Buddhists had to set a good example for others. "Buddhism doesn't deny reality," he argued. "It does not negate the laws of human nature, birth, life, and death."

One of us visitors observed that Marxism dismissed religion as superstition. "Buddhism has the appearance of superstition if it's analyzed one-sidedly," he conceded. "I can only say that it is all part of the spiritual life of a Buddhist."

As Yuan stood there in his unheated stone cell defending the faith, he seemed in communion with the millions of other souls whom the Communists had lost to religion. Because Buddha demanded the greater sacrifice, an idealist like Yuan found him more credible than Marx.

"If you say it is all superstition," the young monk asked us like a Zen master, "why has it lasted until today?"

12

CASTING OFF THE SOILED SHIRT: WHERE COMMUNISM GOES FROM HERE

▄ ▄ ▄ ▄ ▄ ▄ ▄ ▄ ▄ ▄ ▄ ▄ ▄ ▄

Never play with insurrection, but
once it is begun remember that
is must be carried through to the
end.

—KARL MARX, 1852[1]

To someone brought up on Marxism it seems a terrifying step—
suddenly to start living without
the familiar ideology. But in
point of fact you have no choice;
circumstances themselves will
force you to do it and it may already be too late.

—ALEKSANDR SOLZHENITSYN,
1973[2]

THE WINDS OF AUTUMN buffeted the wide steppes of
Siziwang Banner in Inner Mongolia. Peasants, bundled in padded cotton jackets and pile caps with dangling earflaps, were
threshing the grain in their hard earth courtyards. Though it
was only November in 1984, the weather had turned so cold
that I slept in my clothes that night. The weak morning sunlight offered little relief.

The Banner, or county, of Siziwang was known for raising
fine sheep, birthing about 400,000 lambs a year. The county
seat where I spent the night was a gritty little town set in-
congruously amid the seamless expanse of yellow prairie. Even
the air, filled with coal dust, tasted acrid. I had asked local
officials to arrange a meeting with a former Red Guard, and

they sent along an intense young man named Dong, who worked as a deputy director of Siziwang's labor bureau.

Dong was a native of Beijing, but the government had prevented him and thousands of other former Red Guards from returning home to the cities, where there were not enough jobs or apartments. Dong still seemed bewildered by the turn of events that had left him stranded in Inner Mongolia as a reward for his ideological fervor. He had joined the Cultural Revolution in 1966 and was sent off to Mongolia two years later.

"More than a thousand of us came up from Beijing," Dong said. "We came because the slogan of Chairman Mao was 'Go up to the mountains and down to the countryside.' It was Chairman Mao who first proposed going to the countryside. So I came here filled with political enthusiasm to build the frontier of my country."

He was sent with other "educated youth," as the city kids were called, to a commune called Kaipingzhuang. "We educated youth were distributed among the production teams. The living and working conditions were very hard. Our life was far from what we had enjoyed in Beijing and the labor was intense. The climate was completely different from Beijing's. It was colder and higher.

"Our shortest work day," he continued, "was eight hours, and in autumn we worked ten hours or more. Some people got very sick because they couldn't adapt, but nobody died here. If they were too sick, they were sent back to Beijing."

Siziwang, despite its poverty, was expected to accommodate the Red Guards. "Outwardly, the peasants seemed to welcome us," Dong said. "I don't know if they really did welcome us or not, because at the time they didn't need labor in the countryside. We did whatever the local peasants did— ploughing, sowing, hoeing the fields. In the autumn, we harvested the wheat, oats, and potatoes."

Eventually, some "educated youth" were permitted to take blue-collar jobs in the factory towns of Inner Mongolia; but only those in poor health were allowed to go home when the Cultural Revolution ended in 1976. I asked Dong if he regretted leaving Beijing. He put the best face on his fate for a foreigner.

"Personally, I feel that if we had been left in the cities to continue studying and invest our talents, it would have been better for the country. I have thought about returning to Beijing. There are others my age from Beijing who feel the same way too. In Beijing, I still have my mother, brother, and three sisters. . . ."

He cut short his musings. "But after all, Beijing is now a thing of the past for me. We should be looking forward." He had enrolled in a dozen correspondence courses offered by the government. "They send me material by mail and from time to time I take examinations," he said. "Every evening, I study after work, at least three hours a night."

I asked Dong if such gestures satisfied the teenage revolutionaries who sallied forth at Chairman Mao's behest, only to find later that they lost out to those who stayed put.

"It's hard to say," he replied after a short silence. "The present policy of the country is better than it was in the past. And society has created conditions for people like us to study," Dong said hopefully.

Dong's plight seemed a fitting metaphor for what the failed experiment of Communism has done to so many Russians and Chinese. In conversations with some of them, I sensed a desperate hope that their suffering would lead to some kind of national redemption.

One muggy evening in Guangdong, I sat talking with an earnest young man whose father, a wartime veteran of the People's Liberation Army, had been singled out for public vilification as a "capitalist roader" during the Cultural Revolution. My companion recalled how the Red Guards had paraded his father, tied with ropes and crowned with a dunce cap, before a mass rally. "They painted his hands and arms black," he said, "because they said capitalists had black hands." After his release, the son said, his father, a decent man by his loving recollection, had scrubbed the paint from his hands until they bled. The children suffered nightmares that the Red Guards would come in the dark for them too.

Then, almost as an afterthought, my companion volunteered that he had just joined the Communist Party. I asked how he could support an organization responsible for such cruelty toward his family. The Cultural Revolution was an aberration in China's long history, he insisted, and besides, he said, the Party was changing.

For all the pain that the ideology has inflicted upon millions of innocents, the stubborn hope survives, not least among its victims and their heirs, that the system will have to justify itself by abandoning its shabby means while leaving the utopian ends intact. It is a beguiling dream that the evil can somehow be undone and never more be done, but the question is whether the Soviet Union and China can change enough to make an abiding difference to their citizens.

Given Communism's meltdown in places like Eastern Europe, many Westerners are hard put to fathom its residual appeal elsewhere in the world. They underestimate the power of both hope and hate. Marxism-Leninism has responded to individual and collective misery with the panacea of revenge. It entitles the underdog to the sin of class pride. Every injustice finds a ready scapegoat in the capitalist or foreign colonialist. The rhetoric of class struggle offers a catharsis for the wretched of the earth or a pretext for new cruelty. The dictatorship of the proletariat has justified the perpetuation of power by the most banal of despots. Marxism's fatal weakness lies not in the promise but in the delivery. The next time, swears the good Marxist, we will do it right.

While the windy old boasts about the superiority of Communism have been muted, the success of the reforms set in motion, first in China and then in the Soviet Union, looks far from assured. Before China slid back into its conservative mind set, I thought it might evolve into a more authoritarian version of Taiwan. A less-doctrinaire Soviet Union could pattern itself after Sweden, whose socialized welfare system has been inspected by Soviet delegations.

This, however, means giving more than lip service to Chairman Mao's old adage to "let a hundred flowers bloom, a

THE END OF THE LINE 313

thousand schools of thought contend." Creative change entails
an examination of all the alternatives. The most innovative
ideas, including a few since adopted by the leadership in Moscow, have been proposed by Soviet and Chinese dissidents with
a firsthand knowledge of the perils inherent in ideological orthodoxy. Wei Jingsheng, a Chinese dissident in prison since
March 1979 for his enlightened views, called democracy "the
fifth modernization," playing upon Deng's campaign of "the
four modernizations" of China's agriculture, industry, science
and technology, and defense. Without democracy as the lubricant, Wei wrote, "the society will become stagnant and
economic growth will encounter insurmountable obstacles."[3]
In its 1989 suppression of the student democracy movement,
China confirmed Wei's prediction.

Of course, change will not necessarily produce democracy.
To break the political monopoly of the Party apparatus, Mikhail Gorbachev persuaded the Congress of People's Deputies
in March 1990 to invest him as President with even greater
powers than he had enjoyed as Party chief. The Communist
reformers I met wanted to emulate not the United States or
Western Europe but South Korea or Singapore, where author-
itarianism has not inhibited economic prosperity. But even this
requires a tolerance of individual initiative and a laying off of
hands by the Party, whose hacks have been reluctant to share
anything but their rhetoric with the masses. Marxism can
never be regenerated until the influence of this mediocre élite
has been ended.

Economic progress involves more than jacking up industrial output, quality, and productivity. Fundamental issues like
price reform, unemployment, labor mobility, and the free flow
of information have yet to be grappled with. The most astute
Soviet and Chinese Party officials I met saw a long, arduous
march ahead. "You cannot say we are on a paved road with
Adidas shoes on our feet," said Enn Sillari, the Party chief of
Tallinn, as we talked in his sunny office below a portrait of
Lenin. "We are traveling a mountain path in the snow and fog,
and I imagine our progress is slow. But we have to climb this

peak." When I asked Sillari if he was optimistic, he leaned forward in the chair. "Listen, there is no alternative," he said. "If you have one, please tell me."

Though I have not hesitated to offer my opinions in this book, it seems presumptuous for Western observers like me to prescribe what the Soviet and Chinese people need beyond the bedrock democratic freedoms embraced by crusaders like Andrei Sakharov and Wei Jingsheng. Capitalism and a mixed economy contain their own historical inequities that made Communism possible in the Soviet Union and China; from such opposing philosophies some hybrid may grow. "The West can't solve our problems. They can only be solved inside the Soviet Union itself," the Soviet dissident Marxist Roy Medvedev told Piero Ostellino, an Italian journalist, back in 1980. "If Western democrats and socialists really want to help the Soviet Union to become a flourishing democracy, let them create such a society on their home grounds and set our people a good example."

China and the Soviet Union seem unlikely to revert to the totalitarianism of Mao and Stalin; the pendulum may swing backward, but never quite as far. But they are also unlikely to move very far ahead until the Party is shuttled to the sidelines, where it can do as little damage as possible. The impediments to successful reform involve neither ideology nor economics. They are timidity and selfishness, flaws that the early Communists held in contempt. "Let us not imitate those sorry Marxists of whom Marx said, 'I have sown dragon's teeth and harvested fleas,' " Vladimir Ilyich Lenin told supporters after his return from exile in Switzerland in 1917.[4]

My favorite political joke in Moscow posited the resurrection of Lenin from his tomb on Red Square. Lenin ordered his startled heirs to fetch him all the issues of *Pravda* since his death in 1924. Thereupon, he closeted himself in his old study and began to read. After a couple of weeks, the door flew open and Lenin strode out of the Kremlin. "Where are you going?" one of his keepers asked. Lenin snapped, "Back to Switzerland to start over."

If the Soviet and Chinese leaders prove incapable of transforming their societies, the working class may yet do it for them; that is the warning of the popular revolutions that swept Eastern Europe in 1989. It is time for a new vanguard of revolutionaries to dump into history's dustbin whatever no longer works, including the Communist Party itself. Lenin set a precedent more than seven decades ago when he complained that "we are afraid of our own selves. We are loath to cast off the 'dead old' soiled shirt. . . .

"But," Lenin declared flatly, "it is time to cast off the soiled shirt and put on clean linen."

NOTES
AND
SOURCES

▬ ▬ ▬ ▬ ▬ ▬ ▬ ▬ ▬ ▬ ▬ ▬ ▬ ▬ ▬ ▪

SOURCES

To keep abreast of developments since leaving the Soviet Union and China, I have relied upon a number of sources familiar to scholars, among them research bulletins of *Radio Liberty*, extracts from the *Current Digest of the Soviet Press*, the *Moscow News*, and the *China Daily*. When possible, I tried to consult original Russian and Chinese newspaper texts.

I found the dissident journals *Glasnost* and *China Spring*, both of which are now published in New York, invaluable in disclosing what the official Soviet and Chinese press continued to hide.

I am also indebted to the thorough reporting of my colleagues and successors in the Moscow and Beijing bureaus of *The New York Times*, including David Shipler, Craig Whitney, Jim Clarity, John Burns, Seth Mydans, Phil Taubman, Felicity Barringer, Bill Keller, Francis Clines, Edward Gargan, and Nicholas Kristof and his wife, Sheryl WuDunn. Of course, they cannot be faulted for my interpretations and conclusions.

I must thank the Reverend Michael Bordeaux for sharing his insights on religion under Communism and for making available his archives at Keston College in Kent, England. And I appreciate the assistance of Rob McDougall, a sinologist in Canada's Department of External Affairs, in slicing through the arcanities of Chinese internal politics when we were together in Beijing and later in New York. Not least, I am grateful for the enlightenment and courageous witness of three Russian friends who died during the writing of this book, Veniamin and Tanya Levich, and Andrei Sakharov.

These books proved indispensable in matching the theory of Marxism to what I witnessed in practice: *A Documentary History of Communism*, edited by Robert V. Daniels, University Press of New England, Hanover, NH, 1984; *A Dictionary of Marxist Thought*, edited by Tom Bottomore, Harvard University Press, Cambridge, 1983; *Utopia in Power: The History of the Soviet Union from 1917 to the Present*, by Mikhail Heller and Aleksandr N. Nekrich, Summit Books, New York, 1986; *The Portable Karl Marx*, selected by Eugene Kamenka, Penguin Books, New York, 1983; and *Mao Tse-tung Unrehearsed: Talks and Letters 1956–71*, edited by Stuart Schramm, Penguin Books, 1974.

NOTES

Mao Zedong wrote his poem "Ode to the Plum Tree" in December 1961, based on a Sung Dynasty poem by Lu Yu (1125–1210). Translation by Hua-Ling Nieh Engle and Paul Engel appears in *Poems of Mao Tse-tung* published by Dell Publishing Company, New York, 1972.

INTRODUCTION: THE REVOLUTION HAS BEEN CANCELED FOR LACK OF INTEREST

1. Khrushchev's colorful epigraph about shrimp learning to sing—or whistle—has been reported in various forms. The quotation here was cited in *The Life and Death of Lenin*, by Robert Payne, Norton, New York, 1964.

2. Speech by Hu Yaobang on March 13, 1983, commemorating the death of Karl Marx one hundred years earlier, published by Foreign Languages Press, Beijing, 1983.

3. Several years before the crackdown, Deng Xiaoping told the Chinese Party's Central Committee, "I believe that no liber-

alization of any kind should exist." On March 4, 1987, *Ryukyu Shimpo* newspaper in Japan published excerpts of his undated speech.

4. *The Revolution Betrayed*, by Leon Trotsky, Doubleday, New York, 1937.

5. On December 8, 1987, Gorbachev told American visitors to the Soviet Embassy in Washington, D.C., "We are only now realizing what socialism is capable of, what it can yield. We are returning to Lenin."

And on February 18, 1988, Gorbachev said to the Soviet Party's Central Committee, "We are striving in the present conditions to revive the Leninist image of the new system, to rid it of crustations and deformations, of everything that shackled society and prevented it from using the potential of socialism in full measure."

6. This quote from *The Communist Manifesto*, by Karl Marx and Friedrich Engels, and subsequent ones are taken from the English translation by Penguin Books, Middlesex, England, 1967.

7. This quote by Mao Zedong and most subsequent ones are taken from his red-jacketed *Selected Quotations*, published by Foreign Languages Press, Beijing, 1966.

CHAPTER 1 IF IT WORKS, WE'LL CALL IT SOCIALISM: SALVAGING AN IDEOLOGY

1. Gorbachev spoke to Soviet writers about the importance of reading Lenin on June 19, 1986. Excerpts of Gorbachev's remarks, taken down by one of the participants at the meeting, were obtained by Serge Schmemann for *The New York Times*.

2. This quote by Deng Xiaoping and most subsequent ones are taken from his *Selected Works*, Foreign Languages Press, Beijing, 1984.

3. Lenin's belief that an élite Communist vanguard must lead the working class in their revolutionary emancipation was

expressed in his essay "What Is to Be Done?" *(Chto Delat)*, published in 1902.

4. *Selected Quotations of Mao Zedong*, Foreign Languages Press, Beijing, 1967.

5. Ibid.

6. Speech by Milovan Djilas at the Frankfurt Forum in 1987, subsequently published in *Glasnost*, issue no. 12 (1987).

7. In May 1976, the ideological journal *Red Flag* accused Deng Xiaoping of committing heresy in saying, "Any cat that catches mice is a good cat." *Red Flag* quoted Mao Zedong's criticism of Deng: "This person does not grasp class struggle; he has never referred to this key link. His theme still is 'white cat, black cat' making no distinction between imperialism and Marxism."

8. An analysis of the economic ramifications for Beijing in Su Shaozhi's face-saving contention that China was still in the primary stage of socialism may be found in the March 1988 issue of *China Reconstructs*.

9. Marx expressed a broader dislike of ideological dogmatism when he wrote in a letter in 1843 that "I am not in favor, therefore, of setting up a dogmatic standard." Quoted on page 93 of *The Portable Karl Marx*, selected by Eugene Kamenka, Penguin Books, New York, 1983. Most subsequent quotes by Marx are taken from the same book.

10. Victor Serge wrote his description of Lenin in his memoir, *Year One of the Russian Revolution*, smuggled out of the Soviet Union for publication abroad in 1930. Serge, born Viktor Kibalchich in 1890, had returned from Paris to Russia after the Bolshevik Revolution as an ardent supporter of Lenin's policies. Stalin turned against him later and Serge died in exile in Mexico in 1947.

11. *Pravda International*, Vol. 2, No. 6, p. 18.

12. *Liberation Daily*, August 18, 1982.

13. *Liberation Daily*, September 28, 1982.

14. *Soviet Russia (Sovetskaya Rossiya)*, March 13, 1988.

15. *Pravda*, April 5, 1990.

16. On May 7, 1988, Gorbachev asked Soviet editors who took sides in the Andreyeva affair to end their quarrel; Tass reported his remarks on May 10.

17. *Guangming Daily*, November 6, 1983.

18. *People's Daily*, December 7, 1984.

19. *People's Daily*, December 10, 1984.

20. This quote by the Marquis de Custine and subsequent ones are taken from *Journey for Our Time: The Russian Journals of the Marquis de Custine*, Henry Regnery Co., Chicago, 1951.

21. This and subsequent quotes by Karl A. Wittfogel are taken from *Oriental Despotism: A Comparative Study of Total Power*, Yale University Press, 1964.

22. On November 20, 1988, China promised that laws affecting foreigners, including those on contacts with Chinese nationals, would no longer be classified as secret.

23. Boris Egorov, a Leningrad professor, wrote in *Soviet Culture (Sovetskaya Kultura)* on March 15, 1988, that it was impossible to find an accurate map of Moscow in the Soviet Union, but not in Paris. Y. Yashchenko, the chief of the Main Administration of Geodesy and Cartography, told *Izvestia* on September 3, 1988, that Soviet cartographers were finally allowed to draft accurate maps. Summaries by *Radio Liberty*. Also, *The New York Times*, September 3, 1988.

CHAPTER 2 WHAT WAS THE SUBJECT OF YOUR SILENCE? LOSING CONTROL IN A TOTALITARIAN STATE

1. This quote by Fang Lizhi and most subsequent ones were taken from his selected speeches as translated by *China Spring* in its March/April 1987 issue.

2. Open letter by Anatoly Zavernyayev, a Leningrad dissident,

written on July 25, 1987, to the Presidium of the Supreme Soviet and subsequently published in issue no. 7 (1987) of *Glasnost*.

3. Milan Kundera's observation on totalitarianism and paradise was subsequently reported by Roth.

4. George Orwell summed up the bleak terror of totalitarianism in *1984* when the interrogator O'Brien told his victim, "If you want a picture of the future, imagine a boot stamping on a human face—forever."

5. Roy Medvedev mentioned Molotov's treatment of Zhemchuzhina in an interview with Piero Ostellino. The full interview was published under the title *On Soviet Dissent* by Columbia University Press, New York, in 1980.

6. The proverb in Russian is *"Bog vysoko a tsar daleko"*; in Chinese it is *"Tian gao huangdi yuan."*

7. Lenin's and Stalin's views of Russian chauvinism were quoted in *The Language of Communism*, by Michael Waller, Bodley Head, London, 1972.

8. The lyrics for "Without the Communist Party There Would Be No New China" were published in *Red Flag (Hongqi)* on September 16, 1981.

9. Gao Wang, a commentator writing in the *China Daily* on February 4, 1988, used this fable to make the same point. "The same holds true with young people today—the more they are told to believe in the authorities and do only what they are allowed to do in the name of doing them good, the more skeptical and rebellious they will become," Gao wrote.

10. The drunkenness that followed the taking of the Winter Palace was recalled by V. A. Antonov-Ovseyenko in his *Zapiski o Grazhdanskoi Voine (Notes about the Civil War)*, Vol. I, pp. 19–20. This excerpt appeared in Bertram Wolfe's introduction to *Ten Days That Shook the World*, by John Reed, The Modern Library, New York, 1960.

11. Some statistics on moonshining in the Soviet Union quoted

here and later in this chapter came from the Internal Affairs Minister A. V. Vlasov in an interview with *Izvestia* published on March 11, 1987. Translation by *Current Digest of the Soviet Press*, issue no. 10, 1987.

12. The Soviet sugar shortage was discussed in *Radio Liberty*'s research bulletin on August 27, 1987.

13. China's family-planning problems have been a subject of continuous discussion in the Chinese press, notably the *People's Daily* and the *China Daily*.

14. Most statistics cited here, including the popularity of various birth-control devices, were secured through the Beijing office of the United Nations Fund for Population Activities, and unofficial Chinese channels.

15. *Beijing Daily*, February 14, 1984.

16. On June 30, 1988, the *People's Daily* reported that more than one million Chinese children were unregistered by the government. Gu Hailu of the State Family Planning Commission discussed unregistered births in the *China Daily* on September 22, 1988.

17. *Workers' Daily (Gongren Ribao)*, excerpted by the *China Daily* on January 22, 1988.

18. On March 2, 1988, the *People's Daily* quoted Commerce Minister Liu Yi as saying that Chinese would have to change their diets to avoid consuming too much grain.

The 1982 national census reported that meat accounted for only 8 percent of the calories in the Chinese diet, according to the *China Daily*, March 3, 1988.

CHAPTER 3 UNCLE LEI FENG IS DEAD: CASTE AND PRIVILEGE IN A CLASSLESS SOCIETY

1. *Selected Quotations of Mao Zedong*, Foreign Languages Press, Beijing, 1967. Mao's injunction was also quoted by Liu Shaoqi in his essay *How to Be a Good Communist*, Foreign Languages Press, Beijing, 1964.

2. Stories about the woman cook who disrupted the Party cadres' banquet in Shandong appeared in several Beijing newspapers, including the *China Daily*, on February 23 and 24, 1986.

3. *Selected Quotations of Mao Zedong*, Foreign Languages Press, Beijing, 1967.

4. Deng's speech "The Task of Consolidating the Army," July 14, 1975. *Selected Works of Deng Xiaoping*, Foreign Languages Press, Beijing, 1983.

5. Milovan Djilas's quote comes from his book *The New Class: An Analysis of the Communist System*, Harcourt Brace Jovanovich, New York, 1957, p. 39.

6. Deng's speech "Senior Cadres Should Take the Lead in Maintaining and Enriching the Party's Fine Traditions," November 2, 1979. Op.cit.

7. Back in March 1979, Deng Xiaoping criticized junkets by Party officials. "Some comrades have traveled abroad once. They have traveled by jumbo 747 jets, have tried large American sedans, have slept on soft mattresses of luxurious hotels, and have drunk some foreign wine, and they think they know everything," he said. Excerpts of his speech appeared in the Taiwan newspaper *Young Warrior* on April 28, 1979.

8. On May 2, 1988, the *Beijing Review* acknowledged that Fang Lizhi was dismissed in early 1987 as the vice president of the University of Science and Technology in Hefei "for outspokenly advocating bourgeois liberal ideas" but reported that Fang had since "achieved a great deal" in his scientific research. When the pro-democracy demonstrations were crushed in June 1989, the astrophysicist was declared a criminal and sought asylum in the United States Embassy in Beijing.

9. R. P. McDougall, a Canadian diplomat who served in Beijing, analyzed the political importance of *guanxi* in a 1985 paper, "Machiavelli on China: Thoughts on the Tactics of Pragmatism." "*Guanxi* of various kinds is still vital in Chinese pol-

itics. . . . ," McDougall writes. "These networks of personal allegiance, combined with genuine ideological and policy differences, result in a complex mosaic on which political consensus must be built."

10. *Farmer's Daily* newspaper *(Nongmin Ribao)*, reported by Reuters on December 14, 1987.

11. The controversy over Ye Wenfu was covered by the Hong Kong magazine *Cheng Ming*, which reported Ye's harassment in its January and February 1982 issues.

12. Lu Yu's criticism of Ye Wenfu appeared in the army cultural journal *Jiefangjun Wenyi*, November 1981.

13. *People's Daily*, June 12, 1984, and the *China Daily*, June 13, 1984.

14. *Izvestia* reported the criminal case of Janis Sebrinis in Latvia on June 5, 1986. Translation by *Current Digest of the Soviet Press*, issue no. 23, 1986.

15. Lydia Chukovskaya's reply to her expulsion from the Writers Union on January 9, 1974, was obtained in *samizdat* form in Moscow.

16. *Pravda*, February 6, 1975.

17. The effusive birthday tributes to Brezhnev appeared in major Soviet newspapers on December 19, 1976. The awards ceremony at the Kremlin was carried live by Soviet television.

18. Speech by Mikhail Gorbachev to the 27th Soviet Party Congress, January 27, 1987. Translation by Tass.

19. The Supreme Soviet decided at its January 1988 session that towns, neighborhoods, and state enterprises named after Brezhnev could adopt their old names if they requested.

20. The proposal was made by F. Snegirev of Kiev in a letter to *Ogonyok* published in January 1988.

21. Arkady Vaksberg disclosed some of the corruption around Brezhnev in the *Literary Gazette* in October 1987.

CHAPTER 4   NOT A THIEF UNTIL YOU ARE CAUGHT: THE
INEVITABILITY OF CORRUPTION

1. Speech by Mikhail Gorbachev to the 27th Soviet Party Congress, January 27, 1987.

2. The *Beijing Review* reported in May 1988 that customs officials in 1987 handled over 13,000 cases of smuggling with a total value of 166.9 million yuan.

3. Amnesty International's estimate that 30,000 Chinese were executed in the anti-crime campaign since 1983 obviously does not include the new wave of executions that followed the suppression of the democracy protests in June 1989.

4. Arkady Vaksberg indicated in the *Literary Gazette* in December 1986 that some Soviet citizens executed for crimes were subsequently discovered to be innocent, according to *Radio Liberty* research bulletin of July 1, 1987.

Such miscarriages were far more common under Stalin, who espoused the slogan that "Law is what is good for the Party."

5. Three of Georgi Mikhailov's labor camp photographs appeared in *The New York Times* on June 29, 1987. Mikhailov let me examine his other photographs.

6. The extent of the Hainan scandal was reported by *Xinhua* on July 30, 1985. John Burns wrote about the effect of corruption on the island's economy on November 12, 1985, in *The New York Times*.

7. *Izvestia*, May 30, 1986. Excerpts translated in the *Current Digest of the Soviet Press*, Vol. 38, issue no. 23, in July 1986.

8. The corruption scandal in Uzbekistan received prominent coverage by Tass and Soviet newspapers in 1987 and 1988. Some details cited here were translated in the *Current Digest of the Soviet Press*, Vol. 28, issues 35 and 36.

9. On January 23, 1988, *Pravda* reported that the thefts from the state totaled more than $5 billion and that most of the money had not been recovered.

10. The *Literary Gazette* reported on Akhmadzhan Adylov's fiefdom in January 1988, more than three years after Adylov's arrest in August 1984. Details from the *Current Digest of the Soviet Press* and *Radio Liberty*.

11. In August 1988, an unidentified Party official told *Xinhua* that in 1987, 109,000 corrupt Party members were expelled or forced to resign, according to the *China Daily*, August 13, 1988.

12. *Soviet Industry*, reported by Reuters, August 2, 1986.

CHAPTER 5 WATCHDOGS OF REFORM: GETTING TO KNOW YOUR NEIGHBORHOOD SECRET POLICE

1. *The State and Revolution*, by Lenin. Quoted in *A Documentary History of Communism*, Vol. 1, edited by Robert V. Daniels, University of New England Press, Hanover, NH, 1984, p. 61.

2. Decree on the Establishment of the Extraordinary Commission to Fight Counter-Revolution, promulgated by the Council of People's Commissars on December 20, 1917. Quoted in Ibid., p. 90.

3. The futile efforts of the KGB chief Viktor M. Chebrikov to adjust to the new policies of *perestroika* was reported in a *Radio Liberty* bulletin on June 21, 1988, based upon articles in *Pravda, Young Kommunist (Molodoi Kommunist)*, and *Kommunist (Communist)*.

4. Articles polishing the image of the KGB appeared in *Arguments and Facts (Argumenty i Fakty)* from April 1988.

5. Cooperation between the KGB and the Soviet Writers Union was acknowledged by the newspaper *Literary Russia (Literaturnaya Rossiya)* in July 1987.

6. *Pravda* published four articles in January and February 1987 on the KGB's persecution of Viktor Berkhin for investigating mining corruption, and forced a public apology from the KGB for the misconduct of its officials in the Ukraine. Berkhin's death was reported in *Meditsinskaya Gazeta*.

On September 9, 1988, Soviet television reported that regular police had tried to stop investigative reporting by other Soviet journalists.

7. The first of several articles attacking me appeared in the *Literary Gazette* in May 1976.

CHAPTER 6 SEEK TRUTH FROM FACTOIDS: RED TAPE, COVER-UPS, STATISTICS, CONTRADICTIONS

1. Speech by Deng Xiaoping on February 29, 1980, to the Chinese Party's Central Committee.

2. Speech by Mikhail Gorbachev on June 29, 1987, to the Soviet Party's Central Committee.

3. The need for reliable economic information was urged by Grigori Khanin, an economist, and Vasily Selunin, a journalist, in the journal *New World (Novy Mir)* in February 1987. Excerpts translated in the *Current Digest of the Soviet Press*, Vol. 39, no. 25, p. 10.

4. Western agricultural attachés in Moscow usually subtract 10 to 20 percent from the official Soviet harvest figure to take into account moisture, weeds, and even rocks thrown by peasants into the trucks before they are weighed. In May 1988, the *Literary Gazette* confirmed that the 1987 harvest tally of 210 million tons was inflated because it did not subtract the weight of excessive moisture.

5. The deference demanded of ordinary Chinese by Qing Dynasty officials was observed by J. Doolittle in *Social Life of the Chinese*, published in Britain in 1865.

6. *On the Ten Major Relationships* was published by Mao Zedong on April 25, 1956, and appeared in English in the *Beijing Review* on January 1, 1977.

7. Vladimir Kabaidze's remark about bureaucrats was made at the 19th Soviet Party Conference on June 29, 1988, and reported in *The New York Times* on June 30.

8. Igor Prostyakov, deputy chairman of the Bureau for Social Development, was quoted by *Pravda* on January 20, 1988, as

saying that half of the bureaucrats in the ministries of the Soviet republics would have to lose their jobs.

9. *Pravda*, cited in the *Globe and Mail* of Toronto on June 5, 1985.

10. *Economic Daily (Jingji Ribao)*, excerpted by the *China Daily* on August 20, 1984.

11. *Will the Soviet Union Survive Until 1984?* by Andrei Amalrik, Harper & Row, New York, 1970, p. 22.

12. *China Daily*, March 3, 1984.

13. *People's Daily*, excerpted in the *China Daily* on March 23, 1984.

14. *Beijing Review*, April 11, 1988.

15. *Pravda*, March 8, 1988. Dmitri Likhachev, chairman of the State Cultural Fund, disclosed the full extent of the losses from the library fire to the *Moscow News* in April 1988.

16. *Beijing Review*, April 4, 1988.

CHAPTER 7 WHO WILL WATCH MY DUCKS? INDIVIDUAL INITIATIVE, EGALITARIAN SOCIETY

1. *Capital*, by Karl Marx, Vol. 1, Ch. 26.

2. Lenin, *The Tax in Kind*, April 1921. Quoted in *A Documentary History of Communism*, edited by Robert V. Daniels, University Press of New England, Hanover, NH, 1984, Vol. 1, p. 142.

3. Lenin left the door ajar to some capitalism when he wrote in his essay on "Left Infantilism and the Petty-Bourgeois Mentality" that "socialism is inconceivable without large-scale capitalist engineering based on the latest discovery of modern science. . . ."

4. The Chinese government distinguishes between individual businesses, which employ eight or fewer people including family members, and private businesses, which have nine or more employees. The State Administration for Industry and Com-

merce reported that in 1987, China had 225,000 private enterprises employing 3.6 million workers, according to the
China Daily on November 24, 1988. Other statistics released
at the National People's Congress in 1988 indicated up to
twenty million individual businesses.

5. On December 31, 1988, the Soviet government published
in *Izvestia* a decree barring cooperative enterprises from engaging in commercial activity reserved for the state, including
manufacturing alcohol, medicine or narcotics, firearms, and
jewelry containing precious metals, as well as running lotteries
or dealing in foreign currency. The decree affected only a few
of the country's 48,000 cooperative enterprises, but it showed
how vulnerable private enterprise remained to government
whim. Details in *Radio Liberty* research bulletin of February
3, 1989.

6. On October 23, 1987, Novosti Press Agency said only
280,000 Soviet citizens had registered in private or cooperative
businesses, which was .15 percent of the labor force of 131
million.

7. The *Literary Gazette*, August 12, 1977.

8. *Izvestia*, June 6 and 29, 1987. Other obstacles facing cooperatives were discussed by Viktor Yasmann in *Radio Liberty*
research bulletin of August 28, 1977.

9. Lenin's promise that "there will be no more landlords" and
that Russian peasants could keep the land they tilled can be
found in his *Collected Works*, New York, International Publishers, 1943, Vol. 26, pp. 260–61.

10. After Mao's death in late 1976, the *People's Daily* disclosed
that private plots accounted for 6.4 percent of the arable land
in China but produced over 25 percent of all vegetables, fruit,
and sugar cane, and 70 percent of agricultural raw materials.
Noted by Miriam and Ivan D. London and Ta-ling Lee in *Freedom at Issue*, May–June 1983.

11. Speech by Mikhail Gorbachev to the Soviet Party's Central
Committee, June 25, 1987.

12. A survey of nearly 11,000 Chinese farm families published by the *China Daily* on April 23, 1988, reported that 12 percent complained that local officials stopped them from selling surplus produce in the free markets, even though they had fulfilled their state quotas. But nine households in ten agreed that the agricultural reforms improved their lives.

13. The *Peasants' Daily (Nongmin Ribao)* cited the case of thirty-four peasant households in a village in Henan who had to pay 30,000 yuan, or more than 300 yuan a person, for forty different government levies and taxes. An excerpt appeared on October 21, 1988, in the *China Daily*.

14. China's State Statistics Bureau defines specialized households as those where family members work more than 60 percent of their time on a specific business or production activity, gain more than 60 percent of their income from it, and earn at least twice that of ordinary peasant households.

15. On April 9, 1986, the *China Daily* reported that 70 million Chinese still lived below the poverty line of 200 yuan (then about $63) a year.

16. On November 23, 1988, the *China Daily* quoted Lin Yao-chuan, the director of the Department of Rural Economy, as saying the migrant peasants were returning home because of economic cutbacks that eliminated jobs in the cities.

CHAPTER 8 FLOWERS IN THE SUNSHINE OF THE PARTY: MEASURING THE SUCCESS OF COMMUNISM'S SOCIAL SERVICES

1. Lenin to the Komsomol Congress, October 2, 1924. Quoted in *Lenin Through the Eyes of A. V. Lunacharsky*, Novosti Publishing House, Moscow, 1981.

2. "Remarks at the Spring Festival" by Mao Zedong, February 13, 1964. *Mao Zedong Unrehearsed*, edited by Stuart Schramm, Penguin Books, Middlesex, England, 1974.

3. The Chinese journal *Theoretical Information (Lilun Xinxi Bao)* blamed the shortage of hospital beds for the high rate of

the emergency room deaths, which accounted for half of all deaths recorded in Chinese hospitals.

The journal also said Chinese obstetrical wards had 100,000 beds to accommodate a maximum of 5.4 million patients a year, though 17 million women gave birth annually and 5 million underwent birth-control operations. Reported in the April 4, 1988, issue of the *Beijing Review*.

4. On August 5, 1987, the *Medical Gazette* compared conditions in ordinary Soviet hospitals and special clinics for the élite.

5. The unpaid nursing of hospitalized children by their mothers was raised in a letter to Moscow Communist Youth in March 1986, with details appearing in the *Globe and Mail* of Toronto on March 29, 1986.

6. *Trud*, May 6, 1988.

7. *Pravda*, September 28, 1987. Extracts translated in *Radio Liberty* research bulletin, October 12, 1987.

8. On May 27, 1987, the *Liberation Daily* said 40,000 Chinese died annually from traffic accidents and another 40,000 were injured.

9. A. P. Pinkevich in *Outlines of Pedagogy*, 1927, quoted in *A Documentary History of Communism*, Vol. I, edited by Robert V. Daniels, University of New England Press, Hanover, NH, 1984, p. 90.

10. The 1982 survey disclosing poor education among Chinese workers was discussed on December 16, 1985, in the *Beijing Review*.

11. *Izvestia*, January 6, 1987. Translation in the *Current Digest of the Soviet Press*, issue no. 1, in 1987.

12. The *China Daily* reported on November 24, 1988, that over 50 million Chinese were handicapped and that 35 million of these were illiterate. Only 6 percent of blind, deaf, or mentally retarded children attended school compared to 97 percent of normal Chinese children.

13. On June 15, 1988, the *China Daily* also discussed the high truancy rate. *Xinhua* disclosed that in 1987, nearly 1.5 million children quit school in Hubei province alone.

14. Following the June 1989 pro-democracy demonstrations, the Chinese government imposed new restrictions discouraging Chinese students from going abroad, reasoning correctly that many of those already overseas would not return home.

15. Quoted in *Utopia in Power* by Mikhail Heller and Aleksandr Nekrich, Summit Books, 1986.

CHAPTER 9 THE FRAUDULENT FLYING PIGEONS: THE CHRONIC SHORTAGE OF ALMOST EVERYTHING

1. Quote by Leon Trotsky is taken from his book *The Revolution Betrayed*, Doubleday, New York, 1937.

2. Speech by Mikhail Gorbachev in Murmansk, October 1, 1987.

3. James P. Millar's survey of Soviet immigrants was released by the news bureau of the University of Illinois on February 16, 1987.

4. *Will the Soviet Union Survive Until 1984?*, by Andrei Amalrik, Harper & Row, New York, 1970.

5. On November 19, 1988, *Xinhua* said over six million Chinese families were waiting for housing.

6. On May 13, 1988, Mikhail Gorbachev told his Central Committee that "there is no doubt that the food question is a top priority." *Pravda*, May 15, 1988.

7. *Soviet Russia*, as reported by the Associated Press, November 26, 1984.

8. *Izvestia*, October 15, 1987.

9. *Izvestia*, October 9, 1987. Rebuttal by angry readers in *Izvestia*, December 19, 1987.

10. *Trud*, as reported by the *Financial Times of London*, May 9, 1988. On July 6, 1988, *Pravda* disclosed that one million tons of meat were lost annually through spoilage and mismanagement.

11. On May 23, 1988, the Associated Press said the Soviet Union was spending 84 billion rubles ($134 billion) a year on consumer subsidies and this would increase to 104 billion rubles in 1990.

12. On July 8, 1988, the Novosti Press Agency quoted the Soviet economist Nikolai Shmelev as warning that raising prices before enough produce and goods were available in the stores would create serious political and social problems.

13. In 1988, Beijing stores even ran out of salt, despite a 25 percent rise in national salt production. *China Daily*, November 11, 1988.

14. Pork accounts for about 90 percent of Chinese meat consumption. The per capita consumption of pork in China nearly doubled from 17 pounds in 1978 to 31.7 pounds in 1986, according to the *China Daily* on December 3, 1987, when the demand forced the rationing of pork in Beijing, Shanghai, and Tianjin. A decrease in pork production was blamed in part on the rising cost of fodder and low prices paid by the state for meat.

15. *Pravda*, September 27, 1987.

16. *Soviet Culture*, October 25, 1986.

17. *Soviet Youth*, January 9, 1987, and *Komsomolskaya Pravda*, January 31, 1987. Excerpts translated by *Radio Liberty*. On September 16, 1987, Soviet television announced that the fault was traced to a defective transformer.

18. *Economic Daily*, August 23, 1983.

19. In 1974, Mao Zedong's wife, Jiang Qing, tried her hand at designing an ankle-length dress for Chinese women based on the looser Japanese kimono. The *China Daily*, on May 31, 1988, recalled that "city women were asked to wear it as a 'political task.' However, the dress never caught on."

20. *Pravda*, July 1, 1988. Also quoted in *Radio Liberty* research bulletin of July 14, 1988.

CHAPTER 10 IN THE EYES OF THE STATE: SEX, LOVE, AND MARRIAGE WITH YOUR GOVERNMENT AS VOYEUR

1. Quote by Aleksandra Kollontai taken from *Communism and the Family*, Contemporary Publishing Company, New York, 1920.

2. Lenin to Clara Zetkin in Moscow. Quoted in her *Reminiscences of Lenin*, New York, International Publishers, 1934.

3. Article 119 of the Criminal Code of the Russian Soviet Federated Socialist Republic makes sex between men punishable by up to five years in prison.

4. Aleksandra Kollontai recalled her liberated life in *The Autobiography of a Sexually Emancipated Communist Woman*, Herder and Herder, New York, 1971. See also her *Communism and the Family*, op. cit.

5. Viktor Perevedentsev's research on pregnancies and births out of wedlock was quoted in *The Economist* in November 1985. Perevedentsev has written frequently on demographics in the *Literary Gazette*.

6. In its issue of May 30, 1988, the *Beijing Review* reported that venereal disease in China had increased by 3.7 times a year since 1984, in part because of "tendencies toward sexual freedom."

7. Prostitution in the Soviet Union was examined by Lavery Konovalev in *Radio Liberty*'s research bulletin of October 1, 1986. Legislation making prostitution an administrative offense was announced in *Vedomosti Verkhovnogo Soveta RSFSR* in July 1987, with details reported in *Radio Liberty* research bulletin of August 12, 1987.

8. Associated Press, September 11, 1987.

9. *Xinhua*, details in the *China Daily*, July 13, 1988.

10. China News Service, reported by the Associated Press, July 1, 1988.

11. *China Reconstructs*, March 1988.

12. *China Daily*, June 30, 1988.

13. *Xinhua, China Daily*, August 1, 1988.

14. *Health (Zdorovye)*, January, August, and September 1975; March and September 1986.

15. *Ogonyok*, July 1987.

16. *Xinhua*, reported by the Associated Press, December 20, 1987.

17. *Chinese Women* magazine, details in the *China Daily*, February 2, 1984.

18. *People's Daily*, July 5, 1988.

19. *Democracy and Legal System* journal, details in the *China Daily*, May 1, 1984.

20. *Peasants' Daily (Nongmin Ribao)*, reported by the Associated Press, June 18, 1980.

CHAPTER 11 SORE LOSERS: MARXISM'S BOTCHED CRUSADE AGAINST RELIGION

1. Lenin's letter to A. M. Gorky in 1913. Also in Lenin's *Collected Works*, New York, International Publishers, 1943.

2. *China Daily*, April 28, 1986.

3. Mao Zedong's reference to religion as one of the "four thick ropes" constraining the Chinese appears in his *Report on an Investigation of the Peasants' Movement in Hunan*. Mao's call for a competition between religion and Communism is found in his essays, *On New Democracy*.

4. *The New York Times*, June 28, 1987. In 1988, the editors of the dissident magazine *Glasnost* charged in issue no. 13, "It was not just the highest ranks of the Church that were cor-

rupted as a result of the activity of agencies monitoring the Church. Spiritual shepherds of lower rank often function as informers as well, reporting on one another and on the parishioners under their guidance."

5. Because my own notes on Father Dmitri Dudko's sermons are incomplete, the passage on the Young Pioneers is taken from page 116 of the sixth sermon in *Our Hope*, a collection of his sermons compiled by the publishing house of the Russian Orthodox Church in the United States, Crestwood, NY.

6. Father Dudko's recantation appeared in *Vremya* on Soviet television on June 20, 1980. Also, *Izvestia*, June 21, 1980.

7. Kerk in *Nood/Ooostpriesterhulb (Aid to the Church in Need)* in Konigstein, West Germany, circulated a critical analysis by Pietro Modesto of inconsistencies in the recantation.

8. Translation of Father Dudko's letter to Archbishop Vasily of Brussels provided by Keston College.

9. Details on the True and Free Seventh-Day Adventists and Rostislav Galetsky's arrest and eventual release gathered by Keston College.

10. On June 12, 1988 the *Beijing Review* estimated that China had 8 million Christians, 10 million Moslems, and 5 million Buddhists.

CHAPTER 12 CASTING OFF THE SOILED SHIRT: WHERE COMMUNISM GOES FROM HERE

1. Marx's warning to "never play with insurrection" was delivered in an article published on September 18, 1852, in the *New York Daily Tribune*, and later in his collection, *Germany: Revolution and Counter-Revolution*. See *Marxism and Insurrection* in Lenin's *Collected Works*, New York, International Publishers, 1943. Vol. 26, p. 260.

2. Letter to the Soviet Leadership by Aleksandr Solzhenitsyn, 1973; translated in *Marx Refuted*, Ashgrove Press, Bath, England, 1987.

3. *The Fifth Modernization* by Wei Jingsheng, January 1979. In *A Documentary History of Communism*, edited by Robert V. Daniels, University Press of New England, Hanover, NH, 1984, Vol. 2, p. 402.

4. Lenin's recollection of Marx's injunction not to sow dragon's teeth and harvest fleas, as well as his own call to "cast off the old soiled shirt" appeared in *The Task of the Proletariat in Our Revolution*, found in Lenin's *Collected Works*, op. cit., Vol. 24, pages 84 and 88.

INDEX